# Chaining the Hudson

Relic of the Great Chain, 1863.

*Look back into History & you'll find the
Newe improvers in the art of War has
allways had the advantage of their Enemys.*
　　　　　—Captain Daniel Joy to the Pennsylvania
　　　　　Committee of Safety, January 16, 1776

*Preserve the Materials necessary to a particular and
clear History of the American Revolution. They will yield
uncommon Entertainment to the inquisitive and curious,
and at the same time afford the most usefull and
important Lessons not only to our own posterity,
but to all succeeding Generations.*
　　　　　—Governor John Hancock to the Massachusetts
　　　　　House of Representatives, September 28, 1781.

# Chaining the Hudson

## The Fight for the River in the American Revolution

LINCOLN DIAMANT

A CITADEL PRESS BOOK
Published by Carol Publishing Group

First Carol Publishing Group edition 1994

Copyright © 1989, 1994 by Lincoln Diamant

A Citadel Press Book
Published by Carol Publishing Group
Citadel Press is a registered trademark of Carol Communications Group
Editorial Offices: 600 Madison Avenue, New York, N.Y. 10022
Sales & Distribution Offices: 120 Enterprise Avenue, Secaucus, N.J. 07094
In Canada: Canadian Manda Group, P.O. Box 920, Station U, Toronto,
     Ontario M8Z 5P9
Queries regarding rights and permissions should be addressed to
Carol Publishing Group, 600 Madison Avenue, New York, N.Y. 10022

Carol Publishing Group books are available at special
discounts for bulk purchases, for sales promotions, fund-raising,
or educational purposes. Special editions can be created to
specifications. For details, contact Special Sales Department,
Carol Publishing Group, 120 Enterprise Avenue, Secaucus, N.J.
07094

Manufactured in the United States of America
10  9  8  7  6  5  4  3  2  1

Library of Congress Cataloging-in-Publication Data

Diamant, Lincoln

     Chaining the Hudson : The fight for the river in the American
     Revolution / by Lincoln Diamant.
       p.   cm.
     Bibliography: p.
     Includes index.
     ISBN 0-8065-1535-X (pbk.)
       1. United States—History—Revolution, 1775-1783—Campaigns.
     2. Hudson River Valley (N.Y. and N.J.)—History, Military.
     E230.5N4D5   1989
     973'3—dc19
                                              894391
                                              CIP

DEDICATED TO AN EARLY "UNKNOWN SOLDIER"
OF THE REVOLUTION: COURAGEOUS CAPTAIN THOMAS,
HIS FIRST NAME LOST TO HISTORY,
WHO DROWNED WHILE ATTEMPTING TO SET FIRE
TO THE ROYAL NAVY'S *H.M.S. PHOENIX*
ON THE HUDSON RIVER, AUGUST 16, 1776.

# Contents

# Preface to the
# Second Edition

*NOTHING* I have seen, heard, or reconsidered since the initial
clothbound publication of this book has suggested any change in
my fundamental thesis: that the massive chained/boom the Americans stretched across the Hudson River at West Point in the spring
of 1778 played an essential role in the eventual success of the War of
Independence. For five years, until the end of the struggle, the
great chain at West Point, a war contract executed at a speed since
unequaled, checkmated the overwhelming superiority of the Royal
Navy. It reduced the enemy's grand military design in the northern
states to a series of dice-table passes in which Benedict Arnold and
John André were merely high-stake chips. Confronted by
Kosciuszko's (and Washington's) brilliantly evolving West Point
defense-in-depth centered on the rugged wrought iron chain and
its twin water batteries, protected by a great river bank fortress, in
turn protected by four smaller hillside forts, in turn protected by
eleven strategically placed artillery redoubts, the frustrated British
high command was reduced to bribing rather than fighting its way
past such formidable obstacles. Fear of the admittedly untested
West Point Chain and its massed cannon prevented further British
movement to fatally split New England from the other newborn
United States along the hinge of the Hudson and Champlain
Valleys. The enemy's waterborne regular, mercenary, and tory
troops moved instead to Georgia, the Carolinas, and Virginia—a
shift in War Office strategy that climaxed in the total loss of a
second expeditionary army. For the rest of the war, the chain at
West Point—once ruefully saluted by the British commander as
"the key of America"—remained unassailed. One reviewer of this
book has characterized the huge linkage, removed each winter to
barely escape the inexorable grip of tidal ice, as the "American

army's first strategic defense initiative." For this new edition of
*Chaining the Hudson*, the author has corrected the inevitable type-
setting misstrokes, plus a pair of inexplicable howlers in the
*Introduction* (dealing with the density of brackish water, and the
necessary beef ration of the Continental Army) that may have
puzzled earlier readers. Otherwise, the book stands as originally
published, with the author's renewed hope that the surviving links
of what the ragged and occasionally mutinous garrison at West Point
once called "General Washington's Watch Chain" will continue to
inspire Americans everywhere as a symbol of their long and
difficult fight for political freedom.

# Editorial Note

Quotations from original manuscript sources have been transcribed closer to exact reproduction than full modernization. To
retain as much as possible of the character of these crucial
eighteenth-century communications, their irregular capitalization,
spelling, misspelling, grammar, and punctuation have been allowed
to stand—except where they would fail to convey the original
writer's thought. Doubtful cases have been resolved in favor of
modern usage, with slips of the pen and unintentional oversights
silently corrected. The author's comments within a quotation are
thusly [bracketed].

# Introduction

THIS IS a story of the Hudson River from 1775 to 1783, and of the tens of thousands of liberty-loving Americans who—with Frenchmen, Poles, and other European volunteers—fought the British and Germans and their local loyalist sympathizers on the Hudson's surface and along its banks in the bloody eight-year struggle for the political independence of the United States. It was a cataclysm that divided much of the world's past from its future, a revolutionary challenge to the divine right of kings that Robert Graves has called "the most important single event of modern times."

Graves is hardly alone. Closer to the conflict, Thomas Paine declared: "Could we clear away the mist of antiquity, it is more than probable the ancients would admire us, rather than we them." And by the end of the war, Yale's president Ezra Stiles proclaimed: "We have lived an age in just a few years; we have seen more wonders accomplished than are unfolded in a century." One anonymous British pamphleteer quickly understood the great loss toward which his stubborn ruler was heading, and characterized the epic North American struggle as "a war of absurdity and madness" in which every point was a turning point—including major events that would soon sanctify the Hudson River.

The Hudson is not a true "river," but is, loosely speaking, the southernmost fiord in the Northern Hemisphere, a beautiful brackish estuary more than 135 miles long. Flanked by rolling hills, imposing granitic mountains, and an unusual band of basalt "palisades," it has always captured the American imagination. For eons, due to a vast downward geologic tilt of this section of the North American coastline, lighter fresh water that drains into this estuary does not flow "downhill," but blurs midriver with heavier salt waters from the encroaching Atlantic Ocean, in a shifting and swirling tidal interface.

On September 16, 1609 the explorer whose name would eventually bless this unique waterway brought his "jacht *Halve-Maan"* about, some 25 miles south of present-day Albany, and steered back to Europe. Teased north by the river's salty tides, this Englishman, commissioned commercially by the Dutch, had discovered a natural sea level canal that not only penetrated a rugged mountain barrier, but also provided a magnificent military and mercantile highway between the Atlantic coast and the continent's northeastern interior. The beautiful river valley would be a striking example of the effect of geography on history.

The implications of Henry Hudson's two-week voyage of discovery created profound political and economic repercussions throughout northern Europe. The unusually long fiord held the key to easy colonization and development of more than 13 million acres of unclaimed and immensely valuable North American land and natural resources.

In such a strategic setting, conflict—at first between natives and colonials, then between colonial groups using native hirelings—developed quickly. For over a century, North American colonists—aided by native raiders generously supplied with outdated European arms that would occasionally burst when fired—battled for control, commerce, and wealth in New World equivalents of King William's War, Queen Anne's War, King George's War, the Seven Years' War, the War of the Austrian Succession, and other less memorable European military confrontations.

Throughout, the British Crown, asserting sovereignty over the entire Hudson River Valley, adhered to a simple principle: "Hold the valley—win the war."

In the 17th and 18th centuries the population of British North America exploded—from less than 12,000 in 1670 to 2,150,000 in 1770. By that time, colonial rebellion over taxation and trade was teetering on the edge of continental revolution—first, a seaboard boycott of East India Company "bargain" tea; then, general colonial support for Boston and its intolerably interdicted commerce; and finally, Congressional approval for organized American economic resistance. The growing possibility of armed conflict with the mother country forced many forward-looking revolutionaries (and their counterparts among British Ministerial leaders) to weigh theoretical military strategies.

At the actual outbreak of conflict, all sides appeared to accept as a military given the need to control the Hudson Valley. Along the

Atlantic seaboard, the issue was rarely debated. George Washington spoke for everyone in 1777 when he repeated to General Putnam: "The importance of the Hudson River in the present Contest, and the necessity of defending it, are Subjects which have been so frequently and fully discussed, and are so well understood, that it is unnecessary to enlarge upon them.

"These Facts at once appear," the Commander-in-chief said, "when it is considered that the river runs through a whole State; that it is the only passage by which the enemy from New York, or any Part of our Coast, can ever hope to cooperate with an army from Canada; that the possession of it is indispensably essential to preserve the Communication between the Eastern, Middle and Southern States; and further, that upon its Security, in a great Measure, depend our chief Supplies of Flour for the subsistence of such Forces as we may have occasion for in the course of the War."[1] Washington estimated that 100,000 barrels of flour and 20 million pounds of meat were needed to feed 15,000 Continental soldiers for one year.

For his part, the opposing British commander was equally convinced of the importance of this strategic waterway. General Sir Henry Clinton wrote in his memoirs: "The five North American governments to the eastward of Hudson's River teemed with a robust and hardy race of men, seated in a mountainous and strongly defencible country. The southern provinces were alone capable of furnishing the necessary supplies for the war. And these two districts were entirely separated from each other by the River Hudson, forming a broad navigable communication for 170 miles between New-York and Albany.

"The Hudson naturally presented itself as a very important object," Clinton said. If the British could seize and hold the river's highlands, the revolutionaries would find it not only difficult to join forces, but even to feed their troops. "Indeed," continued Clinton, "the inhabitants on each side must in that case have experienced the greatest distresses, on account of the scarcity of bread corn, and of black cattle and horses, with which they had been accustomed mutually to supply each other.

---

[1] GW to General Israel Putnam, December 2, 1777 (*Writings of George Washington*, Jared Sparks, Ed., *Vol. V*, p. 176. Ferdinand Andrews, Boston, 1834–7). Additional footnote references do not occur in the remainder of this work; relevant sources are identified throughout the text, with further explanation in the Bibliographical Notes.

"A ready intercourse," the British general concluded, "would also have been by this means obtained with Canada by the lakes, from whence many importance advantages might have been derived." One can understand the frustrated hyperbole of another British officer, who wrote: "In this whole war, the rebels absolutely prevented us from going 15 miles from a navigable river." On August 16, 1777 Colonel Friedrich Baum and Colonel Heinrich von Breymannn did attempt to lead 1,150 of Burgoyne's German mercenaries, loyalists, and Canadians 35 miles from Fort Miller on the Hudson River towards Bennington, Vermont. Aroused local revolutionaries soon blocked their way; 700 of the enemy were captured and 200 killed. Farther down the valley a relief force under Sir Henry Clinton wisely made no similar effort to penetrate inland.

Washington's military choice, then, was to either defend the waterway, or abandon it. Elsewhere in this vast unsettled land—characterized by one annoyed British commentator as "a country where fastness grows on fastness, labyrinth on labyrinth; a country where a check is a defeat, a defeat, ruin"—the American Commander-in-chief's strategy of "advance when possible, retreat when pressed" would serve successfully. But it could never apply to the Hudson River.

This unusual revolutionary jugular thus became, until the eventual interventions of the French fleet, the conflict's only fixed line of operations. It served both as highway and battlefield, used by British warships and troops to attack the land and water forces of the revolutionaries—and vice versa. Patriotic troops and civilians along the Hudson struggled through eight years of abundance and privation, victory and defeat, heroism and treachery—all the while demonstrating a remarkable capacity for inventive regeneration buoyed up by what London's liberal *Annual Register for 1781* characterized as "an unconquerable resolution and perseverance, inspired and supported by the enthusiasm of liberty."

Such resolution and perseverance in maintaining the sometimes fragile control of this hinge of Revolution also rose from the firm determination and slowly developing strategic abilities of an austere and sagacious presiding officer, George Washington. *"He is the war,"* asserts a Continental officer in a melodrama written 70 years after the Revolution:

> . . . *cool, calm and undespairing,*
> *And like a mighty beacon 'mid the waves*
> *Of revolution, lights us thro' the storm.*

*IT IS* not hard to establish a direct feeling and flavor for those most difficult times. During a much later age, important military communications similar to those reproduced here would be swiftly handled by an urgent telephone call; only an imperfect recollection (or even dissembling) would eventually reflect what a general had actually thought and said. To our good fortune, the telephone was far off; the weightiest matters of the American Revolution are still clearly preserved in writing—on acid-free paper.

"In general," suggests the distinguished Revolutionary scholar Howard Peckham, "the historian should seek eyewitness accounts of events set down in manuscript or print by participants or close observers at the time they occurred." We agree, and wherever possible in this work, secondary interpretations have been eschewed in favor of allowing members of America's founding generation to speak for themselves, describing their long and often stealthy battle against incredible odds.

By the middle of 1776 the British Admiralty had assigned 87 warships carrying more than 6,500 sailors on the North American Station. The 30 enemy warships operating out of New York harbor alone carried 824 cannon. Such an overwhelming naval presence not only effectively paralyzed revolutionary coastal trade, but also caused major shortages and great suffering ashore.

To tip the balance and somehow counter the weight of this great navy, the revolutionaries were forced to master the art of the possible and develop a wide variety of innovative weapons. Within months of Lexington and Concord, slowly progressing from intuitive to exact engineering, the visible and secret struggle for control of the Hudson River offered striking manifestations of what the rest of the world would soon call "Yankee ingenuity."

As if wishes helped, a man who had never built even a house before began work on a monumental fort. Years ahead of the telegraph, a revolutionary general provided the army with almost instantaneous military communication. An ingenious device that helped the Dutch win their own war of independence was adapted for military use beneath the surface of the Hudson. A handful of daring revolutionary seamen updated the ancient technology of naval warfare by fire. Striking fear into the commanders of the Royal Navy, one rebel genius not only developed a harbor mine, but actually invented a torpedo-carrying submarine. He had never built a mine or a submarine or a torpedo before. No one, in fact, had ever built a mine or submarine or torpedo before.

And for the first time in the history of naval warfare—thanks to the fortuitous existence of blast furnaces with substantial iron ore deposits in the immediate vicinity of the Hudson Highlands—this strategic inland waterway was blocked for almost 60 months by one of the longest and largest iron chains ever forged.

Back in 1609 aboard the *Halve-Maan* on its epochal voyage of discovery, Henry Hudson's first mate correctly surmised: "The Mountaynes looke as if some Metall or Minerall were in them." One hundred and sixty years later a Sons of Liberty orator praised America as "a land whose stones are iron, the most useful material in all nature." From such a patriotic perspective, the West Point Chain was certainly the most important bit of ironworking since the ancient Hebrew blacksmith Tubal-cain. It helped insure a naval and military stalemate in the Hudson Valley, and eventually forced the enemy to transfer offensive military operations to the southern colonies, with subsequent defeat.

At its most critical moments, the American Revolution commanded the best efforts of a very unusual group of engineers and artisans. Even so, with the exception of the West Point Chain—which the British chose never to test in battle—none of the revolutionaries' strange new military devices was a great success. But each, considered as an early achievement in what today we would call "psychological warfare," placed a formidable obstacle in the path of a wary and increasingly frustrated enemy. Despite every conceivable disaster, each of the weapons served as a stout nail in the lucky American horseshoe. Without at least one or two of them, the new nation might well have been lost.

As a memento of those dark and dangerous days when our revolutionary forebears were inspired to risk not only their fortunes and sacred honor, but their lives—and therefore ours—we can still pay special tribute to the West Point Chain. Forged in ancient fires of adversity, it continues to symbolize America's historic commitment to visions of a better world, smelted from the common metal of humanity. May the chronicle of these momentous days offer strength and reassurance to face the doubts and crises of our own.

CHAPTER I

# Romans's Fort
## (1775)

---

*In which Congress sets the tone for revolutionary strategy by
sending an ambitious Connecticut engineer to New York to build
a monumental fort on the Hudson River*

---

*ON* May 10, 1775, the Second Continental Congress convened in
Philadelphia to resume its difficult role of coordinating colonial
efforts to win Parliamentary recognition of America's asserted
political and economic rights. At daybreak that same morning,
Colonels Ethan Allen and Benedict Arnold seized the British
garrison and almost a hundred cannon at Fort Ticonderoga.

Congress would not learn of that momentous military success for
several days. With the British army and navy attempting to break
the revolutionary siege lines around Boston by fortifying Dorchester
Heights—as well as a pair of strategic hills, Breed's and Bunker's, on
Charlestown Neck—Philadelphia's concern focused on the
precarious military situation in Massachusetts.

But based on past decades of bloody colonial struggles with the
French, northern delegates forcefully called Congress's attention to
the additional danger posed to the entire revolutionary cause by a
probable British strike at northern and southern New York along the
line of Lake Champlain, Lake George, and the Hudson River.

On that same line in 1755, before being scattered by a
rambunctious colonial army of New Englanders and New Yorkers
led by Sir William Johnson, a circling movement of 1,500 invading

1

French regulars, Canadian militia and Iroquois natives, under French mercenary general Baron Ludwig Dieskau, swept perilously close to the upper Hudson. In 1757, when Montcalm's 8,000 French troops decimated Fort William Henry at the bottom of Lake George, one of his scouting parties actually drove in the colonial pickets at Fort Edward, only 45 miles from Albany.

Now, eighteen years later, the transfer of revolutionary troops and supplies across the Hudson would be intimately affected by this north-south vulnerability. At some point all movement between New England and the other colonies had to cross this important inland waterway. "As the Enemy gains knowledge of the country," New York's congressional delegates warned—and repeated often—"they must be more and more convinced of the Necessity of becoming masters of Hudson's River. It will give them the entire Command of water communications with the Indian nations, effectually prevent all intercourse between our eastern and southern Confederacy, divide our strength and enfeeble every effort for our common Preservation and Security."

With this timely warning, an immediate barrier to block any enemy movement up and down the Hudson became a national rather than a local necessity. In London, Whitehall also recognized the overwhelming military importance of the river, which not only offered the easiest route through New York Province across Lakes George and Champlain to Canada, but whose western tributary, the Mohawk, led directly to the Oneida Carry and key British posts on the Great Lakes.

The British War Office was already planning, in addition to prompt seizure of New York City, stationing several smaller men-of-war and naval cutters along the Hudson. Such vessels, the Cabinet hoped, would "provide safe Intercourse and correspondence between Quebec, Albany and New York, and in conjunction with the Indians, allow continual irruptions into New Hampshire, Massachusetts and Connecticut, and so distract and divide the Provincial forces as to render it easy for the British Army at Boston to defeat them, break the Spirits of the Massachusetts people and compel an absolute subjection to Great Britain."

It was sound strategy; six years and almost an entire war later, when British naval forces still controlled the lower Hudson, Rochambeau's Comte de Deux-Ponts properly puzzled in his diary as to why a lethargic enemy failed to "seize an opportunity so favorable for him as that of our [French] army crossing the river" on

"Northern gate" of the Hudson Highlands.

Martelaer's Rock (Constitution Island) from the south.

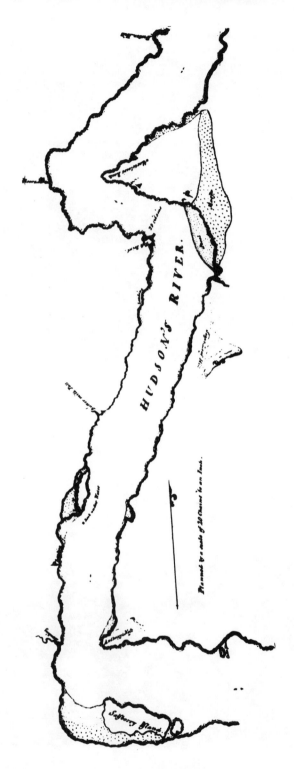

Course of the Hudson River through the Highlands: Clinton/Tappen map, 1775.

the Verplanck-Stony Point ferry route just below Peekskill.

ON May 25, 1775, moving to secure the Hudson from future enemy naval action and spurred by mounting threats of invasion from Quebec, Congress—sitting as a Committee of the Whole to vote its general Declaration of War against Great Britain—unanimously recommended to New York Province "That a post be taken in the Highlands on each side of Hudson's river, and Batteries erected in such manner as will most effectively prevent any Vessels passing, that may be sent to harrass the Inhabitants on the borders of said river."

Receiving that resolution, the New York Provincial Congress immediately named a committee consisting of Colonel James Clinton (older brother of George Clinton, who was in Philadelphia as a member of Congress), James's brother-in-law Major Christopher Tappen, and two militia captains to reconnoiter the Hudson Highlands and recommend a proper place to erect one or more fortifications.

Why choose the Hudson "Highlands"?

Forty miles north of New York City and 90 miles south of Albany, this ten-mile-wide band of rugged Pre-Cambrian granite hills, rising 1,400 feet above the glaciated fiord, offered what appeared to be the best defensive artillery positions against encroaching British warships. Timothy Dwight, future president of Yale, serving in the area during the Revolution as an army chaplain, found the Highlands "majestic, solemn, wild and melancholy." His view was echoed by Major General Samuel Parsons, commanding at West Point during the winter of 1777–78, who wrote bitterly to a friend: "To a contemplative Mind which delights in a lonely Retreat from the world, to view and admire the stupendous and magnificent Works of Nature, 'tis as beautiful as Sharon. But to a Man who loves the Society of the World, it affords a prospect nearly allied to the Shades of Death."

Lonely or not, this rugged area remained the key to military control of the Hudson valley. The location of its fortifications, cantonments, and bloody engagements would soon become a military gazetteer of the American Revolution. By the second year of the war, to control far-flung revolutionary military operations that ranged over a million-square-mile area from Georgia to Canada and as far west as the Mississippi River, Congress established six territorial departments. From late 1776 to the end of the conflict, the tiny Hudson Highlands area—less than 150,000 acres—was considered a de facto seventh department.

*WITHIN TWO* weeks, committee members Clinton and Tappen, drawing a map that exaggerated swings in the actual course of the Hudson, recommended speedy construction of a small revolutionary fort just below the northern "gate" of the Highlands. It was at the deepest point on the river—more than 30 fathoms—where the Hudson not only narrows to less than a quarter mile wide, but also hampers sail navigation with a very difficult S-shaped bend.

The committee's suggested site for the fortification—estimated cost £1,500—was on the lower eastern bank, rather than the higher western bank of the river. From this small decision, taken quickly at a time of crisis, arose many unforeseen consequences.

Next step for the New York Provincial Congress was to locate a skilled military engineer capable of supervising construction of the fortification. But the search for such an individual yielded nothing but frustration. The few professionals who might otherwise have been available were busy reconstructing seaboard defenses that had languished since the Seven Years (French and Indian) War.

Such legislative and military chaos was understandable; the Revolution was just beginning to sort itself out. At one and the same time, it was being fought by independent individuals, military units and government committees. Any knowledge of fortification technology that existed among a tiny handful of revolutionary officers came almost entirely from foreign military textbooks; Colonel Rufus Putnam devised the successful entrenchments on hard-frozen Dorchester Heights from an idea he came across in a book by Clairac that he found in General William Heath's tent.

The engineer-adventurers who subsequently joined the Continental Army were almost all European. Louis le Begue de Presle du Portail, who served five years as Washington's chief engineer, was a French Royal Engineer, whose classic training in siege warfare was not put to decisive use until the 1781 battle of Yorktown.

But this was 1775, not 1781. On July 10 Washington commented bitterly to Congress's President, the immensely wealthy Boston merchant John Hancock: "The Skill of those [engineers] we have is very imperfect, and confined to the mere manual exercise of cannon; whereas the war in which we are engaged requires a knowledge of Fortification. If any persons thus qualified are to be found in the Southern colonies [i.e. west of the Hudson], it would be of great public service to forward them with all expedition." But no such persons were forthcoming, and the New York Provincial Congress may be excused for dragging its feet about what all seemed to agree was a desperate military need to establish a "post in the Highlands."

*A MONTH* earlier, under the protective guns of the Royal Navy, Major General Thomas Gage's troops had finally crossed Boston's Charles River and assaulted the hastily-constructed revolutionary lines on Breed's Hill. In a single afternoon, the British not only suffered 1,150 casualties—40 percent of their entire North American army—but also lost one in four of all their officers killed in the Revolution.

From a military point of view, the months that followed that bloody action on Charlestown Neck reflected an uneasy calm. The enemy lay quiet in Boston, recovering from shock. For their part, more than a few Americans were hoping the revolutionary storm that had arisen so suddenly might yet blow by. It was during that summer of 1775 that word finally reached Hartford that New York was seeking a qualified engineer who could supervise construction of an important fortification along the Hudson River.

Bernard Romans, a distinguished resident of Wethersfield, a town situated a few miles south of the Connecticut capital, heard his adopted country's call. Romans was a Dutch-born former deputy surveyor to the Southern District of British North America, author of *A Concise Natural History of East and West Florida* and *Annals of the Troubles in the Netherlands from 1506 to 1629*. A prolific cartographer, engraver, and self-taught military engineer, he was also the real originator of the march on Ticonderoga.

It was a moment in American history that rewarded Romans's style of aggressive improvisation. He eagerly rode south to Philadelphia to volunteer his services as an engineering contractor. En route, his imagination began to fashion a fantastic, impregnable river fortress, the likes of which North America had never seen. If ships of the Royal Navy were ever to venture as far north as the Highlands, Romans's fort would offer them an unpleasant surprise.

On August 18, with the British still locked up in Boston, the New York Congress temporarily entrusted control of the province to its "Committee of Safety"—but first resolved, after a summer delay that wasted two months of good construction weather, "That the Fortifications ordered by the Continental Congress as proper to be

built on the banks of Hudson's River be immediately [sic] erected."
To implement that resolution, they appointed five *Commissioners for
Fortifications at the Highlands*—increased to seven the following
month.

The Commissioners, with a guard of 24 men, were an important
semi-independent group. Working for 10 shillings a day each, they
recruited laborers, managed necessary payments, and generally
oversaw construction progress on the initial military installations
along the Hudson. This group's establishment by the Provincial
Congress, although belated, marked the first true approach to a
coordinated Hudson Valley defensive military strategy.

As if to underline the seriousness of the situation, the Provincial
Congress voted—18 to 6—to remove several cannon from the Grand
Battery that defended the southern tip of New York City itself, to
send upriver. Despite a vigorous bombardment from Captain George
Vandeput on *H.M.S. Asia*—which wounded three Sons of Liberty,
and for which Vandeput immediately apologized to New York's
mayor—the revolutionaries successfully wrestled the King's guns off
their parapets.

In Philadelphia, Bernard Romans, submitting plans for a fort in
the Hudson Highlands as monumental as his ambition, found
himself in the right place at the right time. He successfully lobbied
the Continental Congress. As delegate Charles Carroll of Carrollton
later remarked to the Maryland Council of Safety, the situation in
which Romans found himself was one in which "we must avail
ourselves of the skill of such [engineers] as we can meet with,
though their Knowledge be not so perfect or complete."

Romans quickly headed back to New York. The Commissioners
for Fortifications accepted his endorsement by Congress and
recommended to the New York Committee of Safety that the
Connecticut engineer be hired to hurriedly plan and construct the
strategic Highlands fort. Romans, however, was envisioning not
some waterside gun emplacement, but a "state of the art"
fortification.

To make matters more difficult, the Safety Committee established
no direct lines of military or civilian authority. Ambitious "Mr.
Romans the Engineer" insisted that he report only to the
Continental Congress. He was delighted to take charge of a major
project that would place him on a level with a host of the
Continental Army's most illustrious officers. Without missing a beat,
Romans asked—fruitlessly, it transpired—for a colonelcy.

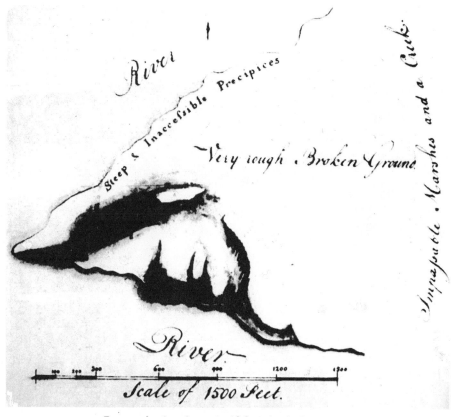

Romans's sketch map of Martelaer's Rock 1775.

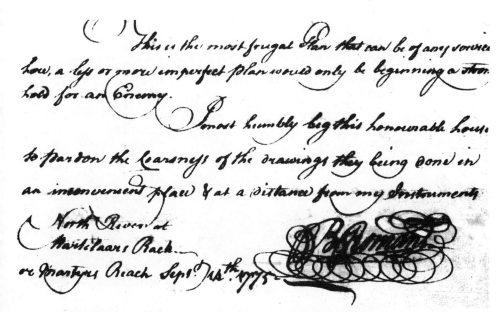

Signature page, Romans's letter of transmittal for his fortification drawings.

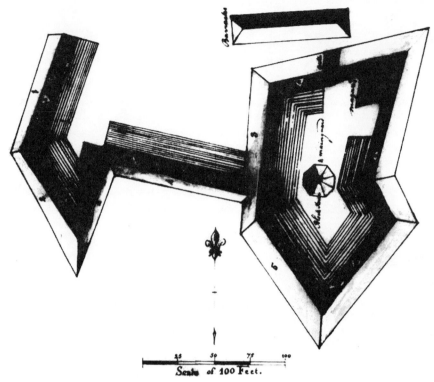

Romans's projected fort on Martelaer's Rock 1775.

Memorial six-pounder marking site of Romans's 1775 unusual blockhouse, across the Hudson from West Point [at right] (1983).

The only site Romans surveyed, following the original Clinton-Tappen suggestion, was a rugged 160-acre Hudson River island in the middle of the Highlands called "Martelaer's Rock." The name was a corruption of *martelaar's reik* (martyr's reach), a fearsome term coined by the early Dutch skippers to describe that extremely difficult tack on the river. The Rock, its highest point only 150 feet above the water, lay a quarter mile across open water from the "West Point." An extensive marsh separated it from the nominal east bank of the river, liberally qualifying it as an island.

Clambering over the southern shore, crossing and recrossing the few level areas that were only several paces wide, Romans began to draw on bits of formal British engineering training. Faced with the greatest professional challenge—and opportunity—of his life, his imagination took flight.

To protect the Highlands and the Hudson River from future British incursion, he drew—and proposed to build with staged payments from the New York Provincial Congress—a very large, complex, and supposedly impregnable stronghold capable of delivering sustained and withering cannon fire against the heaviest man-of-war the Royal Navy would ever be able to send up the river.

Romans's designs—which he purposely kept from the Commissioners—consisted of an unusual octagonal blockhouse/magazine to prevent "mischief" from a vessel's top; five batteries with 81 guns; a fort with bastions ("the soul of the works"); a 200-foot long curtain rampart; several subterranean bombproof chambers for protection and additional magazines; and a 100-foot long barracks with storehouses and guardrooms.

Unafraid to improvise, Romans planned 14 cannon for the curtain, although he said, "according to rule it ought to have only ten." With his total of 81 guns—almost as many as were captured at Ticonderoga—Romans promised "a most terrible Crossfire, to make it totally impossible for a vessel to stand it." In theory, Roman's complicated fortification could have easily damaged and possibly sunk an enemy vessel.

For his four months of involved construction plus additional outworks, Romans planned to charge New York a total of £4,645 4s. 4d., all "computed at the lowest rates available." Romans's estimate was precise, excepting only "150,000 bricks, the price of which I am entirely ignorant of."

Former royal deputy surveyor Bernard Romans apparently had no misgivings about his ability to carry off such a grandiose scheme in the time and with the funds available. His proposed four months of construction, however, should have opened everyone's eyes. In the prevailing military situation, the monumental fort Romans planned was too huge an undertaking for contemporary hand tools, blasting powder, a few yoke of oxen, and an enormous amount of backbreaking labor. Given the country's precarious financial situation, a more practical suggestion would have been to place a few precious revolutionary cannon within hastily thrown-up earthworks at various strategic bends of the Hudson River. Romans's complicated design was far too ambitious for a poor young nation still struggling to break the apparent British stranglehold on Boston.

The only formal explanation Bernard Romans ever made for his flight of fortification fancy was that "a less or more imperfect plan would only be beginning a stronghold for an Enemy." Pacing across the uncompromisingly rugged site of his planned Gibraltar, Romans also ignored many serious problems.

Although the "Grand Bastion" seemed properly indicated on his somewhat distorted sketch map of the river's S-bend at Martelaer's Rock, in reality the planned work was too far west to command the long straight stretch of the river below. Until the moment an enemy vessel came into view and began its own cannonade, it would be masked from the bastion's guns by the rocky "West Point"— something Romans soon had to acknowledge. Inevitably his works would have to be extended to the east.

On September 13 the Fortifications Commissioners came to the Rock to review construction plans. The line-of-sight difficulty along the river was immediately apparent. Romans had also considered placing a separate battery on an easy-to-grade (but far less dramatic) gravel hill to the east—but never seriously worked on it. Perhaps he regarded that location as mere bait to lure enemy ships under an unexpectedly devastating fire from his huge fort.

Another basic problem was the fact that the highest elevation on Martelaer's Rock was still lower than the opposite shore, easily commanded by cannon an enemy might haul by land to the West Point. Romans's 1775 "Grand Bastion" was actually 500 feet lower than engineer Tadeusz Kosciuszko's future (1778) Fort Putnam.

Bitter conflict immediately developed between engineer Romans and the Fortifications Commissioners.

The focus of their dispute reflected the American Revolution— and probably all revolutionary upheavals—in microcosm: high vs.

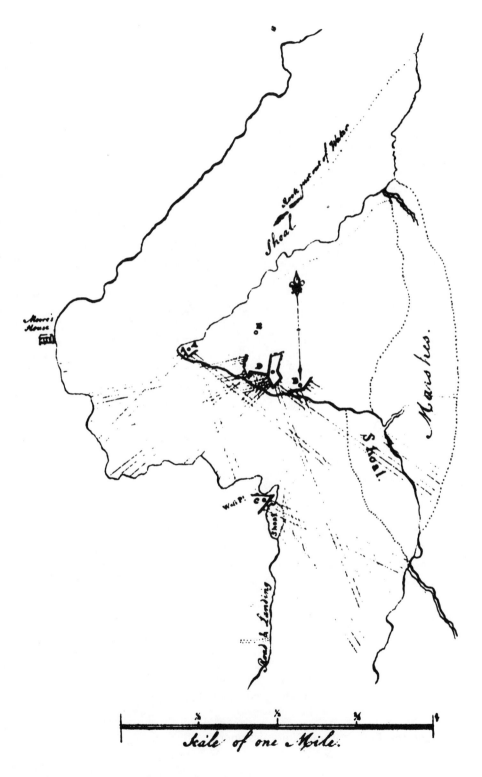

Romans's projected angles of fire, Fort Constitution 1775.

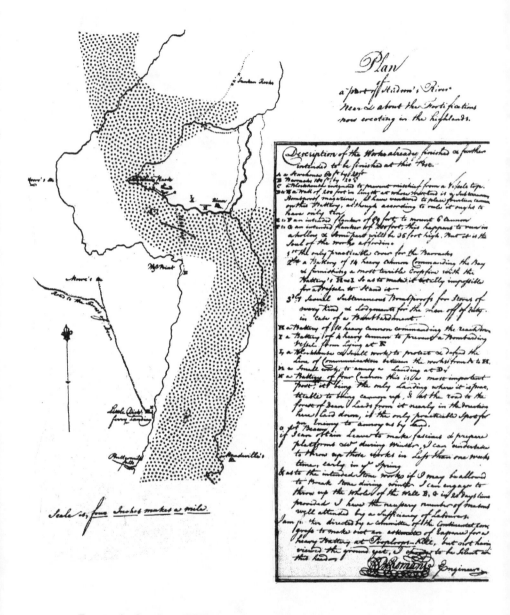

Romans's October 1775 progress report and sketch map (with actual
Hudson River course stippled).

low motivation, sacrifice vs. egotism, organization vs. chaos. Through the critical fall and winter months of 1775, Romans remained locked in dubious battle with the Fortifications Commissioners over construction procedures. Work on the fort—quickly dubbed *"Fort Constitution"* by the Commissioners, after the revered and much-invoked half-written, half-traditional English Constitution—proceeded at a snail's pace.

Amid rising military concern, heated words passed back and forth between Romans and various New York officials. News of the infighting reached Philadelphia and prompted an ongoing Congressional discussion of Romans's plans. A friend of the colonies in London had written that the British were about to move on both New York and Albany in an effort to disrupt essential revolutionary lines of communication. Delegate Samuel Chase of Maryland thundered before an anxious Congress, "Recollect the Intelligence on your Table—defend New York—fortify upon Hudsons River."

Defense of the Hudson was now a serious and growing concern. Thomas Jefferson wrote to his brother-in-law Francis Eppes in Virginia: "By means of Hudson's River, [the British] mean to cut off all correspondence between the Northern and Southern colonies." Four days later Major General Philip Schuyler, commanding the Northern Department, wrote Congress President John Hancock from Albany: "To me, Sir, Every Object, as to Importance, sinks almost to Nothing, when put in Competition with the securing of Hudson's River."

Shorthand notes taken by John Adams during the Congressional debates quote Eliphalet Dyer of Connecticut: "Cant say how far it would have been proper to have gone upon Romains Plan in the Spring [of 1775], but thinks it too late now." There were other places on the river, Dyer insisted, where works might still be thrown up in a few days.

Richard Henry Lee of Virginia, with excellent recall, backed Romans's more elaborate proposals: "Romain says a less or more imperfect Plan would only be beginning a Strong hold for an Enemy." A final argument by Romans's Wethersfield neighbor, Connecticut Congressional delegate Silas Deane, carried the day: "An order went to N. York. They have employed an Engineer. The People and he agree in the Spot and the Plan. Unless We rescind the whole, We should go on. It ought to be done." It was an early example of supposed light at the end of a tunnel.

Responding to Deane, Congress reaffirmed that the Provincial

Convention of New York [the new revolutionary restyling of "Provincial Congress"] should render the Hudson River defensible before winter set in. In deference to skeptical delegates, however, the resolution added, "It is very doubtful whether any Stone work can be properly made at this advanced season; it is submitted to the judgment of the Convention whether it could not be more cheaply and expeditiously done by works of wood or fascines."

Many Congressmen had begun to doubt whether the fort on Martelaer's Rock was being built in the right place. The island had served so long as a wood lot, it now contained little useable timber. So a new Congressional order directed New York "to enquire whether there are not some other places where smaller Batteries might be erected, so as to annoy the enemy on their passage, particularly a few heavy cannon at or near Moore's house [a substantial dwelling on the west bank flats above West Point], and at a point on the west shore, a little above Verplanck's" [a rocky peninsula eventually famous as *Stony Point*].

On October 12 the New York Convention responded to its new Philadelphia instructions by forwarding the text of the Congressional order to its Fortifications Commissioners, urging them to go as quickly as possible "with as much secresy as the nature of the transaction will admit" to the various sites mentioned in the resolution, "taking Mr. Romans to your assistance, and using all possible dispatch in making your Report."

Tracing out a copy of the original Clinton/Tappen map, Romans quickly evaluated a few alternate military sites. He dismissed the suggested battery at Moore's House as useless, and described the point on the west side of the Hudson above Verplanck's as "too easy of access, and in the vicinity of many ill-disposed People."

Always seeking to enlarge his responsibilities, Romans had nothing but praise for additional military construction in the area of "Pooploop's kill [Popolopen Creek], opposite to Anthony's nose [named—according to Washington Irving—for the bulbous nose of Antony van Corlear, Henry Hudson's trumpeter], where the Committee of the Contl. Congress ordered me to make out an estimate for & where I would make a battery of 12 heavy cannon.

"It is a very important pass," Romans observed, "commanding a great ways up and down, full of counter currents, and subject to constant fall winds; nor is there any Anchorage at all except close under the works to be erected." From Popolopen Creek, he wrote, "it is a very easy matter to establish posts with the upper country and Connecticut." Demonstrating rare harmony, two Fortification Commissioners appended their signatures to Romans's report, noting they "fully concur in opinion with the Engineer."

A century earlier, when the Dutch reluctantly relinquished final control of New York and the Hudson River to the British, the natural military strength of the hills above Popolopen Creek had not gone unnoticed: "At Antonios Nose upon the West Coast," a 1672 report stated, "there is in a Corner a piece of ground well watered, low & very strong by nature, where if a Block-house were but erected, & a Breast-work cast up to make a Battery, & but 4 Gunns planted there, it would stop ye Passage of any Vessell or Vessells from passing up the River. This fforte being supplyed with but a douzen Men from Albany & Esopus to manage ye Gunns & to afford some small shott must of necessity give a Stopp to any Vessell from attempting their Designe."

ON November 8 Congress formed a special Committee to the Northward. It consisted of 29-year-old Robert R. Livingston, Jr. of New York (later, in an effort to logroll his conservative state, Livingston was installed on the committee drafting a "declaration of independence"), John Langdon of New Hampshire, and Robert Treat Paine of Massachusetts. None had any real military experience. The committee was dispatched from Philadelphia to confer with Northern Department commander General Philip Schuyler, and visit Ticonderoga and Canada. In passing, it was also charged to "take an accurate view of the state of our Fortifications upon Hudson's River."

The battle on and over Constitution Island swelled to a climax. No one knew better than Bernard Romans how far his grandiose plans were falling behind. The construction delay on the fort turned it into one of the Revolution's worst kept military secrets. Even Royal Governor William Tryon, former governor of North Carolina, who had been posted to New York in 1771, was still circulating freely within the inflamed province, and was bold enough—on September 23—to come upriver with two officers to Haverstraw, 15 miles below Fort Constitution.

There Tryon inquired "with great scrutiny about the new Fortification, the nature of the ground, the state it was in, how many Guns were mounted and how many men watched." He could hardly know that the first snows of winter would signal an inglorious end to Romans's career as a patriotic military engineer. Instead of obstructing the Hudson, Romans and his Commissioners had succeeded in obstructing each other.

On November 15 Romans penned what was surely his valediction; a "petition and memorial" addressed to both the Provincial Congress and its Committee of Safety. In it the engineer complained of "uncertain circumstances" created by the Commissioners, who had made him "contemptible in the Eyes of the Workmen"—a situation that must "grate a man with but a grain of spirit." His orders, he said, were being "continually countermanded" without any "shadow of dignity toward the office he bears," even though "hereafter it would be asked who was the Engineer? but never who was Commissioners?"

After nine hectic weeks, Romans appeared ready to throw in the towel. He asked Congress to take "your humble petitioner and memorialist out of this dilemma where his character cannot fail to suffer & appoint him in the field or elsewhere where his abilities may stand a fair tryal." Toward the Commissioners—"three of them at least"—Romans was suddenly ambivalent, judging them as "honest well meaning men who would sacrifice life and property for liberty," but who suffered too much from "anxious care for the pecuniary affairs of their Country.

"By no means!" Romans insisted, should his complaint "be construed as originating in ill will or other sinister intents against the Commissioners." But the Commissioners got wind of his letter and caught up with Romans that evening. The next morning Romans addressed them with this frigid note:

"*Martler's Rock* [Romans now refused to dignify the Commissioners' rechristening], *16th Nov. 1775.*
"*To the Commissioners for the fortifications in the Highlands.*
"*GENTN.—I forebore to make use of the many polite appellations, such as scoundrel, villain &c., with which Mr. Bedlow was pleased last night, so copiously to honor me in public.*

B. ROMANS."

A week after Romans tossed down that last gauntlet, Livingston's Committee to the Northward, en route to Albany and Ticonderoga, rowed eight miles downriver from New Windsor on the Hudson to his construction site. On November 23 they reported back to Congress that although there were now more than 70 cannon (but still nothing heavier than a 9-pounder) at Fort Constitution, the

Remains of Fort Constitution's southwest curtain rampart—"Romans's Battery"—from: (1) a beach on Constitution Island [West Point at right]; (2) within the lines of Constitution Island [West Point in background] (1983).

Looking north over West Point towards Constitution Island [Martelaer's Rock] (1978). $F$ = ruins of Fort Constitution; $G$ = gravel hill battery site.

Remains of Fort Constitution's southwest curtain rampart—"Romans's Battery"—from West Point's "Flirtation Walk" [Hudson River in foreground] (1983).

installation—with its two-company garrison of 100 militiamen—was "in a less defensible Scituation than we had reason to expect, owing chiefly to an injudicious disposition of the labour, which has hitherto been bestowed on the Barracks, the Blockhouse & the South West curtain. This, Mr. Romans assured us, would be finished in a week, & would mount 14 Cannon, but when Compleated we consider as very insufficient in itself to answer the purpose of defence, tho it is doubtless Necessary to render the whole fortification perfect. But as it is the least useful it should have been the last finished."

Remains of that southwest emplacement, still called "Romans's Battery," survive on a low cliff above the river. The visiting Congressmen carefully noted how "It does not command the Reach to the Southward, nor can it injure a Vessel turning the West point, & after She has got round, a small breeze or even the tide will enable a ship to pass the Curtain in a few minutes. The principal Strength of the fortress will consist in the South Bastion on which no labour has as yet been bestowed.

"The block house is finished," they went on, "& has six 4-pounders mounted in it, & is at present the only Strength of the fortress [after more than two months' work]. The Barracks consist of 14 Rooms, each of which may contain 30 men, but they are not yet Compleated for want of Bricks with which to run up the Chimneys." With freezing blasts beginning to whistle through the Highlands— "high wind & ice made on Oars," noted Committee member Robert Treat Paine—Bernard Romans was still having trouble with the cost of bricks.

"The Fortress," the Committee went on, "is unfortunately commanded by all the Grounds about it & is much exposed to an attack by Land, but the most obvious defect is that the Grounds on the West point, behind which an Enemy might land without the least danger, are much higher than the Fortress. It seems necessary that this Place on the opposite Shore should be occupied & batteries thrown up. Mr. Romans informs us of a place about 4 miles lower down the River where the elevation is much greater. Had we more time, we should have gone & examined it. We cannot help wishing, when we consider the importance of the object," the Committee concluded ruefully, "that Congress send Some persons better versed in these matters than we are."

Everyone in New York and Philadelphia was now convinced that a revolutionary success in driving the British from Boston would immediately result in an enemy attack on New York City, followed by a water-and-land operation up the Hudson. There was a growing belief that Romans's uncompleted work would be powerless to stop the enemy. It spurred fresh Congressional impetus to develop the alternative site six miles to the south.

The Commissioners took another look at "Pooploop's kill" and wrote from Fort Constitution to the Convention on December 7 that they "found its situation the best by much for any defensive work in the Highlands. No enemy [they mistakenly believed] can land at Haverstraw and cross the mountains to annoy it by land. The river is not much wider over to Anthony's nose than here; a battery of heavy cannon would command it down and up, the length of point blank shot. From Pooploop's kill there is a tolerable road to the West Point; an enemy might bring cannons by land against this post."

Based on that report, the New York Convention decided the time had come for a change. On December 14, ostensibly to accommodate the difference between Romans and the Commissioners, the legislators took up the question of whether Bernard Romans had "either Mistaken the Charge committed to him, or as appears from his Conduct, has assumed Powers with which he knew he was not intrusted." Romans's time had run out.

Returning from a fresh survey of the works on Constitution Island, a three-man committee—consisting of Colonel Francis Nicoll, Colonel Joseph Drake, and Thomas Palmer (a civilian member of the New York Convention and chairman of the Ulster County Committee of Safety, who would also serve as a military engineer capable of laying out the lines of Fort Montgomery above Popolopen Creek)—submitted an eight-page report.

In it Palmer documented all the inadequacies of Romans's design of Fort Constitution, and urgently recommended establishment of an additional open barbette battery of eight 18-pound cannon, without fancy parapets, on the gravel hill near the eastern end of the island, commanding the river southward.

After lengthy discussion, the Convention finally decided "Mr. Romans was to blame in refusing to consult the Commissioners on every Matter of Importance, before he attempted to carry it into execution." In company with Fortifications Commissioner Thomas Grenell, Palmer was dispatched to Philadelphia to mollify the Continental Congress in Philadelphia with sketches of his own projected improvements to Romans's original work.

Palmer was also requested to show how Romans had completely

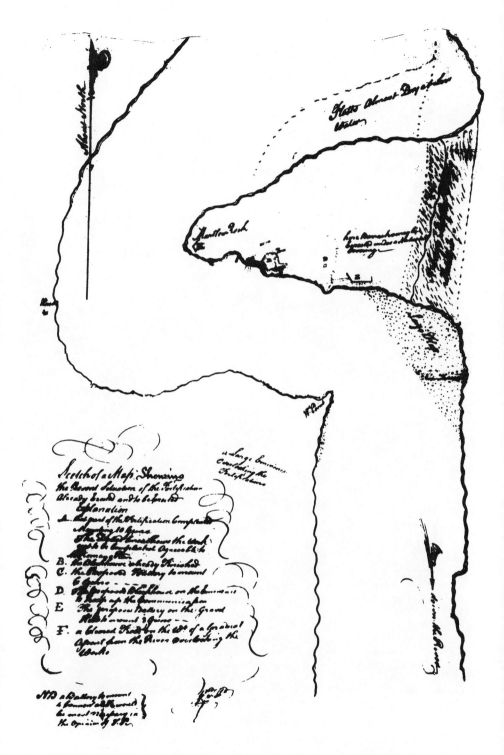

Thomas Palmer's proposed strengthening of Fort Constitution, 1775.

Tablet marking site of Thomas Palmer's proposed 1776 "gravel hill" battery, looking downriver (1983).

ignored "two large Eminences overlooking the works, so situated that an Enemy might improve them much to our damage"; and tell how, when the committee noted to the engineer that "it was his indispensable duty accurately to have observed those matters in his first report to the Continental and Provincial Congresses, he answered that he had 'pointed out the necessity of the one, & the other he had but lately thought of.'" Emboldened by news of Palmer's mission, the Commissioners remaining at Fort Constitution began to override their "master workman" and unilaterally divert construction materials downriver to Popolopen Creek.

The *Report of the State of New York*—with Palmer's own plan for redeeming the situation, or completely abandoning Romans's handiwork in favor of new works at Popolopen Creek—sparked renewed Congressional debate over Fort Constitution. The diary of Richard Smith, delegate from New Jersey, records: "Great Fault found with the Fort now constructing in the Highlands under the Auspices of Bernard Romans the Engineer, as too large and expensive and ill calculated to annoy the Enemy. Maps produced and Proceedings of N York Convention thereon read. Mr. Palmer attending on their behalf, ordered that he be heard Tomorrow Morning."

On January 5, 1776 the Continental Congress, following New York's example, resolved, "That for the reasons contained in the papers hereunto annexed, no further Fortifications be erected on Marteler's Rock on Hudson's river, and that a point of land at Puplopen's kill, on the said river, ought without delay to be effectively fortified." Smith recorded in his diary how Thomas Palmer and Fortifications Commissioner Captain Thomas Grenell had been "called in & examined. This affair took up several Hours. Was at last resolved to abandon the Works at Martilers Rock, with Romans the Projector of them."

By then, eager to defend his professional reputation, Bernard Romans also arrived in Philadelphia, innocently bearing a sealed, derogatory letter from the New York Committee of Safety. The engineer found his reception quite different from that of a few months earlier. The extemporaneous nature of the war was changing. Congress was now establishing a reasonably well-organized pattern of army command; and many ranking early volunteers like Romans, having been found wanting, were asked—or forced—to resign.

Romans, denounced in both civilian and military circles—"He

wants money which he never earned," caustically insisted the New York Committee of Safety—was dismayed to discover what a political pariah he had become. For eight days a special Congressional committee debated (according to Richard Smith) whether Bernard Romans should be called in and examined about his fortifications. The committee decided not to bother. Oliver Wolcott, a delegate from Romans's own state, was asked to advise the engineer that his fort-building services were no longer required.

Eventually Romans was commissioned captain in the Pennsylvania artillery. In his earlier travels among the transplanted Acadians of the Mississippi delta, he had learned French. Now he was ordered north to assist the faltering revolutionary invasion of French Canada. In 1778, after further military misadventures, he left the army.

Robert R. Livingston, whose Committee to the Northward had been so critical of Romans's work on Fort Constitution, now had second thoughts. "I must confess," Livingston wrote to Thomas Lynch, a South Carolina Congressman, "that desisting from the work at Martilars Rock after so much money had been layd out upon it surprized me. The finishing only one Bastion would make it extreamly formidable and indeed impassible unless the Enemy were very much favored by the wind, nor could the expence be very great after what has been already done. At least let a Battery be erected at some little distance from the Fort to the eastward, which may be made of earth by the soldiers, & commands the whole Reach below & must of necessity prove very troublesome to shiping coming up. I wish some Engineer could be found to take charge of this matter at any price."

The New York Committee of Safety paid no heed. On January 16 it ordered all construction materials still at Martelaer's Rock removed at the first opportunity to Popolopen Kill. Roman's dream of a Gibraltar-on-the-Hudson was fading fast.

BRIGADIER GENERAL Horatio Gates, Washington's querulous adjutant at Cambridge, with more than a quarter century of British Army service behind him, noted the obvious: "As soon as our artillery makes the town of Boston uneasie to its present Garrison, so surely will they leave it. Depend on it, the Ministerial push will then be to regain possession of the rivers St. Lawrence and Hudson." Gates hoped aloud that there still could be "a good fort" somewhere above the Highlands to command the channel.

During the winter of 1775, as planned, Colonel Henry Knox loaded the 60 tons of cannon Romans had once helped Benedict Arnold to inventory at Fort Ticonderoga onto "slays." With 80 yoke of oxen, Knox successfully hauled the precious armory more than 300 miles: down the Hudson Valley to Claverack, then eastward across Massachusetts snows and frozen rivers to the outskirts of Boston.

Swiftly installed on Dorchester Heights behind straw-filled breastworks ingeniously devised by engineer Colonel Rufus Putnam, Knox's guns checkmated the British forces and ships in Boston and the harbor below. Meeting at Roxbury, Massachusetts on March 13 with two major generals and three brigadier generals for one of his traditional councils of war, Washington proposed that "the Ministerial troops were about to evacuate [Boston]; that in all probability they were destin'd for New York, and would attempt to possess themselves of that City, by which means they would command the Navigation of Hudson's River—open a Communication with Canada—and cut off all intercourse between the Southern and Northern colonies."

The council resolved that "if the Ministerial troops should totally abandon the Town of Boston, it will be unnecessary to imploy any part of this Army for its defence and Security." Four days later, General William Howe did indeed evacuate Boston, and revolutionary military attention immediately shifted south.

Washington arrived in New York City on April 13.

*TEN DAYS* previous, Catholic Charles Carroll of Carrollton set off from Philadelphia with the 70-year-old—but indefatigable—Benjamin Franklin on a fruitless propaganda mission, attempting to salvage through personal appeal to the independent nationalism of Canadian Catholics, what was rapidly becoming a revolutionary rout along the St. Lawrence River.

Carroll and Dr. Franklin sailed past "Constitution fort" on a wretched trip up the Hudson in sail-shredding early spring winds. They went ashore "from curiousity" on April 5th to see what was actually left at the much-revised and simplified Fort Constitution, now down to only 22 cannon—the remainder had been hauled south to Popolopen Creek. They found not a gunner or artilleryman to serve the guns, and only 102 men fit for duty. There were "81 Quarter Barrells and 1 whole Barrell" of precious gunpowder in spring-soggy magazines that were proving dangerous to dry out, even with controlled fires. The soldiers were demanding hazard pay.

It was a foretaste of many problems that, for the next 18 months, would plague the unhappy island and its discouraged, underfed, ill-equipped, usually unpaid and often drunk garrison. Mainly overlooked, due to miserable living conditions, was the December order of the Convention prohibiting "any Sutler or Retailer of Liquor of any kind to remain at or near the said Fortification, amongst the Mechanicks, Labourers, or other persons." Before long the original garrison of local militiamen rebelled. It was quickly replaced with slightly more dependable Continental regulars.

Carroll was highly critical of both Romans's construction plans and the actual works: "It does not deserve the name of a fort, being quite open on the north-east side. If Lord Howe knew its weak state," Carroll said in an express letter to Washington's newly-opened headquarters in New York City, "he might take the Fort in its present situation with 60 men and without Cannon. He might land his party a little below the Fort on the east side, march over a Marsh, and attack the back"—much as the revolutionaries did three years later at Stony Point.

Carroll also noted how the additional barbette battery ordered two months earlier by the Continental Congress had been "strangely neglected"; only a portion of the gravel hill had been leveled. Understandably, military interest was shifting "lower down the river," Carroll reported, "to a battery to be called Fort Montgomery, and another a little below Cape St. Anthony's nose [Fort Clinton]."

With the British fleet expected momentarily in New York harbor, Washington was taking far greater interest in the Hudson River fortifications. Responding to Carroll's report and doubting whether the New York Convention was truly capable of coping with the difficult problems of defensive construction and disciplined garrisoning along the waterway, the Commander-in-chief sought first-hand opinion from his own experienced officers.

Washington ordered an immediate investigation by a committee that consisted of stodgy but talented Brigadier General Lord Stirling (William Alexander); Colonel Rufus Putnam—who had trod in Bernard Romans's footsteps years earlier as deputy surveyor for West Florida and was by now one of Washington's most dependable engineers; and, standing in for General Henry Knox, Captain Winthrop Sargent, a skilled artillery officer. "I have great reason," Washington wrote Stirling, "to think that the Fortifications in the Highlands are in a bad situation; and the garrison worse." He urged the group to recommend "such alterations as shall be judg'd necessary for putting them into a fit and proper Posture of defense."

Stirling preferred the new fortification site north of Popolopen Creek: "This appears to me to be the most proper Place I have seen on the River to be made the Grand Post, capable of resisting every kind of Attack." His report on Fort Constitution underscored all previous opinion and forever branded Bernard Romans's military engineering work along the Hudson as totally inadequate.

"The westernmost battery," Stirling asserted, "is a straight line constructed by Mr Romans at a very great expence; it has 15 Embrasures which face the river at a right angle, and can only annoy a ship going past." Although other parts of the completed fortification, Stirling continued, "look very neat and picturesque, upon the whole Mr Romans has displayed his genius to very little publick Advantage. The works in their present open condition and scattered situation are defenceless. Everything on the island is commanded by the Hill on the West Point."

Stirling was evenhandedly critical of the manner in which the Commissioners for Fortifications had discharged their own responsibilities—at *"eight hundred dollars a month,"* he stressed to Washington. "One good engineer, with artificers from the Army," he wrote, "might, I think, do the whole business as well."

Stirling's report, suggesting that some new Continental Army broom sweep the contested waterway clean, provided an adequate excuse for Washington—who, when it came to regional authority, always maintained a correct and remarkably effective political posture. He requested a committee from the New York Convention to wait on him; when they returned to the floor of the assembly, it was with a message from the Commander-in-chief that he "will not have occasion for the further service of the Commissioners, as he will take the sole direction of those Fortifications."

The legislators offered no argument. Romans's disappointing performance and the looming enemy invasion of New York City effectively transferred the primary defense of the Hudson River from civilian into military hands.

# CHAPTER II

# Bushnell's Submarine
## (1775–1776)

*In which a secretive Yankee genius trains his sights on the Royal Navy, and builds the world's first submarine to launch the world's first torpedo*

*IN* October 1775, exciting rumors were circulating through the revolutionary lines around Boston. A secret American weapon was being built at Saybrook, Connecticut. It would be brought to camp at Cambridge on a wagon. It could blow up all the British ships in Boston harbor.

At least one of those rumors was true. The object of all the revolutionary excitement—the world's first military submersible—was already undergoing "sea trials" in the Connecticut River. Dubbed *"The Water Machine,"* it was the dream of inventor David Bushnell, a frail and reclusive farmer's son from the west parish of Saybrook.

Bushnell, born August 30, 1740, was a late-blooming mechanical genius. Whenever he found himself free from farm chores, he would read any book he could find. Helping out on the farm barred him from advanced schooling. He was 30 years old when his father died, allowing Bushnell to take advantage of a tiny inheritance to leave the family farm. He boarded in town for two years with Saybrook's aptly-named Congregationalist pastor John Devotion, who tutored him for Yale.

The inventor was 35 and the oldest student in his class when he finally graduated from Yale, where he studied medicine, advanced mathematics and physical science. In his freshman year he demonstrated to a few skeptical instructors—"some personages in Connecticut," as he later called them—the practicality of exploding sizeable amounts of gunpowder under water, something not previously thought possible. Writing to Thomas Jefferson, then U.S. Minister to France, in 1787, Bushnell recalled his dramatic results:

"The first experiment I made was with about two ounces of Gunpowder, which I exploded four feet under water. The second was with two pounds of powder, inclosed in a wooden bottle and fixed under a hogshead, with a two-inch oak plank between the hogshead and the powder. The Hogshead was loaded with stones as deep as it could swim. A wooden tube descending through the lower head of the hogshead & through the plank into the powder contained in the Bottle, was primed with powder.

"A match put to the priming exploded the Powder with very great effect, rending the plank into pieces, demolishing the hogshead and casting the stones, ruins of the Hogshead, and a body of water many feet into the air, to the astonishment of the spectators. I afterwards made many experiments of a similar nature, some of them with large quantities of Powder. They all produced very violent explosions, much more than sufficient for the purpose I had in view."

Even in college, the purpose this deceptively quiet young man had in view was a military mine: he called it "a torpedo," after the stinging crampfish *Torpedinidae*. It was intended to blow hostile shipping out of the water, a dream of undersea warfare that went back eleven centuries to the days of Alexander the Great.

By June 1774 timely targets for such torpedoes had developed—the Royal Navy vessels blockading the port city of Boston. The young patriotic New Englander faced his great challenge—how to design and build a manned submersible, with room enough to permit its navigator to somehow place 150 pounds of gunpowder under the keel of a British warship.

Both at school in New Haven and at home in Saybrook 25 miles away, Bushnell worked closely with his younger brother Ezra to perfect both the submarine and its torpedo. During his senior year at Yale, demonstrating an always elegant mechanical logic, Bushnell came close to sawing, hammering and caulking together, not a working model, but the real thing, the world's first operational submarine.

Within this crude but effective military craft, a lone operator could dive, remain submerged, withstand underwater pressures, slowly steer a compass course, deliver a powerful explosive, and retire unscathed.

Instinctively developing many of the principles still used in contemporary undersea warfare, Bushnell soon found himself regarded as one of America's first great mechanical geniuses. If successful, his challenge to Britain's undisputed rule of North American coastal waters would offer the revolutionaries an incalculable military and political advantage. As an ingenious Yankee snook cocked at the hitherto invincible Royal Navy, Bushnell's revolutionary designs could not have been more perfectly timed.

The exciting news first went forth from Killingworth, Connecticut, ten miles west of Saybrook. On August 7, 1775 with a dispatch rider pacing by his door, Dr. Benjamin Gale—Yale '55—an eminent and inventive local physician whose devotion to science had already been rewarded with a Royal Society gold medal, dashed off a confidential account of Bushnell's efforts to the Great Philadelphia Experimenter, Benjamin Franklin.

"Your [Second Continental] Congress doubtless have heard intimations of the Invention of a new Machine for the Destruction of Ships of War. I now sit down to Give you an Acct of that Machine and what Experiments have Already been made with it. What I relate you may Intirely rely on to be fact.

"I will not at this Time attempt to Give You a Minute Description, as the Post is now Waiting. This Much—it does not Exceed 7 feet in Length, and the Depth not more than 5½ feet. The Person who Navigates it sits on a Bench in the Center of the machine. The Person who Invented it, a student of Yale College graduated this year, Lives within five Mile of me. I was the second Person who ever was permitted to see it, there being no other Workman but himself and his Brother.

"His plan," wrote Gale, "is to place the Cask containing the Powder on the outside of the Machine. It is so Contrived that when it strikes the Ship, which he proposes shall be at the Keil, it Grapples fast, and is wholly Disengag'd from the Machine. He then Rows off. The Powder is to be fired by a Gun Lock fixed within the Cask, which is sprung by Watch work, which he can so order as to have that take place at any Distance of Time he pleases.

"The experiments that has as Yet been Made," Gale scribbled hurriedly, "are as Follows. In the most Private Manner he Conveyd

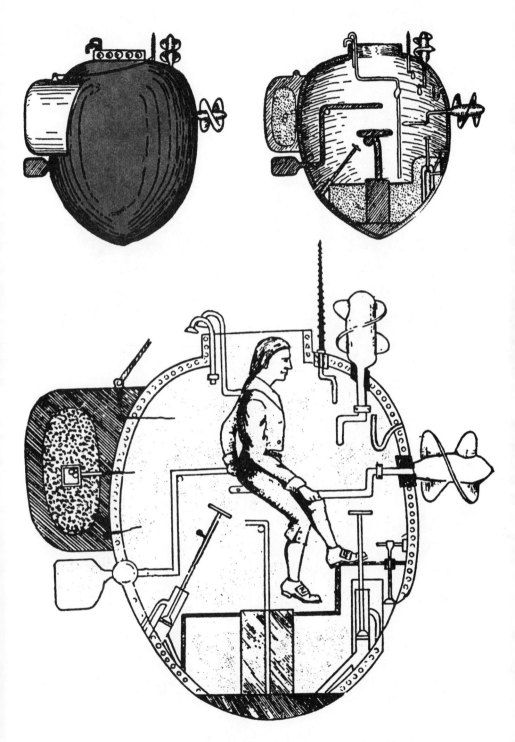

Early 19th century depictions of Bushnell's *American Turtle*.

Full-size operating replica of *Turtle* built 1976 by Fred Frese and Joseph
Leary [Connecticut River Foundation].

Full-sized operating replica of *Turtle* showing powder magazine (torpedo)
[Connecticut River Foundation].

*Turtle* exhibit at Essex Connecticut River Foundation, displaying Frank Tinsley's imaginative (1963) cutaway portrait of Sgt. Ezra Lee operating Bushnell's submarine.

it on Board a sloop In the Night, and went out into the [Long Island] Sound. He then sunk under Water, where he Continued about 45 minutes without any Inconveniency as to Breathing. He Can Row it either Backward or Forward Under water about 3 Miles an Hour, And can Steer to what Point of Compass he pleases. He Can Rise to the top of the Water at any Time he Pleases to obtain a fresh supply of air, when that is Exhausted.

"He has also a Machine prepar'd," Gale continued, "by which he can tell the depth under water, and can then admit water if it is needed to Bring the Machine into a perfect Equilibrium. He has also another Pair of Oars by which he Can Rowe it either up or Down, and a forcing Pump by which he Can free himself from the Water which he admits. At the Top he has a pair of Glass Eyes by which he sees Objects Under Water. I might add he has an Anchor which he Carries on the outside at Bottom of the Machine, by which he Can remain in Place to Wait for Tide Opportunity &c., and again Weigh it at Pleasure. The Whole machine may be Transported in a Cart.

"This story may Appear Romantic," Gale assured Franklin, "but thus far All these Experiments as above related have been Actually Made. He is now at New Haven with Mr. Isaac Doolittle, an Ingenious Mechanic in Clocks &c. [Doolittle constructed the first American printing press in 1769], making those Parts which Conveys the Powder, secures the same to the Bottom of the [enemy] Ship, and the Watchwork which fires it." Bushnell also arranged with Doolittle to fabricate his pumps.

"Give me Leave to Say, it is all Constructed with Great simplicity, and Upon Principles of Natural Philosophy, and I Conceive is not Equall'd by any thing I ever heard or saw. Except," Gale added quickly, "Dr. Franklins Electrical Experiments."

Gale also noted Bushnell's financing: "He Builds it on his own Acct. He was Urged to Ask some Assistance from the Government, but so Inconsiderable a sum was Offered that he refused it, and says he will go through with it at his own Risque. The Only Objections in my Mind is that he Cannot see under Water so perfectly as to fix it right, and whether 100 Weight of Powder will force its way through a ship. I fear the Water will give way before the Bottom of the ship, and the force of the Explosion Eluded." Gale's fear, subsequently shared by Franklin, was groundless.

"I have been Long Urging him for permission to Acquaint You with these facts," Gale concluded, "He at Length has Consented—

with this Condition, that I request You would not Mention the Affair Untill he has made all his Experiments, before he goes with it down to Boston. He is Quite Certain he Can Effect the thing, and his reasoning so Philosophical and Answering every Objection I ever made, that In truth I have great relyance upon it."

Impressed by Gale's glowing description, Franklin asked the Connecticut Congressman Silas Deane to get him more information about the secretive inventor. "I shall be curious to hear Particulars of your new mechanical Genius," he told Deane. En route to a meeting with Washington at Cambridge in October, Franklin took a moment to stop at Killingworth and see Gale. He suggested further experiments with Bushnell's underwater explosions.

But Poor Richard was never closemouthed. News of his Killingworth visit leaked out in Cambridge and rumors began to fly. Samuel Osgood wrote enthusiastically to John Adams in Philadelphia: "The Famous Water Machine from Connecticut is every Day expected in Camp; it must unavoidably be a clumsy Business, as its Weight is about a Tun. I wish it might succeed, and the enemy Ships be blown up beyond the Attraction of the Earth; it is the only Way or Chance they have for reaching St. Peter's Gate."

On November 9 Gale wrote a long letter directly to Deane, assuming that before long "the machine will be in camp. Lately," said Gale, noting Bushnell's not uncommon inventor's paranoia, "he has conducted matters and his Designs with the greatest secrecy, both for the personal safety of the Navigator, and to produce the greatest astonishment to those against whom it is designed."

Gale's letter offered Deane an additional description of the submarine: "The body, when standing upright in the position in which it is navigated, has the nearest resemblance to the two upper shells of a Tortoise joined together." Before long a popular name would be attached to the craft—the *American Turtle*.

"The person who navigates it enters at the top," Gale explained, "It has a brass Top or cover, which receives the person's head as he sits on the seat, and is fastened on the inside by screws. In this brass head is fixed eight Glasses, viz. two before, two on each side, one behind, and one to look upwards.

"In the same head are fixed two brass tubes, to admit fresh air when requisite, and a ventilator at the side to free the Machine from the air rendered unfit for respiration." The two airpipes worked like a modern skindiver's snorkel tube, "so constructed"—Bushnell wrote later to Jefferson—"that they shut themselves, whenever the Water rose near their tops" as *Turtle* descended beneath the surface.

"On the inside," Gale continued, "is fixed a Compass, by which the operator knows the course he steers. In the needles of the compass is fixed 'fox fire,' the [rotting phosphorescent] wood that gives light in the dark. The ballast consists of about 900 wt. of Lead, which he carries at the bottom and on the outside of the machine, part of which is so fixed as he can let run down to the Bottom, and serves as an anchor, by which he can ride *ad libitum*.

"In the bow, he has a pair of oars fixed like the two opposite arms of a wind mill, with which he can row forward; and turning them the opposite way, backward. Another pair can row the machine round, either to the right or left; and a third, either up or down [a pioneer use of the screw propeller]. The Rudder by which he steers he manages by hand, within board. All these shafts which pass through the machine are so curiously fix'd as not to admit water."

Gale moved next to the most important part of the inventor's design: "The magazine for the powder is carried without board on the hinder part of the machine, and so contrived that when he comes under the side of a Ship, he rubs down the side until he comes to the keel, and a hook [actually a long thin auger] is so fix'd that when it touches the Keil, it raises a spring which frees the magazine from the machine and fastens it to the side of the Ship. At the same time, it draws a pin which sets the watchwork agoing, which at a given time, springs the lock, and the explosion ensues."

Gale told Deane how Bushnell was preparing torpedoes to place under three different British ships in Boston harbor, each timed to go off in staggered order to increase the enemy's panic. Thanks to the new underwater experiments suggested by Franklin, "[Bushnell] is now convinced," Gale said, "that his magazines contain three times so much powder as is necessary to destroy the largest Ship in the navy.

"That this projection succeeds I make no doubt," promised Gale, "as I well know the man, and have seen the machine while in embryo. Every addition to it fills me with fresh astonishment and surprize. You may call me a visionary, an enthusiast, or what you please—I do insist upon it that the Almighty has given [Bushnell] understanding for this very Purpose and design. If he succeeds, he should receive a stipend for life; and if he fails, a reasonable compensation for time and expenses is his due from the public."

Good wartime news often travels too fast; Deane's Congressional security was quickly breached. On November 16, only six days after

Gale sent his letter, James Brattle, personal valet to New York Congressman James Duane—and a British spy—conveyed a ciphered message from Philadelphia to New York's Royal Governor Tryon, now fled aboard the British merchantman *Duchess of Gordon* lying in New York harbor.

"The great news of the day with us," confided Brattle, "is how to Destroy the Navy. A certain Mr. Bushnel has compleated his Machine, and has been missing four weeks, returned this day week. It is conjectur'd that an attempt was made on the *Asia* [a British warship in Upper Bay], but proved unsuccessful—Returned to New Haven in order to get a Pump of a new Construction which will soon be completed—When you may expect to see the Ships in Smoke."

Most of that espionage, immediately passed by Tryon to Vice-Admiral Molyneaux Shuldham, was inaccurate; Bushnell and his brother were still busy testing their little craft off Ayer's Point on the Connecticut River. A week later—on the same day that Bernard Romans fired off his last angry letter to the Commissioners of Fortification along the Hudson River—Dr. Gale again contacted Deane: "At the time of my last writing, I supposed the Machine was gone; but since find the forcing pump made by Mr. Doolittle, not being made according to the order given, did not answer.

"Few," Gale noted, "know [except the spy Brattle] the cause of [Bushnell's] present delay. He sets off this day with his new constructed pump, in order to test the navigation, and if not prevented by ice in the River, will proceed soon. He is by no means discouraged in the attempt."

One tiny but crucial difficulty now arose to postpone the entire project. On a cold December 7 Gale wrote again to Deane: "Every trial respecting navigation answers well, but still fails on one account. [Bushnell] proposes going in the night, on account of safety. He always depends on fox-wood which gives light in the dark, to fix on the points of the needle of his Compass and in his barometer, by which he may know what course to steer and the depth he is under water, both of which are an absolute necessity for the safety of the navigator.

"But he now finds that the Frost wholly destroys that quality in that wood; of which he was before ignorant, and for that reason and that alone he is obliged to desist."

Gale was embarrassed both for himself and Bushnell: "I write you this that you and those to whom you may have communicated what

I wrote may not think I have imposed on you an idle story." He appealed to Deane to seek immediate help from Franklin: "Can you enquire whether he knows of any kind of Phosphorus which would give light in the dark and not consume the air? [Bushnell] tried a candle, but that destroys the air so fast he cannot remain under water long enough." Gale had heard that Franklin had experimented with the bioluminescent phenomena of certain glowing fungi and mushrooms.

"The inventor," Gale continued, "now makes all his affairs a secret, even to his best friend. I have liberty only to communicate this much from him, with a view to know if Dr. Franklin knows of any kind of Phosphorus that will answer his purpose. Otherwise the attempt must be omitted until next spring, after the frosts are past. I am therefore to request your strictest silence in the matter."

*IMMOBILIZED FOR* the remainder of the winter by this unexpected turn of events, Bushnell's response was to become more reclusive than ever. His submarine concepts were already too widely circulated in Congress. In the pre-patent era, many enterprising American artisans were quick to appropriate the ideas of others. For example, two weeks into 1776 Captain Daniel Joy, while suggesting to Pennsylvania's Committee of Safety new ways to help defend the Delaware River, concluded a long letter to Samuel Howell with a proposal to duplicate what he had learned indirectly about Bushnell's invention:

"I think an Engin may be made with Copper & Glass Windows (Bulls Eys) in it, properly Ballast'd, so as a man may convey himself (by the help of a compass & a Candle lighted the first to direct him to his object, the other to let him know when he wants a supply of air), under a Man of War's Bottom, & to take with him two or three vessels, charged with 2 or 3 hundred wt of Gunpowder—These vessels to have machinery Locks that may be sett to any time, & on the upper part a pair of Jaws (to go by a spring) large enough to receive a Man of War's kiel.

"Then to proceed," Joy continued unabashed, "unto two other Men of War, leveing one at each. Then to proceed on shore—when the first blowes up it will be looked upon as an accident, the second will cause doubts, and the third confusion.

"If any of the above hints proves of any advantage to the Publick," Joy wound up solicitously, "I shall be happy in executing it, and shall not think my time spent in vain." It was all sufficient justification for Bushnell's increasing silence about his tests with *Turtle*. The inventor would have been more upset had he known that one of his former Yale tutors was already telling friends ("secretly" of course—*in Latin*) about Bushnell's tiny submarine.

Even on February 2, 1776 when influential Governor "Brother Jonathan" Trumbull—the only colonial governor to support the revolutionary cause at the start of the war—invited the inventor to review his progress with the Connecticut Council of Safety, Bushnell first extracted a condition of secrecy. The meeting ended on a positive note; the group agreed to reward Bushnell for his trouble and expense.

"We approve of his plan," the Council stated, "it appearing to be a work of great ingenuity &c., and a prospect that it may be attended with success. It will be agreeable to have him proceed to make every necessary Preparation and Experiment about it, with expectation of proper public notice and reward." The following day the State of Connecticut secretly voted Bushnell £60 to continue his work.

That same week, an increasingly conspiratorial Gale pleaded with Deane to search harder for a foxfire replacement. "With regard to the matter of principal concern," he wrote, "if the Philosopher's Lanthorn may be attained, and will give a better light than what is proposed, I would be glad you would get what knowledge you can from Dr. Franklin. You will well understand my meaning if I am not more explicit."

All this unexpected inaction must have proved a burden to Ezra Bushnell. On March 10 he signed aboard the Massachusetts privateer *Defence* as surgeon's mate—but after a single successful voyage he left the ship and returned to assist his brother.

FROM Boston on March 17, completely outmaneuvered by the surreptitiously-emplaced revolutionary cannon on Dorchester Heights, 11,000 British troops (plus 1,000 loyalist supporters with their few salvaged possessions) began to board royal transports. Only the ships' captains knew whether they were bound for New York—or would sail north to regroup at Halifax. Within a single week there were no more British merchantmen or warships left in Boston harbor; Bushnell's long-stalked prey had suddenly disappeared.

But the inventor was confident that another naval opportunity would soon present itself. Welcoming back his brother Ezra as operator, Bushnell continued to test the tiny submersible, "taking care, before I trusted any person to descend much below the surface, to prove its strength to sustain the great pressures of the Incumbent water.

"I never suffered any person to go under water," Bushnell insisted, "without having a strong Piece of rigging made fast to it, until I found him well acquainted with the operations necessary for his safety, and sufficiently expert to put my design into execution. I found it required many trials to make a person of common ingenuity a skilful Operator [Bushnell himself lacked the brawn and endurance to propel his tiny submarine]. The first I employed was very ingenious and made himself master of the business." Writing that sentence a decade later, the inventor was still not ready to identify the operator as his own brother.

*BY JULY,* the seat of war had shifted south from New England to New York harbor. Less than nine months after George III advised Parliament—"I have the satisfaction to inform you that I have received the most friendly offers of foreign assistance"—Royal Navy transports off Staten Island began debarking not only General William Howe with a huge body of troops, but 8,000 mercenary *"Hessians"* from the German principalities of Hesse-Cassel, Hesse-Hanau, Brunswick, Waldeck, and Anhalt-Zerbst.

Within days, news of their friendly reception by Staten Island residents reached Congress in Philadelphia. "The inhabitants," wrote Maryland delegate Thomas Stone to his state's Council of Safety, "are generally tories, who I suppose will assist [Howe] all they can." John Adams was much less restrained: "The unprincipled, and unfeeling, and unnatural inhabitants of Staten Island are cordially receiving the Enemy. They are an ignorant, cowardly Pack of Scoundrells."

Later that month, eyeing the mass of British sail now filling New York harbor, a skeptical George Washington reluctantly succumbed to importuning from Governor Trumbull and Connecticut's General Israel Putnam, and agreed to permit David Bushnell to hoist his strange "Water Machine" aboard a sloop in Saybrook and bring it down through Long Island Sound to try to assist the outnumbered Continental Army around New York.

To defend the city and the Hudson River from the British—and their thousands of German mercenaries, worth "blood money" to their princes of $35 dead or $12 maimed—Washington was now willing to try undersea warfare. Bushnell, his *Turtle*, and the rewarmed foxfire would finally have their chance.

Arriving in New York early in August, the inventor found the city in turmoil. Not only did "a formidable British fleet—vessells of all size amounting to over 300—lying in New-york bay a little above the Narrows, threaten annihilation to the troops under Washington," Bushnell wrote, but two enemy frigates had already pushed upriver to threaten the revolutionary rear. At this moment, to Bushnell's great distress, his brother Ezra "took sick, before he had an opportunity to make use of his skill."

The inventor begged Brigadier General Samuel Parsons, former member of Connecticut's Council of Safety, for two or three men who could learn how to navigate his cramped little vessel. Parsons supplied three fire ship volunteers for the dangerous service. They included a second Ezra—Ezra Lee, a short, stocky 27-year-old sergeant in the 5th Connecticut Regiment.

Thus Lee became the second man to operate the world's first military submersible. But it was one thing for Ezra Bushnell to propel *Turtle* through the rippling waters of the lower Connecticut River—and quite another for Sergeant Lee to navigate it in the swirling tides of New York harbor.

Lee tells the story: "The party went up into the Sound [via the East River], and on our way practised with the machine in several harbors—We returned as far back as Say-brook with Mr. Bushnell, where some little alterations were made on it, in the course of which time (it being 8 or 10 days) the British had got possession of Long Island and Governor's Island." On the night of August 29, faced with the prospect of annihilation after a disastrous defeat in Brooklyn, Washington withdrew his entire army to New York, and left the entire East River under British control.

"We went back as far as New Rochelle," says Lee, "and had [*Turtle*] carted over by land to the North [Hudson] River." On September 5 General Parsons wrote Major General William Heath, commanding at Kingsbridge in lower Westchester County: "The Machine designed to attempt blowing Up the Enemy's Ships is to be transported from the East to the North River, where a Small Vessel will be wanted to transport it. I wish you to order One for that Purpose. As all Things are now ready to make the Experiment, I wish it may not be delayed. Tho' the Event is uncertain," Parsons asserted, "under our present Circumstances, it is certainly worth trying." On the night of September 6, 1776 the world had its first taste of submarine warfare.

*LEE CONTINUES* the account—here interpolated with the inventor's own wistful comments: "The first night after we got down to New York was favourable (the time for a trial must be when it is slack water & calm, as it is unmanageable in a swell or a strong tide). The British Fleet lay a little above Staten Island. We set off from the City—the Whale boats towed me as nigh the ships as they dared to go, and then cast me off.

"I soon found that it was too early in the tide, as it carried me by the ships-—I however hove about, and rowed for 5 glasses (by the ships' bells) before the tide slacked, so that I could get along side of the man of war, which lay above the transports—The Moon was about 2 hours high, and the daylight about one, when I rowed under the stern of the ship."

Lee's quarry, the 64-gun ship of the line and fleet flagship *H.M.S. Eagle*, anchored just below Bedloe's Island and commanded by Captain John Hunter, was the largest of the two dozen British war vessels in New York harbor. Aboard was Viscount Richard Howe, the General's brother and commander of the British North American Squadron. Says Lee, "I could see the men on deck & hear them talk—I then shut down all the doors, sunk down, and came under the bottom of the ship—Up with the screw against the bottom, but found that it would not enter."

*Bushnell: "He went under the Ship and attempted to fix the Woodscrew in her bottom, but struck, as he supposes, a bar of iron which passes from the rudder hinge and is spiked under the Ship's quarter. Had he moved a few inches, which he might have done without rowing, I have no doubt but he would have found wood, where he might have fixed the screw; or if the Ship were sheathed with copper, he might easily have pierced it."*

"I pulled along to try another place," says Lee, "but deviated a little one side, and immediately rose with great velocity and come above the surface 2 or 3 feet between the ship and the daylight— then sunk again like a porpoise."

*Bushnell: "Not being well skilled in the management of the Vessel, in attempting to move to another place, he lost the Ship. After seeking her in vain for some time, he rowed some distance and rose to the surface of the water, but found daylight had advanced so far that he durst not renew the attempt. He says that he could have easily fastened the Magazine under the Stern of the Ship, above water, as he rowed up to the stern and touched it before he descended. Had he fastened it there, the explosion of one hundred and fifty pounds of powder, the quantity contained in the Magazine, must have been fatal to the Ship."*

"I hove partly about to try again," Lee continues, "but on further thought I gave out, knowing that as soon as it was light, the ships boats would be rowing in all directions, and I thought the best generalship was to retreat as fast as I could, as I had 4 miles to go [actually only 1½ miles—13 cable lengths] before passing Governor's Island.

"So I jogged on as fast as I could, and my compass being then of no use to me, I was obliged to rise up every few minutes to see that I sailed in the right direction, for this purpose keeping the Machine on the surface of the water and the doors open—I was much afraid of getting aground on the island, my course was very crooked & zig zag, and the enemy's attention was drawn to me.

"When I was abreast of the fort on the island, 300 or 400 men got upon the Parapet to observe me—at length a number came down to the shore, shoved off a 12 oar'd barge with 5 or 6 sitters, and pull'd for me—I eyed them, and when they had got within 50 or 60 yards of me, I let loose the magazine, in hopes that if they should take me, they would likewise pick up the magazine, and then we should all be blown up together."

*Bushnell: "Upon his return to N. York, he passed near Governor's Island and thought he was discovered by the enemy on the Island. Being in haste to avoid the danger he feared, he cast off the magazine, as he imagined it retarded him in the swell, which was very considerable."*

"As kind Providence would have it," Lee concludes, "the enemy took fright and returned to the island, to my infinite joy. I then weathered the Island, and our people seeing me, came off with a whaleboat and towed me in." The torpedo, its clockwork still ticking, drifted slowly north into the East River.

An hour later, while Lee was still recounting the reasons for his failure to a chagrined Bushnell, the torpedo suddenly "went off with a tremendous explosion, throwing up large bodies of water to an immense height," to the consternation of the British, but to the great satisfaction of all the revolutionaries—except Bushnell, who bemoaned the loss of a precious torpedo, and the fact that the enemy had now been alerted to his new weapon.

Forty years later, Sergeant Lee—serving as U.S. Customs inspector in Hartford—recounted how General Israel Putnam, a firm *Turtle* enthusiast, had left his quarters in the mayor's mansion at No. 1 Broadway to witness the underwater operation from a nearby Battery wharf. At the explosion, recalled Lee, the general was "vastly pleased, and cried out in his picular way—'God's curse 'em, that'll do it for 'em.'" It was a tiny compensation for the army's fearful loss a week and a half earlier on Long Island.

WITHIN NINE days of Bushnell's abortive attack, the revolutionary army was again outflanked by the enemy and driven out of New York City. But first *Turtle* was safely towed up the Hudson to a point on the shore just below the newly completed Fort Washington. On October 5 against strong river tides, Bushnell relaunched Sergeant Lee on another mission. The target this time was an enemy frigate anchored off Bloomingdale [present-day West 110th Street]— probably *H.M.S. Phoenix,* preparing to run Fort Washington's defenses for the second time that summer. To avoid any possibility of difficulty with copper sheathing on the warship's bottom, Lee tried "a new plan—to go under the ship's stern, and screw on the Magazine close to the water's edge [the backup procedure Bushnell wished that Lee had attempted on *Eagle*]."

"But," says Lee, "I was discovered by the Watch, and obliged to abandon the scheme. Shutting my doors, I dove under her, but my cork in the tube (by which I ascertained my depth) got obstructed and deceived me. I descended too deep & did not track the ship, and I left her.

"Soon after," Lee continues, "the Frigate came up the river, drove our galley on shore, and sunk our sloop." That event was noted by General Heath in his memoirs: "The enemy sunk a sloop which had on board the machine invented by Mr. Bushnell, intended to blow up British ships. Its fate," the general commented wryly, "was truly a contrast to its design."

The British reported that although "a Lieut. and 2 men went aboard" the sunken sloop, they did not recognize the submarine as a potent enemy weapon. Within days, the tenacious Bushnell was able to salvage *Turtle* from the sunken sloop. The little vessel, however, saw no further action and its eventual fate is unknown.

"I found it impossible to prosecute the design any further," the inventor explained to Thomas Jefferson in 1787, "I had been in a bad State of health from the beginning of my undertaking, and was now very unwell." In addition, Bushnell complained, "the situation of public affairs was such that I despaired of obtaining the public attention and assistance necessary. I was unable to support myself and the persons I must have employed had I proceeded. Beside, I found it absolutely necessary that the operators should acquire more skill in the management of the Vessel, before I could expect success. This would have taken up some time," he said, "and made no small additional expence. I therefore gave over the pursuit, and waited for a more favourable opportunity, which never arrived."

Last word on the 1775 underwater episodes belongs to the Commander-in-chief. From Mt. Vernon a decade later, Washington replied to Jefferson's request for more information on Bushnell's many wartime "projects for the destruction of shipping," but warned the new Minister to France that "my memory being treacherous, I may, in some measure, be mistaken in what I am about to relate.

"Bushnell came to me in 1776," the General recounted, "recommended by Governor Trumbull and other respectable characters who were proselites to his plan—Although I wanted faith myself, I furnished him with money and other aids to carry it into Execution—He laboured for some time ineffectually, & though the advocates for his scheme continued sanguine, he never did succeed—One accident or another was always intervening.

"I then thought and still think," Washington noted candidly, "that while it was an effort of genius, a combination of too many things were requisite to expect much from an enemy who are always upon guard." The General conceded the potential of Bushnell's design, "facts which I believe admit of little doubt." But, he added realistically, "it is no easy matter to get a person hardy enough to encounter the variety of dangers to which he must be exposed, 1. from the novelty, 2. from the difficulty of conducting the machine and governing it under water, on acct. of the Currents &ca., 3. the consequent uncertainty of hitting the object of destination, without rising frequently above the water for fresh observation, wch., when near the Vessel, would expose the adventurer to discovery & almost certain death.

"To these causes," Washington apologetically ended his letter to Jefferson, "I always ascribed the non-performance of his plan, as he wanted nothing that I could furnish to secure the support of it."

Bushnell's was not the only secret plan offered to a Commander-in-chief literally plagued by "non-performance." Many less effective Yankee geniuses were constantly "petitioning the Congress for encouragement to destroy the enemy's ships of war by some Contrivances of their Invention"—so wrote Benjamin Franklin to Washington about another inventor, Joseph Belton, less than a month before Sergeant Lee's first attempt in *Turtle*.

Franklin's note introduced Belton to Washington as "a very ingenious Man, now desirious of trying his hand on the ships that have gone up the North River." Equally Important to the thrifty Franklin was an offer from Belton "to work entirely at his own expense, only desiring your Countenance and Permission. I could not refuse this line of introduction to you, and hope his Project may be attended with Success." History tells us nothing of Washington's response—and little more on Joseph Belton.

Despite his operational reservations about *Turtle*, Washington was still willing to acknowledge Bushnell as an inventive genius. When the Corps of Sappers and Miners was formed in August 1779, the Commander-in-chief arranged a commission for Bushnell as one of its three captain-lieutenants. Two years later Bushnell was promoted to captain, and played a role in the siege at Yorktown. By the end of the war he had advanced far enough to command the Corps of Engineers at West Point.

His later years were purposely obscure. He was mustered out of the Continental Army in 1783 after joining the fraternal Society of the Cincinnati—that group of veteran Revolutionary officers who, with Washington as their president, named themselves after the illustrious Roman who twice abandoned his farm to help save the empire.

In 1794, with Bushnell presumed dead (he actually lived until 1826, calling himself *"Dr. Bush"*) Timothy Dwight, president of Yale, composed a long poem on the rising glory of America, in which the former Continental Army chaplain voiced an eloquent if premature eulogy of the gifted inventor who had been his schoolmate at Yale:

> *See Bushnell's strong, creative genius, fraught*
> *With all th' assembled powers of skilful thought,*
> *His mystic vessel plunge beneath the waves*
> *And glide thro' dark retreats, and coral caves!*

But there were no dangerous coral shores that could help defend the Hudson River; the revolutionaries were forced to invent their own unique reefs to frustrate an aggressive enemy.

CHAPTER III

# Fort Washington's
# *Chevaux-de-Frise*
# (1776)

*In which the revolutionaries build two additional forts and a new version of a hundred-year-old Dutch weapon, to keep the British Navy from ascending the Hudson River.*

THROUGHOUT THE early summer of 1776, as Washington uneasily awaited the arrival of the British fleet in New York harbor, he kept his ten thousand "ragged boys" occupied with pick and shovel, throwing up widely scattered earthworks across lower Manhattan, and on the heights of Brooklyn across the East River. Anticipating a possible enemy landing on the Battery, which the revolutionaries feared might turn Fort George into a "Citadel to keep the Town in subjection," the inland-looking northeast and northwest bastions of that stronghold were completely demolished.

Once the enemy fleet appeared, it seemed clear that naval control of the waters around New York, in particular Upper Bay and the lower Hudson River, would pass to the British. During the last week of June, the Commander-in-chief apparently confided to Reverend William Gordon that "at least 2,000" troops were still "destitute of arms, and near as many with arms in such condition as to be rather calculated to discourage than animate the user." Nevertheless,

Congress insisted the city be defended. Washington's men kept loose order among 20,000 New York residents of sharply divided political sympathies. Hardheaded Connecticut revolutionary Isaac Sears had predicted that the coming of spring would see half the population of New York City turn against the Continentals. Nevertheless, the army continued to lay out fields of cannon fire that would make an amphibious enemy attack on Manhattan as costly as possible.

Congress had earlier detached General Charles Lee of Virginia from the siege of Boston to undertake some professional organization of New York's defenses. Lee was a revolutionary volunteer who had been a British major, a colonel in the Portugese army, and an aide-de-camp to the King of Poland. At the moment, the experienced but quixotic Lee was outranked only by Washington and cantankerous Massachusetts General Artemas Ward. Thirty months later—after insubordination, capture, exchange, and further insubordination—Lee would be court-martialed and suspended from the revolutionary army. At this moment, however, he was riding high—although he confessed he found his Congressional assignment baffling.

"What to do with the City, I own, puzzles me," Lee wrote in frustration to Philadelphia on February 19, 1776, "It is so encircled with deep navigable Waters that whoever commands the Sea must command the Town." While Lee was willing to acknowledge that Manhattan's narrow interior lines offered a potentially strong field of battle, "so advantageous it must cost the Enimy many thousands of men," the island's 30 miles of irregular shoreline exposed the city lying at its southern tip to unpredictable British assault, and made it an essentially untenable fortress.

Despite such misgivings, in less than three weeks Lee prepared a complex military plan that included new forts on both sides of the East River at Hell Gate. It also called for erecting a battery at Catherine and Cherry Streets; a stronger work just above it on Rutgers Hill; another at Coenties Slip, below Wall Street; a chain of redoubts thrown up on Jones's and Bayard's hills, and at Lispenard's House on the Hudson River, with "the whole Island redoubted in certain regular steps quite to Kings Bridge." Lee also planned heavy barricades on all the important roads leading inland from the river, plus a breastwork around King's College—already serving as a military hospital.

Lee advised Congress that King's Bridge—at the far tip of

Manhattan Island 14 miles north of the Battery—should be strongly fortified to maintain free and open communication with Connecticut, "on which Province," he counseled, "you can alone depend for succours of men, for the Breadth and depth of the North [Hudson] River renders the Communication with Jersey too precarious. The possession and security of Long Island," the general added, "is certainly of still greater importance than New York."

By then Congress had decided on another transfer for Lee—to Charleston, where he was placed in command of the Southern Department. Responsibility for implementing his New York defense plans devolved on General Lord Stirling. Washington wrote Stirling to complete the initial work as quickly as possible, paying special attention to fortifications along the Hudson River.

*NINE MONTHS* earlier, as we have seen, the New York Provincial Congress took first steps to defend the waterway by ordering its four-man committee to sound the Hudson from New York City to New Windsor, 50 miles upriver. On October 7, 1775 the Continental Congress requested further suggestions on the most effective way to obstruct navigation on the river, but there was no immediate response.

That lack of political coordination was hardly surprising; only a tiny handful of revolutionaries barely qualified as engineering officers, and none of them possessed the skills required for the desperate concept of blocking a huge river. Their contributions could only be guesswork—with some brilliant improvisation.

So by June 1776 the best the New York Congress could offer Philadelphia was the following committee report: "Obstructing the navigation of Hudson's river, although a difficult and laborious undertaking, is nevertheless in our opinion practicable, an Object worthy of public attention, and proper to be submitted to the consideration of His Excellency George Washington."

During the first week of July, the revolutionaries began work on two important artillery positions 11 miles north of the Battery. The posts were on cliffs on either side of the Hudson, where the river is more than 3,000 feet wide (those matching heights now serve as anchorages for the George Washington Bridge). To honor the Commander-in-chief, the 220-foot-high eminence on the east bank was christened *"Mount Washington."*

Pausing only to read the freshly-printed Declaration of Independence to his revolutionary troops, Colonel Rufus Putnam,

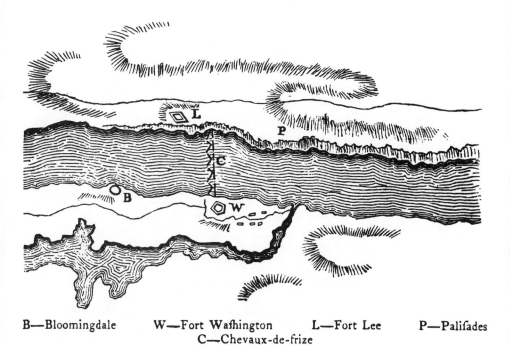

B—Bloomingdale     W—Fort Waſhington     L—Fort Lee     P—Paliſades
C—Chevaux-de-frize

Sketch map of revolutionary defenses at Forts Washington and Lee (1860).

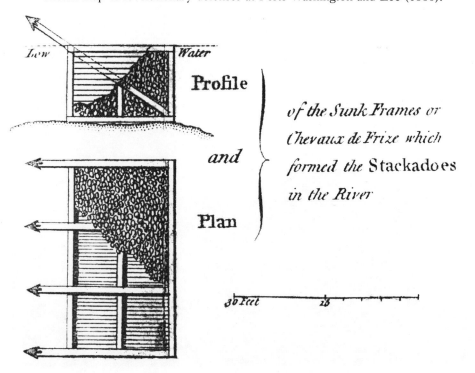

Profile

and

Plan

*of the Sunk Frames or Chevaux de Frize which formed the* Stackadoes *in the River*

William Faden's sketch of a revolutionary *cheval-de-frise* (London, 1779).
[*Low Water* line belongs above iron "beak."]

Washington's August 17, 1776 handbill urging evacuation of women and children from New York City.

By His EXCELLENCY

## GEORGE WASHINTON, Efquire

General, and Commander in Chief of the Army
of the United States of North-America.

WHEREAS a Bombardment and Attaek
upon the City of New-York, by our cruel,
and inveterate Enemy, may be hourly expected:
And as there are great Numbers of Women,
Children, and infirm Perfons, yet remaining in
the City, whofe Continuance will rather be prejudicial than advantageous to the Army, and their,
Perfons expofed to great Danger and Hazard:
I Do therefore recommend it to all fuch Perfons,
as they value their own fafety and Prefervation,
to remove with all expedition, out of the faid
Town, at this critical Period,—trufting, that with
the Bleffing of Heaven upon the American Arms,
they may foon return to it in perfect Security.
And I do enjoin and require, all the Officers and
Soldiers in the Army, under my Command, to
forward and affift fuch Perfons in their Compliance with this Recommendation.

GIVEN under my Hand, at Head-Quarters, New-York,
Auguft 17, 1776.

### GEORGE WASHINGTON.

NEW-YORK,—Printed by JOHN HOLT,-in Water-Street.

Dominique Serres's 1779 *The Forcing of the Hudson River Passage, Oct. 9,
1776;* the river is unrealistically narrow [U.S. Naval Academy Museum].

now acting Chief Engineer of the Continental Army, laid out the necessary lines on both sides of the river for three fortifications with outworks. The fort on the east side, also named after Washington, was rapidly shoveled up and garrisoned by the men of Colonel John Shee's and Colonel Robert Magaw's 3rd and 5th Pennsylvania Regiments.

Despite its massive appearance, this pentagonal earthwork, lacking a ditch, casemates, palisades, and a barracks, represented a surprising departure from the elements of traditional military design. Making matters worse was the lack of drinking water atop Mount Washington, while all working water for the fort had to be carried in buckets from the salty Hudson, a backbreaking climb more than 200 feet straight up over rocky cliffs. Control of the strong point was dangerously dependent on control of the surrounding area.

Argument arose. If and when the British army pushed its way up Manhattan Island, could this east shore fort withstand a massive enemy assault? Repeated councils of war listened to Washington's openly expressed misgivings, but continued to vote with Generals Nathanael Greene and Israel Putnam, who considered the new post impregnable.

Additional fortifications were under construction on the opposite 300-foot Palisades cliff in New Jersey. One was called *"Fort Constitution."* The other, nearer the river, was named *"Fort Lee"* (the name persists today)—honoring the still untested revolutionary general. The new *Fort Constitution* soon created confusion with Bernard Romans's similarily-named work 40 miles upriver; within four months, *both* Jersey fortifications were denoted *"Fort Lee."*

*WASHINGTON, MEANWHILE,* occupied himself with a new defensive Hudson River strategy. On June 13 he advised John Hancock in Philadelphia that, with the cooperation of the New York Provincial Congress, he soon would begin sinking a series of *cheval-de-frise* in the river, "one of which is already begun."

These *chevaux-de-frise*—"Frisian horses"—were an offshoot of the traditional military abbatis. They were ingenious shallow-water obstructions cleverly adapted by the revolutionaries from a century-old Dutch anti-cavalry device, to fill gaps in a line of hulks to be sunk across the Hudson River from Fort Washington to Fort Lee.

*Chevaux-de-frise* were originally developed on land by the northern provinces of the Spanish Netherlands during their war of independence against foreign domination. Lacking cavalry mounts, soldiers and civilians in the province of Friesland—which coincidentally became on February 26, 1782 the first of the seven Dutch provinces to formally recognize the United States of America—devised bulwarks of protective timbers linked by chains, with projecting iron spears. These heavy contrivances were wrestled into position to protect the province's narrow village streets and fortified gaps from Spanish cavalry charges.

After Bunker Hill, similar land defenses against marauding British dragoons were improvised by the revolutionary infantry guarding the neck between Boston and Roxbury—and would later be used by the British to protect their own evacuation of the city.

The apparent success of such roadblocks led Philadelphia carpenter Richard Smith to develop an ingenious design for a similar *cheval-de-frise*—underwater. He presented his plans to Benjamin Franklin and the Pennsylvania Committee of Safety on July 24, 1775. The submerged river channel obstacles, Smith argued, could prove effective against even good-sized ships; they would help the revolutionaries adjust some badly lopsided naval odds.

Patriot strategy was to place a line of *chevaux-de-frise* "cassoons"—so-called from the sunken caisssons in which the pointed spears were fixed—across an apparent channel, with their iron picks (or pikes) hidden two or three feet below the surface of the river at low tide. The true channel was blocked by hulks scuttled end to end, with a secret gap left open for passage of friendly vessels.

Maneuvering around properly located *chevaux-de-frise* required some delicate navigation. Attacked head-on, the obstruction would rake and even open the bottom of a hard-driving vessel, making it an easy target for shore batteries.

One British officer carefully described the revolutionaries' initial Delaware River obstructions: "This kind of *Chevaux de Frise* consists of a large timber, like the main mast of a Ship, at the top of which are three branches, armed and pointed with Iron, spreading out fanwise 15 foot asunder. The main boom is fixt at an elevation to the frame of a float or stage composed of vast Logs, bound together as fast as possible; then covered with plank to top and caulked.

"When this Machine is towed to its place," the officer continued, "it is loaded with about 30 tuns of stones secured in cases, which by taking the Plugs out of the deck to admit the water into the float, sinks it down and keeps it firm and steady. It then makes this appearance in profile: the points of the Branches six or seven feet under the surface of the Water, and spread in front 30 feet. A row of these *chevaux de frise* are sunk 60 feet asunder from each other, and another row behind to form a range."

Indestructible Joseph Plumb Martin—a foot soldier from Connecticut later nicknamed *"Private Yankee Doodle"* for his record of fighting through the entire Revolution—witnessed at least one early Delaware demonstration, against the ill-fated *H.M.S. Augusta.* Sailing upriver a few miles below Philadelphia, that 64-gun British ship-of-the-line found herself hooked on *chevaux-de-frise* sunk to guard what Martin called "that Burlesque upon the art of Fortification," Fort Mifflin.

"As soon as she was discovered in the morning," Martin recounts, "we plied her so well with Hot shot that she was soon in flames. Boats were sent from the shipping below to her assistance, but our shot proving too hot for them, they were obliged to leave her to her fate. In an hour or so she blew up, with an Explosion that seemed to shake the earth to its Centre, leaving a volume of smoke like a thunder cloud, which as the air was calm, remained for an hour or two. A 20-gun ship which had come to the assistance of the *Augusta* in her distress, shared her fate."

Once the basic *chevaux-de-frise* design was worked out in the Delaware, anxious revolutionaries farther north picked it up. By the end of October 1775, Josiah Quincy was writing to Washington from Braintree suggesting the weapon be used to blockade the narrow channels of Boston harbor. By May of the following year Benedict Arnold was advising the Carroll/Franklin mission to Canada: "I have in contemplation the sinking of *chevaux-de-frise* at the islands five miles below [Sorel], where the channel is very narrow, but the water so high we cannot fortify at present."

Along the banks on the Hudson, simple but heavy work was soon begun on what General Israel Putnam identified with some orthographical difficulty as *"Shevrord fres,"* another revolutionary officer called *"Shiver de freeses,"* and a British Navy captain identified as *"Chiverd'friezes."*

When sunk in relatively shallow water, the obstructions were obviously effective, but the Hudson was deeper than the Delaware. Off Fort Washington the river's navigable channel was almost 2,400 feet wide, with from three to eight fathoms of water. As Sergeant Ezra Lee had discovered to his frustration in *Turtle*, it was also subject to powerful tides.

*IN* July 1776, before an adequate barrier of hulks and *chevaux-de-frise* could be extended across the shallower western half of the river, the two new revolutionary forts were passed by the 5th Rate 44-gun British frigate *H.M.S. Phoenix* under Captain Hyde Parker, Jr., and the 6th Rate 24-gun *H.M.S. Rose* under its draconian Captain James Wallace, fresh from harassing the coastal towns of southern New England. The enemy vessels weighed anchor in New York's Upper Bay on July 12, ignored a lightweight revolutionary cannonade from a dozen miles of shore batteries along both sides of the river, and ran almost unscathed up the Hudson.

The enemy warships—mounting 4- and 6-pound cannon—shepherded three tenders, leading the revolutionaries to suspect the flotilla was aimed 80 miles upriver towards Poughkeepsie, at that time the third largest city in New York State and home of Shipyard Point—the dockyard where *Congress* and *General Montgomery* were taking shape on the ways. The two frigates were the largest of 11 authorized by Congress December 13, 1775.

A worried Elizabeth Tappen wrote her husband July 19: "We have news of the ships moving up the river, Troops flocking in here like swarms of Bees, People that live at the river moving everything away." But despite such fears, the initial British naval foray up the Hudson made no effort to go above Tappan Zee and Haverstraw Bay, where the river is 2½–3½ miles wide.

The War Office had been advised, according to a London newspaper, that "Mr. Washington's Magazines are all in Cortlandt Manor; to get Possession of them must surely be an object of Gen. Howe's serious Attention, and an additional Inducement to attempt a Landing in the Rear of the Provincial Forces." As their shore parties pillaged local farmers, the two enemy warships remained in the American rear, effectively blocking any water transfer of supplies to Washington's army on Manhattan.

The distressing news of the British naval passage alarmed Congress: "About half after three O'Clock," Washington advised Hancock on the evening of July 12, "two of the Enemy's Ships of War, one of 40 and the other of 20 guns, with three tenders, weighed anchor in the Bay opposite Staten Island. Availing themselves of a brisk and favourable breeze with a flowing Tide, they run past our batteries up the North River without receiving any certain damage that I could perceive. They on their part returned the fire as they run by." It seemed obvious that forts alone could not block the waterway. Other obstructions were essential.

Within days, responding to clamor from Congress, a thoroughly aroused "Convention of the Representatives of the State of New-York" voted unanimously to establish a new and powerful "Secret Committee." This group was charged with executing "such Measures as to them shall appear most Effectual for Obstructing the Channel of Hudson's River, or annoying the Enemy's Ships in their Navigation up the said River."

The Secret Committee, operating on a parsimonious initial budget of only £5,000, was chosen with care from among the 40-odd members of the Convention sitting in White Plains. Chairman was 37-year-old radical Whig Robert Yates, originally a member of the Sons of Liberty from Albany County.

Serving with Yates on the committee were Christopher Tappen of Ulster County, Dutchess County patricians Robert R. Livingston and Gilbert Livingston, William Paulding, and the conservative young lawyer John Jay from Westchester County.

Only a few weeks earlier Jay had assisted in the treason trial of William Hickey, who had deserted the British army to enlist in Washington's bodyguard. Hickey was found guilty of "mutiny, sedition, and treachery" for participating in a plot by several tavern keepers and prostitutes, masterminded by ex-Governor Tryon, to deliver up the Commander-in-chief—dead or alive—to the British.

Hickey was hanged June 28 in a field near Bowery Lane. All four Continental brigades in Manhattan were paraded before a tumultous crowd of thousands of New Yorkers to view the execution. Washington took advantage of the occasion to warn his susceptible young troops to "particularly avoid lewd women, who by the dying confession of this poor criminal, first led him into practices which ended in his untimely and ignominious death."

FOR MONTHS to come, Yates's powerful civilian Secret Committee—which later included former New York Congressman Henry Wisner and erstwhile King's College classics professor Robert Harpur—struggled to coordinate revolutionary defense strategies along the Hudson River.

Wisner missed most of the Committee meetings; long before there were any covert 100,000-pound French gunpowder shipments from overseas, he had written the how-to pamphlet, *Essays Upon the Making of Salt-Petre and Gunpowder,* and was busily engaged in establishing a powder mill located safely inland in Ulster County, to produce the desperately needed munition. The last American mill at

Canton, Massachusetts, had gone out of business in 1770; for the necessary saltpetre ingredient, the Americans were forced to fall back on collecting and processing human urine.

The Secret Committee actively used its mandate to "impress boats, Vessels, Teams, Waggons, Horses and Drivers when it shall find it necessary for the publick service, as well as call out the Militia if occasion should require." It apparently missed out on one revolutionary invention. Robert Erskine was ironmaster of Ringwood Furnace in northern New Jersey; his cartographic skill and knowledge of the lower Hudson Valley soon brought him the job of "Geographer and Surveyor-General to the Army of the United States," and he became Washington's most trusted New York area mapmaker.

On July 18 Erskine sent a model of a new type of river obstacle—ingeniously constructed from long iron-tipped spikes in the shape of a tetrahedron—to his friend John Morin Scott of the New York Convention, to show to General Israel Putnam. But Putnam was busy constructing his wooden *chevaux-de-frise*, with no time for either Scott, or Erskine's model. Despite the rebuff, Erskine did produce a sizeable number of his 400-pound iron-shod devices, and shipped them to Fort Lee.

On July 19 Washington acquainted the new Secret Committee, sitting in Poughkeepsie, with an item at the top of his military agenda—an effort to attack *Phoenix* and *Rose* upriver. Hidden in the relative safety of Spuyten Duyvil Creek at the north end of Manhattan, Continental Army Lieutenant Colonel Benjamin Tupper—who distinguished himself under fire by destroying harbor lighthouses during the British occupation of Boston—was busily mounting 18-pound cannon on several oared galleys, each manned by 12 to 16 army "watermen" from Connecticut and Rhode Island.

"It is a matter so purely confidential, if it can be effected," the Commander-in-chief cautioned the committee, "that I must desire the most profound Secresy be observed on the Subject."

The transit of the two enemy warships "exhibited proof of what I had long most religiously believed," Washington wrote privately to his brother John in Virginia at the end of the week, "that a vessel, with a brisk wind and strong tide, cannot, unless by a chance shot, be stop't by a battery, unless you can place some obstruction in the water to impede her motion within reach of your guns." It would be 21 agonizing months before the revolutionaries developed such adequate obstructions.

Meanwhile, other important information was being funnelled to the Secret Committee by members of the Convention. On July 21 William Duer, a delegate from upstate Charlotte County, reported to Robert Yates that "Genls Putnam and Mifflin have made an Exact Survey of the River opposite Mount Washington, and find that the Depth in no part exceeds 7 fathoms [42 feet]—The Channell is from 3 to 7 Fms—*G.W.* expresses himself extremely anxious about the Obstruction of that Channell [through which the 856-ton *Phoenix* and 448-ton *Rose* slipped] and Means are daily used for executing that Purpose."

Seeking hulks to block the river, the Committee found itself limited to older vessels trapped in the port of New York since June 25 when the Royal Navy arrived off Sandy Hook to bottle up the harbor. It was still early in the war, and even the most ardent revolutionaries had trouble bringing themselves to scuttle sound ships.

"It is impossible to procure Vessells enough at New York," Duer complained in frustration, "so that the Measure must be delay'd till such Time as more Vessells can be brought through the Sound from Connecticut. However I am not without apprehension that this Resource will be cut off, as I understand that some of the Enemys Vessells have sail'd out of the [Sandy] Hook, with an Intention (probably) of cutting off our Communication with the Sound.

"For god's Sake," said Duer, "exert yourselves to Secure the Sea Vessells which are still in the [upper Hudson] River. It is an Object of so much importance that no Difficulties, however great, ought to deter us from our Attempts to carry it into Execution. If we succeed, the Designs of the Enemy in this Campaign are effectually baffled. If we fail, we cannot be in a more lamentable Situation than we are now.

"Exclusive of the great Advantage we should reap in obstructing the Channel so far to the Southward," Duer went on—hoping, like so many other revolutionaries, to trap *Phoenix* and *Rose*—"it is, I fear, the only Place we can depend on shallowing, south of the Highlands, whilst the enemy Men-of-War are in the River. For if proper batteries are erected near the Water at Mount Washington and on the opposite Side, mounted with Guns of 18, 24 and 32 Pounders, it will not be practicable for any Vessels to be so near as to prevent our working under Cover of these Works.

"I have strongly urg'd Genl Washington to send Genl Mifflin some heavier Metal, and though he seems half inclined, this necessary Operation has not yet taken Place. I had almost forgot to tell you," Duer cautioned, "that this Design of obstructing the Channel near Mifflin's is under the Pretext of preparing Vessels for obstructing the East River—It will therefore be adviseable that your Conversation should give a Colouring to this Matter."

Duer was an English-born speculator who was also Lord Stirling's son-in-law; he soon became an important Continental Army contractor. Later in the war, when Duer's revolutionary ardor slackened, Lafayette called him a "tory" and a "rascall"; afterwards the ex-Congressman spent six years in jail for embezzlement.

On the same day Duer wrote to the Secret Committee, Washington advised Connecticut's Governor Trumbull of his unsuccessful efforts to locate any of the "heavier metal" Duer had mentioned, without seriously weakening the fortifications under construction around the city itself. "By letter received from the five-Gentlemen Committee appointed by the Provincial Convention of the State to reconnoitre and report the situation of the High Lands and Forts on Hudsons River," Washington advised Trumbull, "I find them in great want of Cannon; the two men of war and three tenders being in daily expectation of attempting to pass the [upriver] Forts Montgomery and Constitution to burn the two Frigates [*Congress* and *General Montgomery*] building at Poughkeepsie.

"In this situation," the Commander-in-chief continued, "they have mentioned sending to your Honour a request for those [cannon] now at the Salisbury Furnace [in Connecticut, about 30 miles northeast of Poughkeepsie] which I am fully perswaded you will, if possible, readily comply with, as it is not in my power to lend them any assistance from this Quarter."

The strategic ironworks at Salisbury—which came into being with the discovery of "Ore Hill" by a Massachusetts surveyor in 1731—was confiscated for war use by the State of Connecticut on February 2, 1776, whereupon the Salisbury workers struck successfully for a wage increase. The recalcitrant furnace and foundry owner, tory Robert Smith, quickly fled to England (but returned after the war to reclaim the works). Meanwhile, the State turned over his hematite ore beds, 14-year-old blast furnace (originally constructed by Ethan Allen), forges, and cannon foundry to ironmaster Colonel Joshua Porter.

Under Porter's supervision, with superintendents Hezikiah Fitch and Lot Norton, Salisbury manufactured more than 800 cannon during the war, with many tons of cannon balls and grapeshot—as

well as hundreds of cooking kettles for the army. Its ordnance—
solid-cast vertically, then bored—ranged from 191 light swivels to
200 18- and 20-pounders. The Continental Army was not the major
beneficiary of Salisbury production; two-thirds of the indispensable
heavy weapons were diverted to naval use, including many sold for
privateering.

The New York Convention's resolution to Connecticut requested
"20 of the heaviest cannon that can be had," plus "eight 6 pounders
and eight 4 pounders," with "a proper Quantity of Shot & Trux
[cast iron gun carriage axles and wheels] for the sd. cannon,
absolutely necessary & wanting for the Defence of Hudsons River
as well as the forts erected on its shores and armed Vessels ordered
to be prepared for its Defence—the whole to be borne to Coll.
Hoffman's Landing [on the Hudson above Poughkeepsie]."

This essential order was carried direct to Salisbury by 31-year-old
Secret Committee member John Jay, who had been given carte
blanche to deal directly with the State of Connecticut. Arriving from
Poughkeepsie on the afternoon of July 22, accompanied by
carpenter David Hand "to take the Dimensions of the Trux in order
that carriages may immediately be made for the sd. cannon," Jay
discovered that Porter was away; and his two superintendents "were
not authorized to dispose of, or part with, several Cannon, & a
considerable Quantity of Shot" to the State of New York "without
License from Governor Trumbull." In addition, there were "no
Trux made, nor could they order any to be made without
[Trumbull's] direction."

Galloping along the rough roads of western Connecticut, Jay
found Trumbull at Lebanon; the governor had by then also received
Washington's letter. Trumbull convened his Council on July 27th, a
Saturday, and expressed "his Readiness to do all in his Power
towards the Good of the American Cause and the Safety of this
State." Agreement was quickly reached to "lend the State of New
York Twenty Cannon, *(viz)* ten Twelve pounders & ten Six
pounders, Also a Suitable Proportion of Shot for Said Cannon, to be
replaced and said Shot to be Returned or Accounted for by said
State when requested." The Salisbury furnace "overseers" were also
"Directed to Cast a sufficient Number or as many as Can be, of Iron
Trucks and Carriage Wheels for said Cannon, to be loaned to said
State and returned or accounted for with the Cannon."

Jay was formally asked to sign "proper Receipts." And to protect
himself from religious zealots in western Connecticut, he in turn

requested Trumbull to endorse the bottom of his cannon order: *John Jay Esq. is a Gentleman friendly to the United States of America. It is necessary for him to travel on the morrow, being Lord's Day. Permit him to pass without let or molestation.*

When Jay returned to the ironworks, Colonel Porter was back. "He agreed to prepare the Cannon mentioned with the greatest expedition," Jay reported to the Secret Committee, "several of them not being as yet bored or drilled. Four twelve Pounders were soon made ready, together with fifty rounds of Shot for each of them." Porter insisted that casting "trux" would "impede the casting of Cannon," and persuaded Jay to lodge that request with Colonel Livingston's ironworks at Ancram, New York, offering to lend "some sand-moulders and give every other assistance in his Power."

"For these Reasons," wrote Jay, "I did not think it either reasonable or prudent to insist on a Compliance with the Governor's order respecting the Trux." Jay arranged for the ordnance at hand to be shipped on heavy carts through the Taconic mountain passes to Hoffman's Landing, where a sloop waited to carry the guns downriver.

The "Teemsmen" carrying the cannon were paid 35 shillings per ton; attached to Jay's report to the Secret Committee was a neat August 3 receipt from Hezikiah Fitch for "Twenty Eight pounds four Shillings lawful money of Connecticut," which would also cover transportation costs. Jay rode back into New York State to locate Robert Livingston at Ancram and ask him to supply or manufacture the necessary carriage hardware.

On August 16 Livingston was able to send downriver "10 Carriages, four of which have the Truck with them, the others will soon follow." He included a complaint that Connecticut had not honored its promise to supply Ancram with additional molders. One reason may have been Livingston's reputation for poor employee relations; the death of an ore digger during a 1755 labor dispute at Ancram had provoked a long strike. "Contented with no indulgance, bound by no contract," the ironmaster wrote Governor Clinton, "[the workers] desert my service at thair pleasure."

*ROBERT YATES* was soon able to report to Washington on the successful outcome of Jay's mission to Salisbury: "We have the pleasure of informing your Excellency that we have obtained ten 12-pounders and ten six-pounders, with 50 rounds of shot for each cannon," for use at Fort Washington and elsewhere.

Earlier, on July 26, General Putnam brought his old comrade-in-arms General Horatio Gates up-to-date on the defensive measures in the lower river: "We are preparing *Shevord fres*, at which we make great despatch by the Help of Ships, which are to be sunk—a Scheme of Mine which you may be assured is very Simple, a Plan of which I send you. The two Ships' Sterns," Putnam told Gates, "lie towards each other about seventy Feet apart. Three large Logs, which reach from Ship to Ship, are fastened to them; the two Ships and Logs stop the river 280 Feet. The Ships are to be sunk, and when hauled down in the Channel the Picks will be raised to a proper Height, and they must inevitably stop the River, if the Enemy will let us sink them."

With Royal Navy warships lying out of range only a few thousand yards away in Upper New York Bay, construction of the unusual-looking *chevaux-de-frise* along New York City's waterfront was hardly a secret. Early in August, 34-year-old Ambrose Serle, secretary to Admiral Lord Richard Howe aboard *H.M.S. Eagle*, noted in his journal: "The Structures which we supposed yesterday to be Fire Stages, were towed up the North River this morning.

"They seem to be intended for *Chevaux de Frize* to block up the Passage," Serle continued, "either to prevent the Ships that are now above from coming down, or our Fleet from getting up without being raked by their batteries. It is of a peculiar Construction, and all the Industry of malevolence, which is the most active Sort of Industry, has been used to complete it. Our People don't seem to regard it, and fancy they can easily run it down, or remove it out of their way."

ON August 2, four miles above Dobbs Ferry in the shallow western waters of the Tappan Zee with depths of less than a fathom, *Phoenix* was blown hard aground on a falling tide. That information spread swiftly downriver. Without delay, Lieutenant Colonel Tupper, hoping to catch Captain Parker's flotilla at this sudden disadvantage, next morning led his armed Connecticut and Rhode Island row galleys, accompanied by two schooners, out of Spuyten Duyvil to attack the British. For nearly two hours, the enemy exchanged long-range fire with Tupper. The rolling hills on either side of the river echoed the cannonade, as the outgunned revolutionaries gave almost as good as they received.

News of that spirited upriver confrontation quickly reached Philadelphia. Within the week Thomas Jefferson candidly reported to his brother-in-law Francis Eppes in Virginia: "Our galleys at New York have had a smart engagement with the men-of-war which went up the river; it is believed the enemy suffered a good deal. The galleys are much injured, although we lost but two men. The commander writes us word that he retired, that he might go and give them another drubbing, which in plain English means, I suppose, that he was obliged to retire." Jefferson was close to the mark; Colonel Tupper complained privately that Connecticut crews did not adequately support the two leading Rhode Island galleys.

"General Washington commends the behavior of the men much," Jefferson continued, "They lay pretty close to the enemy, and two of the galleys were exposed to the broadside of their ships almost the whole time. The damage done them proves they were in a warm situation."

"We saw many Splinters drifting down," reported Tupper—who served throughout the Revolution and eventually became a Brigadier General. But Captain Parker on *Phoenix* laconically logged only "two shott in our Hull." According to *Rose's* log, it suffered a bit more: "The Starbd Quarter Gallery shot away, some of the Rigging hurt & several Shot in the Hull." One British sailor was killed and four wounded.

American propagandists were soon hailing the affray as a decisive American victory. Nine days after the engagement James Rivington's *New-York Gazetteer*—with only a month left to serve as the revolutionaries' mouthpiece—printed a colorful eyewitness report that included the "call of one of our mortally wounded Tars to his mess mates: 'I am a dying Man, revenge my Blood, my Boys, and carry me along Side my Gun, that I may die there.'"

"Judge then—" the *Gazetteer's* patriotic account continued, "let the World—let our Enemies judge, if the Sons of Connecticut and Rhode-Island, from which States our Gallies were almost wholly officered and manned, did not behave with Spirit and Intrepidity becoming the Descendents of such noble Ancestors, in fighting, for two Hours, an Enemy of at least four Times their Force.—O! ye despicable ministerial Bawlers!—it could only have entered into such servilly dastard Souls as your own, to believe that the brave Americans were cowards."

THE DAY after that naval engagement on the Tappan Zee, Washington happily reported to an anxious Hancock in Philadelphia that "the Hulks and three *Chevaux de frieze* that we have been preparing to obstruct the Channel, have got up to the place they are intended for, and will be sunk as soon as possible." The Commander-in-chief was apprehensive lest additional shallow-draft enemy vessels follow *Phoenix* and *Rose*, and even get into twisting Spuyten Duyvil Creek to trap the refitting Tupper and destroy King's Bridge—critical crossing for the long revolutionary supply line into New York City.

On August 10 British Lieutenant Stephen Kemble, an aide to General Sir Henry Clinton, noted in his journal: "A very large float was carried from Town to be sunk in the North River, the Passage of which the Rebels are endeavouring to stop in such a manner as to oblige our Ships to come nearer their batteries in their course up."

Responsibility for sinking those completed *chevaux-de-frise* was given to Washington's aide Captain Mathew Cooke. But Cooke was soon enmeshed in a bitter debate as to whether the Fort Washington-to-Fort Lee line—3,300 feet wide—was actually the best place to obstruct the river. A few days earlier, Brigadier General Thomas Mifflin diplomatically withdrew from that controversy, advising Washington that "as I had no orders respecting the *Chevaux-de-Frise*, and as the artists appeared willing to take their own way, I did not presume to interfere."

That excuse hardly sat well with the Commander-in-chief, whose patience was running out. On August 10, he ordered Mifflin to begin sinking any materials available, to obstruct the channel as quickly as possible. The next day he urged his dependable engineer Colonel Rufus Putnam to hasten *chevaux-de-frise* construction.

The passage of *Phoenix* and *Rose* had left Washington concerned that his right flank might be turned by a massive amphibious operation on the Hudson. Successful blockage of the river, on the other hand, would not only put an end to that possibility, but would also trap the two enemy frigates in the Tappan Zee. British Captains Parker and Wallace were aware of their vulnerability; they regularly dispatched picket boats down to Fort Washington to keep a watchful eye on the revolutionaries' activity.

Within a few days of Washington's order, Major General William Heath noted in his journal that a large number of *chevaux-de-frise* were finally sunk near Fort Washington. "A line of these, and hulks," he wrote, "was formed across the river; some were sunk very well, others irregular. Some of the hulks were strapped together with large Timbers, which separated on going down. A passage was left open for Vessels to pass through."

On August 13 Captain James Wallace confirmed in *Rose's* log:

"Saw several Vessels sunk in the Channel Abrest the Fort, with 4 Brig's ready to sink." Although the revolutionaries misjudged the depth of the Hudson—and, more important, the strength of its tides—the potential danger from the new obstacles was not lost on the enemy. Royal Navy Captain George Collier wrote home: "I know not what Mr Washington & his army are doing, but ours have been totally inactive—The Enemy have now Time to breathe & to throw up fresh Works—I understand the Ships will not be able to go close to their Batteries from their having placd sharp Stakes pointed with Iron (called *Chevaux de frise*) by way of sinking our Ships if they should strike against them."

Washington, meanwhile, was grappling with a new problem—how to remove women and children to a place of safety when the enemy finally attacked the city—there might even be fighting in the streets. He appealed to the New York Convention: "When I consider that the city will in all human probability, very soon be the scene of a bloody conflict, I can not but view the great numbers of women, children and infirm persons remaining in it with the most melancholy concern. When the men of war passed up the river," the Commander-in-chief reported, "the shrieks and cries of these poor creatures, running every way with their children, was truly distressing: and I fear will have an unhappy effect on our young and inexperienced solidiery. Can no method be devised for their removal?"

The Convention returned the problem to Washington, who immediately issued a handbill announcing that a "Bombardment and Attack upon the City of New-York, by our cruel and inveterate enemy," was "hourly expected: And as there are great Numbers of Women, Children and infirm Persons, yet remaining in the City, whose Continuance will rather be prejudicial than advantageous to the Army, and their Persons exposed to great Danger and Hazard: I Do therefore recommend it to all such persons, as they value their own safety and Preservation, to remove with all expedition out of the said Town, at this critical Period,—trusting, that with the Blessing of Heaven upon the American Arms, they may soon return to it in perfect Security." A great many of New York's revolutionary families took the opportunity to leave—not to return again for seven difficult years.

After a month of pillaging farms on the shores of Haverstraw Bay, and surviving a revolutionary fire ship attack on August 16, *Phoenix* and *Rose* were finally recalled to New York harbor to join the British invasion of Long Island. The two enemy frigates hoisted anchor on August 18; to the dismay of the revolutionaries, they were both able to again thread their way, almost unscathed, through the sunken hulks and obstructions between Forts Washington and Lee—the *chevaux-de-frise* "beaks" faced the wrong way.

Captain Parker led in the 141-foot long *Phoenix:* "At ½ past 5 passed through the Channell on the East side of the Vessels &ca Sunk by the Rebels to block up the Channell between Geffrey's Hook and Berdetts Mountain [Fort Lee]." "At ¾ past 5," echoed Captain James Wallace in the 110-foot long *Rose:* "We past the *Chiver'friezes,* within the Musquet Shot of the Rebel Battery on the Eastern Shore."

"Not one of all their Shots struck the *Phoenix,*" Ambrose Serle recorded jubilantly in his journal—although General Heath wrote Washington that same afternoon that "the *Phoenix* was thrice hulled by our shot from Mount Washington." "One or two struck the *Rose,*" Serle continued (with Heath's corroboration) "and those did but little Damage. One man only was wounded by a splinter in the Leg."

News of the enemy frigates' departure from the Tappan Zee spread quickly upriver; on the 20th, John Nicoll wrote to Governor George Clinton from Red Hook, above Poughkeepsie: "I am Sorry To Heare Them Pirats have Got Oute of The River; was in hopes They wass Oure Own."

Still worse was to come. Within two days, in the greatest amphibious operation the world had yet seen, more than 22,000 British and German troops came ashore on Long Island in 88 prefabricated flatboats, bateaux and galleys. Before long they were engaged with 10,000 Americans in the first full-scale battle of the Revolution. It was a lopsided contest in which the revolutionaries suffered 1,400 casualties and soon lost control of Long Island and Brooklyn. On the fogbound night of August 29 Washington deftly withdrew all his surviving troops across the East River to Manhattan.

The British fleet now indisputably dominated the waters around New York City; the Continental Army lay exposed to flank attack. Revolutionary councils of war debated immediate evacuation of the island, with the entire city put to the torch. "Last spring," John Jay wrote to Robert Morris in Philadelphia, "I would have devastated all Long Island, Staten-Island, the City and County of New York, and all that part of the County of Westchester which lies below the mountains. I would have stationed the main body of the army in the mountains on the east, and eight or ten thousand men in the highlands on the west side of the river."

It was a brave but belated assertion from a provincial patrician who in a quarter year had become a highly effective revolutionary; only three months earlier, Jay had introduced the resolution in the New York Congress that insisted "that the good people of this Colony have not, in the opinion of this Congress, authorized . . . this Colony to be . . . independent of the Crown of Great Britain."

But in the end, any scorched-earth policy was rejected; instead, the Continental Congress voted to strengthen the city's defenses. Hugh Gaine, publisher of New York's only remaining newspaper, the revolutionary *New-York Gazette: and the Weekly Mercury,* reflected the city's growing fear and tension by fleeing across the Hudson to Newark with a printing press and most of his type.

New problems had arisen with the river obstructions at Forts Washington and Lee. At the end of August General Heath received a disquieting report from Colonel Israel Hutchinson of the 27th Continental Infantry: "I am to inform your Honor that a *Chevaux D Fries* sunk by Capt Cooke is now floating down the River. He has been with me this Morng and tells me that it is His Opinion that the current is so rapid that all Endeavours of this Kind will not stop the River."

On September 12 Peter Livingston, President of the New York Convention, received more news that some of the *chevaux-de-frise* at Fort Washington "intended to be effectually sunk, were a few Days ago floating with the Tide." Before long the former college professor and Convention secretary Robert Harpur was caustically inquiring of George Clinton as to "the Probability of the Permanence of these Machines, and whether you conceive the Navigation of the Enemy's Fleet is thereby Obstructed?"

*CLINTON HAD* no chance to reply—the final British assault on New York City came on the morning of September 15. Mounting a well-coordinated amphibious operation (the kind General Charles Lee had warned about half a year earlier), General Howe swept most of his Long Island troops ashore at Kip's Bay (present-day East 34th Street), a few miles above the American defense positions. With the password of the day *"Wolfe,"* and countersign *"Quebec,"* the enemy also celebrated the 18th anniversary of the defeat of Montcalm and the British capture of French Canada. But it was that defeat—and the American political and economic expansion it unleashed—that led to the revolution the British were now forced to suppress.

Again, Washington miraculously extricated his entire army, establishing a temporarily defensible line across the Heights of Harlem on the northern part of the island.

In his detailed journal, British Lieutenant Colonel Stephen Kemble enumerated all the laboriously prepared and hastily abandoned revolutionary entrenchments—from Kip's Bay south to the Battery, and north to Bloomingdale along the Hudson River. They included a "sod Fort called Bunkers Hill, the only Work of any consequence and strength on the Island, and tolerably well finished. All the rest of their Works (which are innumerable)," Kemble recorded, "appear Calculated more to Amuse than for use." His opinion was soon echoed in Colonel John Peters's *Toriade:*

> *The Island's width & length, full fourteen Miles*
> *Was full of Ditches, Forts, Redoubts, & Piles . . .*
> *On each side, up & down, is ditch and Fort,*
> *It seems that labour was their daily sport.*

Reporting to his former employer Lord Dartmouth, Ambrose Serle related his own colorful version of the dramatic events of the 15th. Serle, later to serve as British press censor for New York City, pictured the invasion as "awful & grand; I might say, beautiful, but for the melancholy Seriousness which must attend every Circumstance, where the Lives of Men, even the basest Malefactors, are at Stake. The Hills, the Woods, the River, the Town, the Ships, Pillars of Smoke—so terrible and incessant a Roar of Guns, few even in the Army & Navy had ever heard before—all heightened by a most clear & delightful morning, furnished the finest Landschape that either art and nature combined could draw, or the Imagination conceive."

While the revolutionary families who remained in New York prepared for a difficult and perhaps shadowy existence, their loyalist counterparts reacted with unrestrained joy. They passionately celebrated their rescue by King George's troops, after five months under the revolutionary heel—five months in which the loyalist population of the city had more than doubled. The grim and muffled evacuation of many of those same people from New York to Nova Scotia in 1783 must have stirred bitter memories of that joyous September day in 1776.

Serle sent Lord Dartmouth a glowing description: "Nothing could equal the Expressions shewn by the Inhabitants upon the arrival of the King's officers among them. They even carried some of them on their Shoulders about the Streets, and behaved in all respects, Women as well as Men, like overjoyed Bedlamites.

"A Woman pulled down the Rebel Standard upon the Fort," related Serle, "and a Woman hoisted up in its Stead His Majesty's Flag, after trampling the other under Foot with the most contemptuous Indignation. I espied both Circumstances from the Ship, and could not help paying the first Congratulations to Lord Howe upon the Occasion. The Admiral sent a Party of Marines to take Possession of the Fort.

"The Happiness of the Inhabitants upon the Occasion drove them about like madmen," Serle continued. "They have felt so much of real Tyranny since the New England & other Rebels came among them, that they are at a Loss how to enjoy their Release. They would have rung Bells, but the Rebels carried them off with many things of Value, some Days before their departure." During the previous fortnight, under a resolution of the New York Convention, the bronze bells of all New York City's churches and public buildings were indeed taken down and shipped across the Hudson to Newark, lest "the State be deprived at this crucial Period of that necessary, though unfortunate, resource" for cannon. The Convention also authorized collection of "all the Brass Knockers in the city of New-York, the same to be sent to some careful person" in New Jersey, for similar purpose.

To the liberal Dartmouth—former British Secretary of State for the American Department—Admiral Howe's secretary added: "Great Numbers of Emigrants, particularly Irish, are in the Rebel Army, some by Choice, and many for mere Subsistence. They have also many transported Felons who have exchanged Ignominy and Servitude for a Sort of Honor and Ease.

"This is a further Argument against the Transportation of such People from England in future," Serle wrote. "Confinement to hard Labor at Home might answer some valuable Purpose. Here, they do Great Britain much Injury by bringing over Numbers, and Trades, and so adding Strength, already too great, to the Force of America against her." To provide liberated New York with at least one operating newspaper, Serle was soon assigned ashore to publish the abandoned *New-York Gazette: and the Weekly Mercury*. Within two months, however, printer Hugh Gaine reaffirmed his royal allegiance, returning to the city to continue his journal.

Captain Duncan of *Eagle,* also going ashore at the Battery on September 15, reported: "At the landing-place I was met by the mob, who gave me three cheers, took me on their shoulders, carried me to the Governor's Fort, put me under the English colours now hoisted, and again gave me three cheers, which they frequently repeated, men, women and children shaking me by the hand and giving me their blessing, and crying out 'God save the King!' "

Lower Manhattan Island was now securely in British hands, and the Hudson River provided the enemy with an easy route to the American rear. That fact frightened the New York Convention, and gave fresh impetus to revolutionary efforts to block the waterway. On September 17 the Convention, sitting in safety at Fishkill just above the Highlands, resolved "that Hudson's river at and about Fort Washington is not yet sufficiently obstructed." The Convention ordered Captain Thomas Grenell to requisition a whaleboat with "a sufficient number of hands whose attachment to the American cause may be relied on," to repeat Generals Putnam and Mifflin's soundings in the Hudson off the fort.

As the pace quickened, Continental officers put their men to work on the river obstructions, abandoning the niceties of using only old ships. From Washington's headquarters north of the city on Harlem Heights, "hurried and surrounded with a thousand things [the Commander-in-chief gently complained on September 20]," Quartermaster General Stephen Moylan was ordered to purchase and sink any ships necessary to fill out the line of hulks.

Within two days the Secret Committee also voted "in consequence of the Power invested in them by the Convention of the State of New York, to impress for the Use of the Publick two new ships found near Esopus Landing"—belonging to John and Samuel Franklin—as well as two brigs berthed at Poughkeepsie.

The Committee, requesting "assistance from all commanding Officers on the River," ordered each vessel to be loaded with as much timber and oak plank as possible (charged to QMG Moylan), and to sail for Fort Washington. The need for lumber was urgent, not just for additional *chevaux-de-frise,* but also for cannon platforms at Fort Washington, and a broader military bridge at the head of Spuyten Duyvil Creek.

To keep everyone honest, the Convention appointed a seven-man subcommittee of "unexceptionable Character and great Experience" to appraise the seized Esopus ships and offer the Franklins equitable compensation. Together with the two less expensive brigs, the total cost was £7,844. Secret Committee Chairman Yates advised the Convention: "Our Stock of Money is now very low, our Contracts and Expenses far exceeding the Sum we were furnished with, and the Demands on this Committee are frequent and urgent. Upon these Considerations we hope the Convention will by some Means or other furnish us with a farther Supply."

Typified by John Jay's neat receipts for the borrowed Connecticut cannon, all the Committee's confiscatory activities were conducted on a very businesslike basis. Before ships were sunk in the Hudson, their rigging was removed, carefully labeled and carried back to Poughkeepsie for storage until after the war. But the thrifty Secret Committee members were still bothered by the idea of sinking a pair of perfectly sound ships from Esopus—vessels that had "never been out at sea, and by the report of Masters of Vessels and Ship Carpenters, well built and of the very best Materials."

If it eventually turned out that such ships were being wasted, Chairman Yates cautioned Washington, "it would become a matter of concern, unless the Interest of the Public renders the Measure absolutely necessary and unavoidable." The Commander-in-chief assigned his 32-year-old military secretary—later Lieutenant Colonel—Tench Tilghman (son of an ardent tory) to reassure the Committee and speed work on further Hudson obstructions at Fort Washington. Assisting Captain Cooke, Tilghman raced to help block the river, before British commander Howe, ominously quiet since his seizure of lower Manhattan, was again on the move.

On October 3 Tilghman requested that Cooke, who had sailed upriver to cut additional timber for *chevaux-de-frise*, come down immediately, "as he is much wanted here to sink the Vessels. We are at a Stand for want of him, for as he has Superintended the Matter from the beginning, he best knows the properest places to be Obstructed."

Cooke arrived at Fort Washington—too late.

*A FEW* days earlier Vice Admiral Richard Lord Howe had advised the Admiralty that in order to prevent the revolutionary forces from bringing further supplies down the Hudson to New York City, he would lead from strength and again order "a Detachment of Ships above their Works at Jeffrey's Hook [Fort Washington] on York Island and the opposite shore of Jersey; between which they had lately been making fresh Attempts to block the channel with sunken frames and Vessels." It was twelve weeks since *Phoenix* and *Rose* had first run upriver; the revolutionaries had obviously strengthened their forts and obstructions. The question was: to what degree?

Royal Navy Captain Andrew Snape Hamond—later governor general of Nova Scotia—commanding *H.M.S. Roebuck,* described the situation: "As the Rebel Army was chiefly supplyed by the North River, and placed great dependence upon it, they had taken a great deal of pains to throe a Boom a cross by sinking Vessels & and frames of Timber to prevent our ships from passing up. They had placed these obstructions in the narrowest part, where the River is about 12 hundred Yards wide between two High Lands, having Fort Washington on the Right and Fort Constitution on the Left.

"Each contained several batterys of heavy cannon," Hamond continued, "placed at some distance along the shore. Six row Galleys [Tupper's], each with a large Gun in their prow, guarded the boom in front, so that, we understood, they looked upon it to be perfectly secure; and it is possible, from seeing the great preparation they had made, we might also have thought so, if an American had not come into our Camp & stated that he was Brother to the Ferry Man who plyed from Fort Washington on the York side to Fort Lee on the Jersey shore, who had informed him that there was an opening in the Dam by which ships might pass, and had showed him where it was. Being asked if he would undertake for a Reward to Pilot a ship through the opening, he assented.

"Upon this Information," Hamond went on, General Howe "very strongly & officially pressed the Admiral to take advantage, conceiving that if ships could be got up the North River—embracing the first opportunity & flood Tide, each ship following in a Line after the other—the Rebel's supplys would not only be cut off from Albany & that country, but even their Communication with the Jerseys would become very uncertain & unsafe, which could not fail of distressing them, and would very much assist in the intended operation of surrounding their army."

Such turncoat espionage helped lessen the anxiety of Royal Navy captains planning to maneuver up an unfamiliar river filled with tidal shoals. Earlier that summer at the treason trial of Washington's bodyguard Hickey, John Yates, a river captain from Ulster County, told presiding judges John Jay and Governeur Morris that tory Governor Tryon had offered him a dollar a day and £5 a foot for every man-of-war he would pilot up the river—plus "200 acres of land at the determination of the American war."

On October 9 from Washington's headquarters at the Roger Morris mansion on Harlem Heights—three days before General William Howe launched a new attack on the revolutionary left flank that eventually carried the British army deep into Westchester County—Tench Tilghman ruefully reported to John Hancock and the Continental Congress in Philadelphia that the several vessels and *chevaux-de-frise* sunk in the Hudson opposite Fort Washington had once again proved incapable of blocking the Royal Navy.

On that day all those obstructions were again breached, this time by Captain Hyde Parker, Jr.'s ubiquitous 44-gun frigate *Phoenix*, followed by Captain Hamond's 44-gun *Roebuck* and Captain Cornthwaite Ommanney's 28-gun *Tartar*, with tenders.

"About 8 o'Clock this Morning," Tilghman reported, "the *Roebuck* and *Phoenix*, and a frigate of about 20 guns, with Three or Four Tenders, got under way from about Blooming dale, where they had been lying some time, and stood with an easy Southerly Breeze towards our '*Chevaux de frise*,' which we hoped would have intercepted their passage while our Batteries played upon them. But to our Surprise and Mortification, they all ran thro without the least Difficulty, and without receiving any apparent Damage from our Forts [Tilghman was mistaken; the three enemy ships suffered substantial damage, with nine British sailors killed and 18 wounded]."

From the relative quiet of "Tapan Bay" 15 miles upstream, Captain Hamond of the 5th Rate 886-ton *Roebuck* wrote Vice Admiral Shuldham to praise 36-year-old Captain Parker's spirited leadership during the action—a role for which Parker was eventually knighted. (Two years later, Parker—son of a Royal Navy rear admiral and by now a commodore—supported Lieutenant Colonel Archibald Campbell's successful 3,500-man amphibious assault against General Robert Howe that resulted in the capture of Savannah. Subsequently, Parker was accused of allowing several hundred American prisoners Campbell placed aboard his fleet to die of starvation and disease. In a later war Parker served as Nelson's Commander-in-chief at the Battle of Copenhagen).

"Hyde Parker," wrote Hamond, "showed great merit in coming up on the *chevaux de frise*, as the Pilot proved to be totally ignorant of the place where the opening was supposed to be at the moment when it was necessary to look out for it. As soon as Parker found this, he determined at once to steer the same way that he came down [on August 18th], which was cloase to the eastern shore where we found a broad Channel of twelve fathom water."

In his personal journal, Hamond elaborated the story: "Having previously considered what would be best to be done in the Event of the Guide proving Treacherous, Capt Parker had pistols laying on the Binnacle, telling the guide that would be his Fate if the ships should stop in their passage. On the near approach, the Pilot, in great confusion, told him the marks which then appeared were not those that had been described to him, and he was totally at a loss.

"Fortunately this had been so strongly suspected," Hamond continued, "that Capt Parker immedty hauld up to the side where it was known the deepest water lay—and the ships all passed within 40 yards of the Muzzles of the Enemy's Guns in the Batterys of Fort Washington—amidst the fire of 100 Cannon from both sides of the River—in little more time than about 20 minutes.

"The shots that did the ships the most damage was from the Jersey shore," Hamond recounted, "The guns from those batteries were so well served that very few missed striking some part of the ship; and by its falling very little wind (perhaps occasioned by the firing), we were upwards of an hour in passing. Eight men were killed in the three ships, four of which unfortunately came to my share, who could least spare them, as indeed is generally the case. Among them was poor Leake, my first lieutenant.

"I have the pleasure," Hamond wrote to Admiral Shuldham, "to tell you that we have taken two of their galleys. When they found they could not escape us, they ran them on shore, and left them so precipitately that no man would stay long enough to set them on fire." Admiral Howe also reported to London that one of the captured galleys "mounted a Thirty-two Pounder, with swivels; the other two Nine-pounders and two four-pounders. The two remaining Gallies with some small Vessels being favored by the Tide and Weather, escaped the Ships in shoal Water, where they had sufficient Protection from the Shore, which was in the Enemy's possession."

Excerpts from enemy logs tell a fierce if laconic story: "AM. at 4 barrocaded the ship. At 7 weighed and made sail. At 8 Five Batterys on the York and two on the Jersey Shore began to fire on us. Likewise hove a number of Shells with a Continual Fireing. At ½ past 9 got through the Passage by the *Chevaux de Frieze*; hoisted two Flags at the Main Topgt Mast Head as private Signals, which was Answer'd by the [32-gun] *Repulse*.

"*[Phoenix:]* In passing the Forts a Mid, two Seamen and a Boy were Kill'd and twelve others wounded, Our Mizen Mast & Mizen Topmast entirely disabled, Main Stay and Several of the Lower & Topmast Shrouds Cut; The Sails & Running Rigg very much damaged; The Spare topmt some other Sparrs & the Boats very much Shatter'd. We also received 4 Shot through our Hull."

"[Tartar:] After Hulling us several times, wounding our Masts and cutting a great deal of the Rigging and Sails, a Shott went thro the Mizen Mast and afterwards killed a Midshipmn. The Splinters of the Masts wounded the Captn Lieut of Marines & Pilot."

"[Roebuck:] In passing the Battery the small Cutter was Shatter'd to pieces; found it Necessary to Cut a drift. Lieut Leek & Mr Hitchcock Mid were killed & 7 seamen wounded." [Two of Roebuck's wounded subsequently died.]

On board the revolutionary galley Independence, Lieutenants Jeremiah Putnam and Nathaniel Cleves "about 7 A M Observed the Ships Below to Be moving. We Imeadetly Cauld all Hands. After seeing the Other Galley [Crane] Under way, We hove Up and stood Up the river after them. When We got Above the Chevax De free, spoke with Cook [Captain Mathew Cooke] and askt what he intended to Doo. He answerd that he Did not know, and said there Was Not Warter Enough to Go in to the Creek [Spuyten Duyvil].

"The Wind being Moderate," the two lieutenants' report to Washington continues, "we gained a head of them wich gave Us Encoregment to keep along. It soon after Breezd up & the Ships Gaind Upon Us fast; and at about 11 A M they Began to fire Upon Us With theire Bow Chasers. At About twelf they Over reacht Us, wich Causd us to Bare in Shore, and at ½ P M We run her On shore Just Above Dobsey Ferry.

"We had not time Enough to Git Our People and things On shore in the Boates, and the shiping Began to fire, Wich Obligd Us to Swim On shore But no Lives Lost. I Observd the Enemy to man theire Boats and fire a Bradside of Grape Shot as we Ley in the Bushes, and Emeadetly sent theire Boat on Bord With a Warp and hove her a long side."

Enemy logs of that chase recount the capture of Independence, Crane and a schooner. They also cover more mundane (and sadder) matters: "Open'd a Cask of Beef No. 17, Contg 86—Short 2 Pieces. At 6 Committed the Bodies of the Deceased to the Deep." In the action, the British also sank a sloop carrying (unbeknownst to them) Bushnell's Turtle.

Tilghman, for the Commander-in-chief, reported to the New York

Convention: "How far the enemy intends to go up, I don't know, but His Excellencey thought fit to give you the earliest Information, that you may put Gen. Clinton on his Guard at the Highlands; for they may have Troops on Board to surprise those Forts. If you have any Stores on the Water side, you had better have them removed a Second Time; Boards especially, for which we shall be put to great Straits if the Communication is cut off. The Enemy have made no Move on the Land side.

"While I was writing the above by His Excellency's direction," Tilghman concluded, "he went to bed. I thought it a pity to disturb him to sign it. I therefore have the Honor to subscribe myself (&c.)

TENCH TILGHMAN

Admiral Howe's secretary-cum-newspaper-editor Ambrose Serle rejoiced in his diary that, "The North River is now in full Possession of His Majesty's Fleet, and the Retreat of the Rebels entirely cut off. They are deserting apace, and very sickly and much dispirited. They are also retiring backward, destroying Corn & Hay as they go, further into New Jersey from Bergen & Newark and the adjacent parts."

On October 10 Robert R. Livingston wrote privately from Fishkill to South Carolina Congressman Edward Rutledge about the apparent ease with which the enemy had passed the river obstructions. Livingston told his friend in Philadelphia: "I am not surprized at it, having long ago, from the manner in which that work was conducted, predicted what has hapned, & proposed to the Genl what wd have secured us agt the whole navy of England, at Less expence than this has cost us—the sinking of blocks [additional hulks]. Tho' he inclined to it, it was over ruled at head Quars."

The New York Convention's Committee of Safety acknowledged Tilghman's letter. Fearing the enemy naval vessels once again loose in the Hudson, they told Washington: "Nothing can be more alarming than the present Situation of our State. We are Daily getting the most Authentic Intelligence of Bodies of Men Enlisted and Armed, with orders to assist the Enemy.

"We much fear that those co-operating with the Enemy will seize such Passes as will cut off all Communication between the Army and us, and prevent your Supplies," the Committee continued, "We dare not Trust any more of the Militia out of this County [Dutchess]. We have called for some Aid from the two adjoining ones, but beg Leave to suggest to Your Excellency the Propriety of sending a Body of Men to the Highlands or Peekskill, to secure the Passes, prevent Insurrection and overaw the Disaffected.

"We suppose," the Committee warned, "Your Excellency has taken the necessary Steps to prevent the Landing of any Men from the [enemy] Ships, should they be so inclined, as no Reliance at all can be placed on the Militia of Westchester County."

Again late in the day, the Continental Congress suggested that Washington, "by every Art and whatever Expence, obstruct effectually the Navigation of the North River between Fort Washington and Mount Constitution, as well as to prevent the regress of the Enemies' Frigates lately gone up, as to hinder them from receiving Succors."

THREE DAYS after that second successful naval passage of the Hudson defenses, the British moved 13,000 troops by water up the East River and into Long Island Sound, landing them on the eastern edge of Westchester County. The revolutionary forces immediately retreated from Manhattan, leaving behind the 3,000-man garrison of Fort Washington. When Charles Lee in Westchester learned that Washington's final war council had voted to continue defending the fort, he reportedly exclaimed, "Then we are undone." Extensive land maneuvers in Westchester between Washington and Howe culminated October 28 in a pitched but indecisive battle at White Plains.

The previous day a small body of British troops tested Fort Washington's defenses from both land and water. Revolutionary marksmanship was improving; the enemy parties were easily turned back. On November 2 however, traitor William Demont, adjutant to Colonel Magaw at Fort Washington, slipped through the lines—"in the Service of my King & Country, thus saving the Lives of many of His Majesty's Subjects"—and delivered to Lord Percy a plan of the fort's defenses.

The British net began to close. Within three days, H.M.S. Pearl accompanied by Joseph and British Queen, were ordered up the river to join Phoenix, Roebuck and Tartar in harassing the revolutionaries from the Hudson side of Westchester County. This time, however, the American cannoneers at Forts Washington and Lee found the range.

Captain Thomas Wilkinson of Pearl logged his upriver passage of the riverside forts: "At 3 Weigh'd and came to Sail. At ½ past the Rebels opened their Batteries on us from both shores. At 5 running throw the *Shive de frise*. They fired Cannister, Grape and Musquet shot at us. We return'd Round & Grape Shot, with Musquetry. At ½ past 5 sent all our Boats to assist the *Joseph*.

"We recd a number of shot in our Hull," Wilkinson's account continues, "& several between Wind & Water. Found the Ship to make [water] at the rate of 5 inches p hour. Had the Major part of our running Rigging & a great part of our lower Cut to pieces. Found Wm Brown, Seaman, Kill'd & several wounded. The Sails much torn, our Mizen & Mizen topmast shatter'd & the Boats much damaged. At 6 Anchd about ½ a Mile above Kings bridge in 8 fm water."

On November 8 Washington sent a worried letter to Nathanael Greene: "The late passage of the three vessels up the North River is so plain a proof of the inefficacy of all the obstructions we have thrown into it, that I cannot but think it will fully justify a change. What valuable purpose can it answer," Washington cautioned, "to attempt to hold a post from which the expected benefit cannot be had?"

But Greene was adamant about defending Fort Washington, and replied the following day: "I cannot conceive it to be in any great danger; the men can be brought off at any time if matters grow desperate." Twenty-four hours later the Commander-in-chief took a fateful step. He divided the Continental Army, ferrying most of his troops across the river near Haverstraw, leaving only a small force under General Heath to guard the passes through the Highlands. Howe could now turn immediate military attention to the revolutionaries lately bombarding his warships from the safety of Forts Washington and Lee.

On November 16 the British general ordered 8,000 men—including most of his Hessian mercenaries—to attack the 3,012 Americans left in and around Fort Washington. In some of the bitterest fighting of the war, the vastly outnumbered revolutionaries gave better than they received, but the two-pronged enemy attack slowly pushed all the defenders south of the fort back into an earthwork originally designed to hold only a thousand men; 154 were killed or wounded before Colonel Magaw ordered a surrender, to avoid senseless slaughter.

Until the British officers stepped in, the Hessians were efficiently stripping Magaw's men to their underclothing. The freezing revolutionary soldiers were then marched to hellish confinement in New York City's windowless warehouses and prison ships; half would not survive that notoriously inhuman enemy treatment.

An officer aboard *H.M.S. Emerald* lying in the Hudson off the fort, wrote contemptuously to a friend in Halifax: "Our situation afforded us a sight of the Engagement. Let it suffice to Remark that the Rebels flew on all sides from Redoubt to Redoubt like so many Sheep. This mighty & indeed strong place, which, with Real Military Men, could have held out a two month siege, was Reduced by our brave Troops in six or seven hours. Out of Curiousity I went the next day to the Fort. It was erected on an Exceeding lofty Hill & contained 23 pieces of Cannon, with a great quantity of Arms & Ammunition, and upwards of 3,000 prisoners. Washington either was not in the Action or Else made his Escape privately.

"We are now Masters of Hudsons River," the naval officer crowed, "Whereby a Communication is open'd to Albany & the Lakes."

It was a major crisis of the Revolution. On a single November afternoon the Continentals lost both a key post and more than twenty per cent of their effective fighting strength. Captured American war materiel included 146 brass and iron guns ranging up to 32-pounders, 12,000 shot and shell, 2,800 muskets and 40,000 cartridges, not to mention tents, entrenching tools, and other essential equipment. The enemy also counted 200 of Robert Erskine's unused tetrahedrons.

"I am sorry to inform you," Washington wrote sadly to the New York Convention upriver, "that this Day about 12 o'Clock the Enemy made a general Attack upon our Lines about Fort Washington, which having been carried, the Garrison retired within the Fort. Col. Magaw finding there was no prospect of Retreating across the North River, surrendered the Post. We do not know our own loss [it was 54 killed—100 wounded—2,858 captured] or that of the enemy in forcing the Lines [67 killed—335 wounded—6 missing], but I imagine it must have been considerable on both sides, as the Fire in some Parts was of long continuance and heavy; neither do I know the Terms of Capitulation. The Force of the Garrison before the Attack was about 2,000 men."

That night, in a private letter to his brother John Augustine Washington, the Commander-in-chief confided: "This post, after the Ships went past it, was held contrary to my Wishes and opinion, as I conceived it to be a dangerous one. Knowing that the Channel of the River (which we had been laboring to stop for a long time at this place) could not be obstructed unless there were Batteries to protect it, I did not care to give an absolute order for withdrawing the Garrison till I could get round and see the Situation of things, and then it became too late."

Four days later Fort Lee also fell—to a flank attack by Lord Cornwallis, who ferried 4,000 British troops across the Hudson at Yonkers and clambered up the Palisades. Now wracked by growing strategic dissension between General Lee and the Commander-in-chief, the Continental Army fled south through New Jersey. With it travelled a volunteer aide-de-camp to General Nathanael Greene, Thomas Paine, scribbling away at an immortal pamphlet he called *The Crisis*.

On December 1 rambunctious Colonel Anthony Wayne, commanding at Fort Ticonderoga, finally received news of the unnerving disaster around New York City. "Is the Genius of America fled our arms?" he railed in dismay to Secretary of War Richard Peters in Philadelphia. "Is she Ashamed to Associate with her Degenerate sons; or does she Esteem them as Aliens, unworthy her protection: are not the Enemy as vulnerable as us—cuts not our Swords as keen—pierces not our Balls as deep as theirs—*they do*— why then this terror—why shrink as from a Gorgen head, whenever they appear?"

At that moment in England, King George III, as if aware of his successful capture of one-fifth of the revolutionary army, proclaimed December 12 and 13 as days of fast and prayer for the British Isles. The King invoked the deliverance of "our loyal subjects within our Colonies and Provinces in North America from the violence, injustice, and tyranny of those daring Rebels who have assumed to themselves the exercise of arbitrary power."

Had the American Revolution been a traditional 18th century European war, the collapse of Fort Washington would have brought it to a rapid conclusion. As far upstream as Dobbs Ferry, the Hudson was now a British river. All that remained of the costly and unsuccessful revolutionary attempts to blockage the waterway were a few shattered masts in the water off Fort Washington—a post swiftly renamed *"Fort Knyphausen"* to honor the Hessian mercenary general commanding the right wing of the November 16 attack.

As Washington's remaining troops slipped slowly through the gently falling snow towards Trenton and the Delaware River, the shattered revolutionary cause held hardly a glimmer of hope for the future.

CHAPTER IV

# Stirling's Beacons and Hazelwood's Fire Ships
## (1776–1779)

---

*In which Congress presses for a secret signal system and Lord*
*Stirling designs a chain of flaming towers, while brave Captain*
*Thomas meets a watery death attacking* H.M.S. Phoenix

---

FIRE, THAT most ancient and frightening of military weapons, was
used with good effect by the revolutionaries along the Hudson.

Throughout history, nighttime signal fires on mountain peaks
relayed simple, instantaneous messages; by day, depending on wind
and weather, smoky pyres could be seen for a considerable distance.
Now, synchronized cannon fire created additional attention.

Since the British seized New York from the Dutch in 1664,
colonial militia service had been required from every "male above
the age of 16, provided with a good serviceable gun." As
Revolutionary fighting spread to the Hudson Valley, the Continental
Army invariably counted on swift militia support; some quick means
of communication was needed to summon these indispensable
"home guards" into battle.

That need for an early warning system led Congress to resolve on
October 7, 1775—nine months before General Howe's troops came
ashore on Staten Island—that joint efforts be undertaken by the

Conventions of the states of New York and New Jersey, and the Connecticut Assembly, to "establish, at proper Distances, Posts to be ready to give Intelligence to the Country in case of any Invasion, or by Signals, to give Alarms in case of Danger."

Ten days later the New York Provincial Congress "Resolved, That in order to give a General Alarm throughout the Colony, Beacons be erected at convenient Places and Distances, and that some fit Person be employed under the Direction and Advice of the several Country Committees to make a proper Arrangement for this business."

As military tension in New York mounted, the Convention forwarded its resolution to the legislatures of New Jersey and Connecticut. Connecticut's Governor Jonathan Trumbull approved the plan, and promised to establish "proper Persons in readiness at a Minute's Warning to carry any Intelligence of Alarm or Invasion."

But revolutionary security was quickly breached; tory sympathizers informed ex-Governor William Tryon of a new patriot system being developed to signal arrival of the British fleet outside New York City, with "Beacons erected all the Way up at proper Places, to give the Alarm." From the safety of the *Duchess of Gordon*, Tryon quickly passed that information to London.

Arriving in New York from the successful siege of Boston in the spring of 1776, Generals Nathanael Greene, Lord Stirling, and John Sullivan immediately sought Washington's counsel to develop a distinctive pattern of signals, 20 yards apart and 200 feet above the sea at New Jersey's Navesink Highlands.

During earlier colonial wars, a signal station on that same steep Atlantic cliff had given warning of foreign privateers nearing the Sandy Hook entrance to the port of New York—in the 19th century, Navesink would become the site of famous twin lighthouses signalling to immigrants the end of their long Atlantic crossing.

On April 20 the Commander-in-chief ordered the army to "establish good lookouts on the Heights and Headlands at the Entrance of the Harbor, and upon the appearance of a Fleet, make such signals as being answered from place to place shall convey the earliest intelligence to Head Quarters of the strength and approach of the Enemy; these signals for greater Certainty to be followed by Expresses."

A week later the three generals agreed to the use of huge red-and-white striped flags by day, with bonfires by night: "Upon the Appearance of any Number of Ships from one to six," a single bonfire to be lit (or flag displayed); "from six to 20," two; "for any greater number," three.

An identical set of signals was established 16 miles farther north on Staten Island's Todt Hill, 380 feet above Lower Bay —the highest point on the Atlantic littoral between Maine and Central America. This station would relay the Navesink warning nine more miles to the Battery at New York City.

On May 19 Colonel John Glover gave additional orders for two invasion signal cannon to be fired by day from the ramparts of Fort George at the Battery, plus a flag hoisted atop Washington's headquarters to alarm the regular troops and militia, as well as all inhabitants of the city. If the British fleet appeared by night, his signals included the two cannon, plus "two Lanthorns hoisted." Two days later, Glover reminded Fort George sentinels to keep a sharp lookout towards "the Narrows, Staten Island, Red Hook, &c.—to observe if any signals are given from thence, and acquaint the Officer of the Guard immediately therewith."

Even with the most powerful spyglass, 16 miles was a considerable distance through the summer sea haze that usually hangs over Lower Bay. But a smudge of smoke or a hint of flags at the proper point on the horizon—even a pinprick of fire by night— could alert the city.

Even so, the New York Convention still displayed doubts about this new signal technology. Preferring express riders, the legislators peevishly noted: "We have not been entirely inattentive to the Subject. Every Regiment of our Militia has its Place of Rendezvous appointed, and Riders are fixed to alarm the Country in case of an Invasion. If upon consideration we shall judge that Signals may be of Service in calling in our Militia more speedily, we shall communicate to you our own Determination on that Head."

Ignoring this lack of legislative enthusiasm, Washington advised General Putnam on May 21: "Delay not a Moments's time to have the Signals fix'd in such a manner and at such distances as to be easily discerned, day or Night. Nothing can be attended with more signal advantages than having timely notice of the Enemy's approach. A brisk Wind and flowing tide will soon produce them, when they are once on the coast; everything should be in readiness for immediate action."

By the end of June, more than a quarter year after sailing out of Boston's Nantasket Roads, General Howe and his troopships were sighted once more—off Navesink. The alert revolutionaries soon

One of Navesink, New Jersey's Twin Lights, erected 1862 on the site of the original Navesink Highlands Revolutionary beacon (1985).

19th century lighthouse on Todt Hill, site of the Staten Island
Revolutionary relay beacon (1985).

Palisades on west bank of the Hudson River.

The "PHOENIX" and the "ROSE" Engaged by the ENEMY'S FIRESHIPS and
GALLEYS on the 16 of Ag.st 1776.

warned of his arrival with flags and flaming pyres. "For two or three days past," the Commander-in-chief wrote John Hancock on the 29th, "three or four Ships have been droping in, and I just now received an Express from an Officer appointed to keep a look out on Staten Island, that 45 arrived at the Hook today, some say more. I suppose the whole fleet will be in within a day or two."

Lieutenant Colonel Samuel Webb, Silas Deane's stepson, noted in his journal: "This morning at 9 o'Clock we discovered our Signals hoisted on Staten island. A fleet of more than one Hundred Square rig'd vessels had arrived and anchored [inside Sandy] Hook." On July 3 Washington again reported to Hancock: "There remains no doubt of the whole of the Fleet from Hallifax now being here."

The revolutionary militia in New Jersey mustered swiftly but could offer no opposition to the enemy's disembarkation on Staten Island. On July 12 Admiral Richard Howe arrived, adding his North American squadron to brother William's transports in the harbor; 8,000 additional German mercenaries under Lieutenant-General Philip von Heister were ferried ashore on August 16.

A week later, under the overall command of Sir Henry Clinton, almost all the British and German troops were transported across Upper Bay to Brooklyn, to begin the battle for Long Island—as already noted, an action that turned into a revolutionary military disaster. Despite Washington's most adroit wartime maneuvering, the British were soon in control of all of lower Manhattan Island, and a new set of revolutionary beacons became necessary to signal the focus of further enemy attacks.

Lord Stirling ordered immediate construction of a chain of alarm posts on the highest hills of the countryside surrounding New York City. These new beacons, 15 to 20 miles apart, extended in an arc from the foothills of western Connecticut through New York and New Jersey.

In the Hudson Highlands, the relay anchored itself on both Constitution Island and 1,355-foot-high Butter Hill (present-day Storm King Mountain). An additional post was established five miles upriver on the 1,530-foot summit of Mount Beacon—after more than two centuries, that sobriquet still persists. Its signal fire could be seen by militiamen on both sides of the Hudson as far north as Poughkeepsie. Spaced several miles apart, Stirling's chain of beacons extended south from Butter Hill along the crest of the Ramapo and Watchung Mountains—by way of Morristown, Pluckemin and Middlebrook—to Navesink.

The General relied on simple engineering to erect uniform beacons on all these various hills and mountains. A good army manual writer, Stirling left as little as possible to a private's imagination: "Each of the Beacons are to be of the following Dimensions: at bottom 14 feet square, to rise in a pyramidal Form to about 18 to 20 feet high; then to terminate about six feet square, with a stout Sapling in the centre about 30 feet high from the Ground, with the part of its Top about ten or 12 feet above the whole Work." Thus a large signal flag flown by day could also be detected by spyglasses.

"The Officer who oversees the Execution," Stirling specified, "should order the following sized Logs to be cut as near the Place as possible [thus clearing the area around the beacon]; 20 Logs of 14 feet long and about one foot Diameter; two Logs of about 12 feet long; ten logs of about nine feet long; ten Logs of about eight feet long; 20 logs of about seven feet long; 20 Logs of about six feet long.

"He should then sort his longest Logs as to diameter, and place the four longest on the Ground parallel to each other and about three feet from each other. He should then place the four next Logs in size across these at Right Angles, and so proceed until all the Logs of 14 feet be placed.

"Then he is to go on in the same manner with Logs of 12 feet long, and when they are all placed, the two upper Rows of Logs should be fastened in their Places with Wooden Plugs or Trunnels, taking Care as he goes on"—Stirling finally gets to the combustibles—"to fill the Vacancies between the Logs with old dry split Wood, or useless dry Rails [the soldiers were apparently expected to drag old fence rails to the tops of local mountains] and Brush, not too close, leaving the fifth Tier open for Firing and Air." Once ignited, these 2,000-cubic-foot pyres of partially green wood would provide an impressive mass of smoky fire visible over miles for more than an hour.

IN THE months that followed, as the enemy maneuvered in and around New York City, Stirling's beacon system saw continued use. From Fort Montgomery on July 10, 1777 General James Clinton issued an order coordinating the beacon signals with cannon fire. Six alarm guns were to be discharged by the revolutionary detachments along the Hudson at Peekskill, to be answered by two at Fort Independence (just north of Peekskill), two at Fort Montgomery (four miles farther north), two at Fort Constitution (six miles farther north)—"with the Beacon there to be fired as usual."

Fort Constitution's guns and beacon were to be answered by two rounds from a brass 24-pounder near New Windsor (six additional miles north). "Upon this Signal," Clinton continued, "the Militia are to march by Detachments, without further Notice, as Reinforcements of this [Fort Montgomery] Garrison."

Discipline at lower levels in the signal service was never foolproof. Following one incident on Mount Beacon, Captain Abraham Williams—acknowledging what may have been an act of tory sabotage—embarrassedly reported from Fishkill to Governor Clinton: "By some unaccountable negligence in the Guard, the Beacon on the east side of the River, either by accident or design, unfortunately took fire about one o'Clock this day & burnt to the ground. As it is probable this accident will be taken by the Country for a signal of alarm, I have taken the liberty to give you this information to prevent the movement of the militia."

FIRE ALONG the Hudson could also be a terrifying offensive weapon.

For centuries prior to the American Revolution, the Royal Navy had drifted fire ships downwind to set enemy vessels aflame—much as Samson tied firebrands to the tails of 300 foxes and sent them into the Philistine corn fields. In 1588 the British used fire ships successfully against the Spanish Armada, rewarding that dangerous service with £100 or a gold medal.

Weighing the same techniques, Congress authorized Washington on May 30, 1776 to build fire rafts to defend the Hudson River. "This Art," John Adams rejoiced, "carries Terror and Dismay along with it, and the very Rumour of Preparation in this Kind may do more service than many Battallions."

Early in July the Commander-in-chief requested the New York Convention's Secret Committee to start work on such rafts at Poughkeepsie's Shipyard Point. "If properly constructed and executed with Spirit and Intrepidity," Washington told Governor Clinton, "rafts are the most dangerous and alarming Enemies to Shipping. Expense ought not to be regarded if the Prospect of Success is in any Way encouraged."

On July 14, 1776 from Fort Constitution, Colonel James Clinton reviewed the Secret Committee's military objectives: "I approve of much of your Plan for Making Fire Rafts, and doubt not you will carry the same into Execution with the utmost Expedition. I think it advisable to purchase two other old Sloops, or more if necessary, for the Purpose. But let it be done at the cheapest rate," Clinton added, "for the Oldest and Worst Sloops will do."

Within two days, the Committee was able to advise Clinton that four fire rafts were almost ready: "We propose to fix them in the best manner we can, with dry Wood, Tar and such other combustibles as we can procure at this place. Two or three old Vessels we shall fix as fast as possible for the same Purpose. We shall send the Fire Rafts down as soon as completed."

The unusual speed with which the hastily recruited carpenters were able to complete those four rafts encouraged the Committee to order six more. All were destined downriver for Fort Constitution, together with the converted sloops/fire ships. The plan was to equip this little offensive flotilla—loaded with as much "Light Wood and Pine Knots, Pitch, Turpentine, Tar-Tubs and Barrels as can be got"—with grappling irons and 1,000 fire arrows (to set fire to enemy sails).

On July 12 Convention member William Duer wrote from White Plains to John Jay and Robert R. Livingston in Poughkeepsie: "I hope to induce one of you to repair immediately to New York. The Committee of Safety in Philadelphia have sent three Persons to New Jersey in Order to assist us in making Fire Ships—one of them, with whom I have convers'd, is peculiarly clever." Duer was speaking of Captain (later Commodore) John Hazelwood of Philadelphia. Hazelwood had developed all his fire ship experience in less than two months, by attacking British shipping on the lower Delaware.

It was the Pennsylvania Committee of Safety that first brought Hazelwood to Washington's attention. "Understanding that fire-vessels and rafts are preparing at New-York in a method different than ours," they wrote, "we are induced to send Captain Hazelwood to your Excellency to offer his services in this business. We have the highest confidence in his skill and abilities, having given him command of all our Vessels and Rafts. He has already sent forward a quantity of useful materials, which he is told do not make any part of the composition at New-York.

"The Committee do not mean he shall obtrude his opinion of advice upon those to whom your Excellency may have committed the direction of this species of defense," the Philadelphia group concluded modestly, "but they thought upon the comparison of different modes, some real improvements might be struck out."

Duer gave the newly arrived Hazelwood high marks. "The Fire

ships charged in his Manner," Duer told the Secret Committee, "must, I am confident, prove Destructive to any Vessell they fix upon—I have spoken concerning our Wish to destroy the *Phoenix* and *Rose* now in this River, and he is ready to undertake it. Not doubting but he will meet with generous Encouragement, I applied to Genl Washington to get Leave for him to come up the River; but his Presence is still wanted in Town, loading Ships 'till this Day Week, when he will wait upon your Committee if You send him Notice by Express; he lodges at Mrs. Graham's in Broad Street." Several days later, Hazelwood received a letter from Henry Wilmot, Deputy Chairman of the New York Convention, asking him to come up to Poughkeepsie immediately, bringing combustible materials required to charge the upriver fire rafts and ships.

On July 23 Governor Clinton at Fort Montgomery voiced concern to the Commander-in-chief: "I am happy to find the Measures taken here for the Reception of the Enemys Shipping approved. [Yesterday] some of the carpenters from Poughkeepsie arrived at this Place with the Fire Rafts. They are constructed on the Plan lately transmitted to your Excellency by my Brother—We are busy preparing & hope to be able Tomorrow or next Day to draw them across the River, tho I fear we will be put to great difficulty in procuring Anchors, Cables &c for securing them. The Combustible Matter with which they are filled will, I apprehend, hardly be quick enough, for want of Spirits of Turpentine & Salt Petre. We have neither," Clinton continued, "& I don't know where to apply for or how to secure these necessary Articles."

On August 26, having delayed a month in the city on more urgent business, Captain Hazelwood finally arrived from New York, bringing to Poughkeepsie the badly-needed "2 Brls of Spirits of Turpentine and 6 gals of Spirit of Wine," as well as "60 Hand Grenade Shells complete, 12 strong Port Fires, 10 lbs. Slow Matches and 10 lbs. Spun Cotton." He eagerly demonstrated to Committee members his practical procedures for charging "Firerafts," applying principles developed on the Delaware—and carefully described by Daniel Joy to Samuel Howell and the Pennsylvania Committee of Safety in the same letter in which Joy put forward Bushnell's submarine designs as his own.

Joy advised Howell to begin by dipping "all inflammetery Matter in boil'd turpentine. Lay a tier of faggots supported here & there with billots of wood to give a free passage for the air. Then put Shingle shavings, Billots of wood & faggots alternately, untill the

Body of the Raft is full; Then lay three false Gutters charged with quick-match, prepared in the following manner:

"Take several clear thrids of woostard or yarn, slack twisted together, & dip it in a compound of pounded gunpowder & salt-peter, well mixed up with Spirits of Turpentine, & then well Dryed. Lay it in the whole length of the gutter, over which put a length of tow, oakem or straw dipt in Spirits of Turpentine & Dryed, & tack it down with a few Nails to keep them both fast.

"Then lay several wisp of straw as before cross-ways, & some to be carried off through the Middle from the intersection of the others, in order that the whole may be on Fire by the time they get's alongside the Enemy. Then raise the remainder with ceder rails or dry sparrs—first a tier one way, kept apart by here & there a faggot, then a tier crossways, & so alternatively untill high enough. Then the whole should be secured together by two Small chains crossing on the top, to secure it from being pulled to pieces by the enemy.

"Towards that part where you Judge the Enemy will come with their boats to tow them off, place Rocket & Pistol barrels charged with Serpent composition, all inclining toward the Enemy, that when they take fire, they shall continue blowing off the matter they are charged with, amongst the Ships rigging & sails. Over them raise a ridge of straw like a roof, on which scatter a quantity of powdered rosin. Next secure it from the weather by Thatching it with rye straw, & pay it well with Turpentine. After that is hardened, give it a coat of hot tar."

Anyone following Joy's instructions could scarcely go wrong. Secret Committee members Christopher Tappen and Gilbert Livingston were so impressed by the way Hazelwood fitted out the Poughkeepsie rafts that they urged the New York Convention to issue him a certificate of commendation, proudly adding "we think we can now carry on our Works without further Assistance." The Convention gave Hazelwood the "Thanks of this House," plus $300 for expenses.

Left unstated was everyone's enormous disappointment over the event that had delayed the Pennsylvania consultant so long in New York City. With Hazelwood's participation, the initial use of fire ships on the Hudson River had actually been a distressing failure.

ON July 8 with the revolutionary forces still in control of all of New York City except Staten Island, General William Howe, perhaps eager to commence naval operations before the arrival of his older brother, suggested to Vice Admiral Molyneaux Shuldham "that it would be attended with many salutary consequences if Two of His Majesty's Ships were Stationed up Hudson's River, to cut off and intercept any supplies coming to New York, and answer many other good purposes."

In response, Shuldham advised the Admiralty: "I have given orders to Captain Parker of the *Phoenix* [44 guns], taking the *Rose* [24 guns] under his command, to proceed at the first favourable opportunity upon this service."

On July 12, the day Admiral Richard Howe arrived in New York harbor with the rest of his North American Squadron, *Phoenix* and *Rose* with three smaller support ships were detached from the fleet, running upriver—as we have seen—through almost 200 cannon shots from Forts Washington and Lee. They sailed 16 miles up the Hudson to interdict Continental supply lines and rearm many loyalists stripped of their weapons by local revolutionary safety committees.

Washington wrote directly to Governor Clinton: "I am apprehensive that they design to seize the passes in the Highlands by Land, which I am informed may be done by a small Body of Men."

News of the enemy incursion reached the New York Convention by way of a copy of a warning letter from Washington's aide-de-camp Richard Carey, Jr., to Colonel James Clinton at Fort Montgomery: "Two Men-of-War have this Afternoon passed by our Forts and gone up the River past Kings Bridge. You will therefore take such Measures as to put the Forts under your Command in the best State of Defence possible to Annoy the Enemy. You are also to Dispatch Expresses along the River, that no Vessels may fall into their Hands, and to give Notice of this Manoeuvre to the Commanding Officer at Albany, with all Expedition possible.

"I have it in Command farther to desire you," a postscript by Carey continued, "to take the Carpenters from the Vessels which are building at Poughkeepsie, and prepare those vessels which were taken from the Torys and are now at Esopus, Kingston, to be made use of as Fire Rafts, or to make Rafts in any other way Expeditiously, that will Answer the purpose of Harrassing the Ships which are gone up the River." The Convention immediately ordered all New York militiamen to safeguard public and private stores along the river.

*Phoenix* and *Rose* continued to operate in insolent isolation on the Tappan Zee for more than a month, exchanging occasional cannon fire with roving revolutionary artillerymen. Shore parties from the flotilla's bomb ketch and two well-armed tenders harried patriotic farmers on both sides of the river.

The Royal Navy now lay both in front and in back of Washington's army on Manhattan Island. A group of smaller American vessels, bypassed when the enemy ran past Fort Washington on July 12, was quickly assembled and armed. On August 3—as noted—it sailed upriver to attack the two British frigates in a spirited engagement that did little except reinforce revolutionary morale.

A week later an American council of war decided the two enemy warships represented a prime target for whatever American fire vessels could be brought into immediate action. On the whisper of such revolutionary activity, the British captains cautiously shifted their anchorage to a deeper part of the Hudson opposite the mouth of Yonkers's Saw Mill River.

Two of the fire ships constructed at Poughkeepsie and sent downriver were now ready; on July 31 Ephraim Anderson, working with Hazelwood, advised John Hancock in Philadelphia that both ships were "complete and hauled off in the Stream. In my next," Anderson promised the President of Congress, "I hope to give you a particular account of a general Conflagration in the demolition of the Enemy's fleet. I expect to take an active part, and am determined (God willing) to make a conspicuous figure by being a 'burning and shining Light' to my Country."

*Phoenix* and *Rose* had only a short time to wait. After two postponements, late on the drizzly moonless night of August 16, the two fire ships, a converted sloop and schooner—accompanied by three row galleys manned by Connecticut watermen—slipped out of Spuyten Duyvil creek and moved north.

Favored by wind and tide, the tiny flotilla edged slowly through the darkness towards the British warships anchored four miles away. In order to witness the dramatic midnight confrontation, a group of Continental Army officers, including General William Heath, rode through the soft summer rain up the east bank of the Hudson to a spot near present-day Yonkers. Their vantage point was not far from the grand Hudson Valley manor home where John Jay's loyalist friend Frederick Philipse III was being held under protective house arrest by the New York Committee of Safety; Philipse, from one of the wealthiest families in America, would flee to England after losing everything in the Revolution.

General Heath's memoirs describe the suddenly illuminated river: "The Gallies and Fire Vessels were silently moving up with the Tide, and almost immediately after the Sentinels on Board the English Ships had passed the Word, '*All is well*,' two of the Fire Vessels flashed into a Blaze; the One close on the side of the *Phoenix*, and the other grappling one of the Tenders. To Appearances, the Flames were against the side of the *Phoenix* and there was much Confusion on Board. A Number of Cannon were discharged into the Fire Vessel in order to sink her. A number of Seamen ascended and got out on the Yard-Arm, supposedly to clear away some of the Grapplings.

"The Fire Vessel was alongside near Ten Minutes when the *Phoenix* either cut or slipped her Cables, let fall her Fore Top sail, wore round and stood up the river, being immediately veiled from the Spectators by the Darkness of the Night. The *Rose* and the other two Tenders remained at their moorings; but it was said that one of the Tenders was deserted by her Crew for a while."

Fifty years later, Joseph Bass of Leicester, Massachusetts, captain of the 100-ton Poughkeepsie-built fire ship *Polly*, recalled his role in that midnight foray. Attached to the Continental Water Service, Bass commanded nine men aboard the converted sloop. A Captain Thomas from New London—history is silent as to his first name—commanded the smaller schooner.

The holds of both vessels were crammed with faggots of combustible wood and bundles of straw, both dipped in melted pitch—with a dozen more barrels of pitch placed around the deck. Foot-wide canvas strips dipped in turpentine hung down from the spars and rigging. A powder match was inserted in this mass of combustible material, ready for firing by the captain—as he escaped from his cabin through a specially-cut door directly into a whaleboat lashed alongside the sloop. One of Bass's men stood forward as pilot, four more sailors were forward with grappling irons, and three waited in the whaleboat, ready to cast off and pull for shore and safety.

With *Polly* in the lead, both fire ships dead-reckoned their way up the dark river. First indication that they had reached their target was the nearby sound of a ship's bell, and—as Heath recounted—the enemy watch's cry, "*All's well*" echoing in the night. In the rain under the looming Palisade cliffs, it was impossible for the American captains to determine which enemy ship was which.

Nonetheless, at the sound of the bell Bass swung *Polly* to port without hesitation, and bore down on the nearest shadow. It was the tender *Shuldham*—in the darkness Bass had unwittingly passed *Phoenix* and *Rose*. As the two ships closed, *Polly's* forward grapplers swung their hooks into *Shuldham* and cleated them fast.

Bass fired his match and jumped through the makeshift cabin exit, leaving both vessels "almost immediately in a blaze." A mile away at Philipsburg Manor on the opposite side of the Hudson, everyone was suddenly awakened by the rattle of musketry, followed by cannon fire on the river. "Words Cannot Express the anxciety I was under," Frederick Philipse wrote to his wife Elizabeth in New York City the next morning, "I heard fireing and saw the lights of the fire ships. One of our company heard a cannon. We all immediately got out of bed and sat at the door for two hours until the firing and lights ceased and disappear'd, but words cannot Express my uneasiness."

Joseph Bass remembered (inaccurately) how a panic-stricken enemy crew—including a few loyalist men, women, and children fleeing from Westchester and Rockland County revolutionary safety committees—poured onto *Shuldham's* deck, either to perish in the flames or in the river. The abandoned tender soon parted her moorings, drifted slowly towards shore, and burned to the water's edge.

Captain Thomas's lagging fire ship was quickly revealed by the brightly burning *Shuldham*. It came under an instant and vigorous British cannonade. But now Captain Thomas could see his quarry. He swung to port and bore down on *Phoenix*. Applying his grappling irons, Thomas lit his match.

The entire cabin took fire, with Thomas unable to reach the whaleboat through the flames. With five of his men, the commander dove into the Hudson—and was drowned.

Sailors on *Phoenix's* 37-foot-wide deck cut away the burning rigging. The frigate slipped her cables, while her longboats, aided by the tide, slowly towed her into the darkness (it was not *Phoenix's* night to die—she would go down four years later in a Cuban hurricane).

The following day, 45-year-old James Wallace, captain of *Rose*, logged his version of the night's action: "PM at ½ past 11 saw some vessels close on board of us. took them to be Rebel Gallys two of which prov'd to be fire vessels, our tender *[Shuldham]* being on our

Larbd quarter ½ a Cable distance, one of them fell Athwart her on fire, which set the Tender instantly in a Blaze but hindred her from faling on board our Ship, we veer'd away but finding we could not get clear of her cut the Cable. She driving clear of us fell Athwart the *Phoenix's* Bow; which near set her on fire, they got Clear by Cutting their Cable and Towing her off, Our people from the Tender all got safe on board."

Captain Hyde Parker, commanding *Phoenix,* logged a simpler story: "At 11 PM discover'd a Vessel Standing up the River, she being near the *Rose's* Tender, hail'd her and gave order's to Fire into the Vessel; in Five Seconds the Rebel Vessel boarded her Tender and was set fire to. By the light of this Vessel we discover'd another standing toward us at a Cables length distance.

"Immediately order'd the Cable to be Cut & Commenced Firing upon the Fire Ship; in Ten Minutes afterward she Boarded us on the Starboard Bow at which time the Rebels set fire to the Train and left her. Set the Fore Topsail and Head Sails which fortunately cast the Ship and disengaged her from the Fire Ship, after having been Twenty Minutes with her Jibb Boom over our Gunwale. The *Rose's* Tender was totally consumed; the same fate must have Attended the *Phoenix* had not the Steadiness of the Officers & Ship's Company saved her."

The next day the hulk of the grounded *Shuldham* was boarded by revolutionary militia lieutenant John Langdon and two of his men. Under fire from the British frigates—a cannon ball passed within a few inches of his head—Langdon succeeded in towing what was left of *Shuldham* down to Fort Washington.

One six-pounder, three smaller cannon, ten swivel guns, two cutlasses and a crowbar were salvaged by "the adventurers," as General Heath called them when he commended them to Washington with the suggestion that "Some Reward Proper to be Given, Perhaps Prompting others to Daring Actions."

Writing to Governor Trumbull two days later, Washington recounted the manner in which *Phoenix* had "unluckily cleared herself. The only Damage the Enemy sustained," the Commander-in-chief noted, "was the Destruction of one Tender." He did not pass along Heath's private observation—"I wish I could say that our other [Connecticut-manned] galleys did anything at all; a very considerable advantage would have been reaped."

Instead, Washington wrote: "It is agreed on all Hands that our People engaged in this Affair behaved with great Resolution and

Intrepidity. One of the Captains, Thomas, it is to be feared, perished in the attempt or in making his Escape by Swimming, as he has not been heard of. His bravery entitled him to a better Fate."

One trained observer, former schoolteacher Captain Nathan Hale, wrote in a valediction to his brother Enoch in Canterbury, Connecticut: "The night was too dark, the wind too slack for the attempt. The Schooner which was intended for one of the Ships had got by before she discovered them, but as Providence would have it, she ran athwart a bomb-catch, which she quickly burned. The Sloop by the light of the former discovered the *Phoenix*—but rather late— however she made shift to grapple her, but the wind not proving sufficient to bring her close or drive the flames immediately on board, the *Phoenix* after much difficulty got herself clear by cutting her own rigging." Thirty-three days later Hale himself would become a martyr to the revolutionary cause.

"Though this Enterprise did not succeed to our wishes," Washington noted philosophically to Governor Trumbull, "I incline to think it alarmed the Enemy greatly; for this morning the *Phoenix* and *Rose* with their two remaining Tenders, taking advantage of a brisk and prosperous Gale and favourable Tide, quitted their Stations, and have returned and joined the rest of the Fleet."

In the midst of all his other correspondence, the Commander-in-chief squeezed in a long letter of instructions to his 29-year-old cousin Lund Washington, who was managing Mount Vernon while the general went to war. Still disturbed by Captain Thomas's death, Washington noted to Lund, "We have not heard of him since, but it is thought he might have made his escape by swimming." General Orders that same day announced as an "award of merit to each of those who stayed last and were somewhat burnt, Fifty Dollars; and Forty to each of the others."

Soon thereafter the Connecticut galleys were sunk; on October 14 Trumbull sent a request to Washington that their crews "be admitted to return" to the regular army. This time the Commander-in-Chief was less forgiving. He had Adjutant General Joseph Reed write with some asperity that "the very critical state of our Army and frequent movements of the Enemy render it almost impossible for the General to write himself, wthout neglecting more important duties."

Reed noted how only the hope at headquarters that the "Captains of the galleys from your State would retrieve their reputation, prevented your having an earlier information of their behaviour.

They misbehaved, invariably," Reed complained, "from the first moment they came, to the time of their departure about a week ago." Reed saved his most distressing news for last: "They are now under sentence of a Court Martial for misbehaviour in the first [August 3] attack made on the ships in the North River. And on every other Occasion since, they have manifested such want of spirit and judgement as to be despised by the whole Army."

GENERAL HEATH, meanwhile, was urging that Washington immediately follow up the August 16 attack. He wrote: "From the confusion which was apparent, I am confident that if an attempt should be made on the fleet below, and but one or two ships set on fire, their confusion would be beyond description." While the failed revolutionary attempt on *Phoenix* and *Rose* was hailed by the British as their own striking victory—with a celebratory dinner for the two captains aboard *H.M.S. Eagle*—it did not keep Royal Navy Captain George Collier of *H.M.S. Rainbow* from (unknowingly) agreeing with Heath.

Collier candidly observed: "The present Situation of this numerous Fleet is extremely critical, as the Rebels have Six Fire Ships now in sight lying close under the Cannon of the Town; the first dark night when the Wind blows strong down the River, they probably will send them in Flames to burn us, & I forsee if they attempt it the loss of half our Transports & Mercht Ships—who from Terror will cut their Cables, fall aboard of one another, & if not burnt will be wreckd on Shore." Collier related how during this period, while holding the fleet's "Post of Honor, lying advanced above all the Shipping & nearest to the Enemy," he slept only by day.

As Collier predicted, even in the midst of the revolutionary retreat from lower Manhattan, fire rafts were drifted against British shipping in the harbor. At 3:00 a.m. on the morning of September 16 Captain Thomas Wilkinson on *H.M.S. Pearl* logged the "sudden approach of four Fire Ships, which obliged us to Cut our small B[owe]r Cable and drop lower down. Two of the Fire Ships were tow'd on shore by our Boats, and the other two drove on shore."

Capt. Henry Duncan on *Eagle* also logged "the appearance of a fire Vessel driving down the No River with the Ebb. At ½ past Saw a Second fire Vessel on fire in the No River, and soon after a third." Duncan's private journal records how he was "called by the officer of the watch and informed that a fire-vessel was close on board of us. I immediately run on the forecastle, and perceived that the light approached us but slowly. By daybreak we perceived them plainly to be four fire-vessels. By slipping or veering, the ships escaped them."

On *H.M.S. Fowey* Captain George Montagu logged dodging the same group of fire rafts; the first was "close on board the *Repulse*, but drifted clear of her & coming down on me, Cut my small Br Cable, let go the B[es]t Br & Veer'd to a Cable; Soon after the Guard boats made the Signl for more Fire Vessels. Perceiving Three to be drifting directly in my Hawse, Cut the Bt Br Cable & made sail."

And on *H.M.S. Preston* Captain Samuel Uppleby, seeing "two Fire Ships on fire coming down the stream, got out all the Boats & mann'd them. The Fire Ships were intended to burn the *Renown*, *Repulse*, and *Pearl* but past them & drove onshore without doing any damage."

Five days later on September 21, a fire of a different sort began to burn out of control in New York City; more than a fifth of its homes were consumed before the wind shifted. The British always insisted revolutionary incendiaries caused that scorched-earth catastrophe; "It is not to be doubted it was done by design," Lieutenant Colonel Stephen Kemble wrote in his journal on September 27. Several patriotic citizens remaining in the city were assaulted or thrown into the flames.

The next day the British seized a young man slipping north towards the American lines on upper Manhattan with a list of British troop dispositions on his pocket. They "hung him immediately to a tree," Rear Admiral Bartholomew James recorded in his journal, noting how Captain Nathan Hale "died with great heroism, lamenting only that he could not communicate his intelligence to his commander-in-chief, as he had done with success twice before."

CHAPTER V

# Fort Montgomery's Chain
## (1776–1777)

---

*In which a new pair of powerful forts are built at the southern gate to the Highlands—while the revolutionaries, after much difficulty, string the first of two great chains across the river*

---

*THE WIDTH* of the lower Hudson varies dramatically. At Haverstraw Bay below the Highlands, the estuary stretches almost three miles between shores. Yet only a few miles farther north, at four separate locations—Iona Island, Anthony's Nose, Con Hook, and Constitution Island/West Point, the river narrows to only 1,500 feet wide. The strategic importance of those four constrictions was not lost on military-minded members of the Continental Congress. On May 25, 1775—only five weeks after Lexington and Concord—they "Resolved, that experienced persons be sent to examine Hudson's River, to discover where it will be most adviseable and proper to obstruct the navigation."

Within only a few days of that Philadelphia resolution, as we have seen, Colonel James Clinton and Major Christopher Tappen were busy identifying for the New York Provincial Congress potential fortification sites in the Highlands. Forty-two-year-old Clinton, Tappen's brother-in-law (and father of New York's future brilliant

85

governor De Witt Clinton), was the older brother of George Clinton, then sitting in Congress as a delegate from New York. James was a native of New Windsor, on the west bank of the Hudson just north of the Highlands.

James was no stranger to New York warfare. Part of his adult life had been spent leading local militiamen in colonial wars against the French; he gained particular distinction at the capture of Fort Frontenac on the headwaters of the St. Lawrence River. At the beginning of the Revolution, Congress quickly appointed Clinton colonel of New York regulars.

Within two weeks, Clinton and Tappen recommended construction of a major fortification on Martelaer's Rock—to which the colonel appended an observation that eventually would change the course of the war in the Hudson Valley: "By Means of four or five Booms chained together on one Side of the River, ready to be drawn across, the Passage can be closed up to prevent any Vessel from passing or repassing." Clinton's vision was the first formal suggestion to block enemy ships with a chained obstruction across the river. The New York Congress immediately conveyed the suggestion to Philadelphia.

The revolutionaries could only guess whether Clinton's proposed barrier would be able to withstand not only enemy action, but the enormous pressure of maximum ebb tides that drained twice a day through the river constrictions, at velocities in excess of one knot. Perhaps recalling the successful chain boom during the Great Siege of Malta two centuries earlier, no one seemed to doubt that cut-and-try engineering, coupled with heroic ironworking on a scale not previously attempted on this side of the Atlantic, would prevail over both the Royal Navy and the tidal Hudson.

Primitive man had always created rough fibrous connections, supports, or barriers from twisted vines, later weaving braided plant fibers into tougher ropes. The concept of obstructing a watercourse with a roped boom to impede the passage of enemy vessels is as old as defensive warfare, but as ships grew larger and heavier, something stronger than rope was required.

Looking back in history, chains of metal—*"two fore and two aft"*—were used more than 4,000 years ago by the Chinese emperor Yu to moor his ships. In 950 B.C., Hiram, a *"cunning worker in brass,"* was fetched out of Tyre *(I Kings 7)* to decorate the Temple with *"wreaths of chain work";* Hebrew legend suggests Hiram also crafted metal chains for King Solomon's ships.

Aristophanes mentions Athenian naval cables made of iron. Alexander used metal cables around 320 B.C. to prevent early enemy frogmen from cutting his ships adrift in the dark. In *Book III* of Caesar's *De Bello Gallico*, we read *"pro funibus ferreis cateris revinctoe"*—fastened with iron chains instead of ropes. The invention of such strong, flexible chains of metal links represented a quantum leap forward to an ironworking technology that continued long past the middle of the 19th century—at which time wire cable, once again a kind of braided rope but this time with many thin steel wires, would offer even greater flexibility, durability and length.

At the start of the second millenium A.D., the emperors of Byzantium finally realized an ancient dream—control of navigation along the Bosphorus; they succeeded in stretching three metal-chained booms across that strategic waterway. One boom ran between the castles of Imzoz Kalesi and Yoroz Kalesi at the entrance to the Black Sea. A second carried 4,000 feet from below Constantinople's present Topkapi Palace across the narrow strait to the rocky islet of Kiz Kulagi (Leander's Tower) near the Asian shore. The third and most important chained boom protected shipping in Golden Horn bay; this was finally snapped by the Venetian fleet during the Fourth Crusade in 1203. Much of that chain was carried back to Venice—together with four bronze horses from Constantinople's Hippodrome to grace St. Marks's cathedral.

A very successful wrought iron chain was made by Venetian blacksmiths in the 16th century for the Maltese Knights of St. John of Jerusalem. At the cost of ten gold ducats a link, they forged a 650-foot chain to protect a shallow but strategic arm of the magnificent Grand Harbour on Malta's northeast coast.

The southern end of that chain was secured by a huge anchorage on the rocks of the Senglea peninsula, while its northern end was warped around an enormous waterside capstan beneath the guns of Fort San Angelo outside the city of Birgu, across from present-day Valletta. Normally the eased-out chain lay quietly on the bottom of Birgu harbor. But in wartime it was wound to the surface while boatmen slipped wooden pontoons and rafts underneath the links.

For three summer months in 1565 while tens of thousands of Turks and Christians battled and died in the "greatest siege of history," that Maltese harbor chain succeeded in keeping Suleyman I's fleet out of Birgu, and thus brought an end to Turkish expansion in the western Mediterranean.

In England, chains were used as early as 1428 to block the

narrow entrance of Portsmouth harbor. They were replaced regularly; Portsmouth city fathers paid for a new "chene overthwart the haven" in the same year Columbus discovered America. A large chain/boom was also used to protect the Channel port of Dartmouth, and during the Second Dutch War in 1667 the Admiralty's Surveyor of Victualling, Samuel Pepys, chronicled in his *Diary* the spectacular failure of the British naval chain across the river Medway.

During the American Revolution, the English harbor entrance at Portsmouth was resealed, against a 1779 Franco-Spanish invasion fleet cruising the Channel.

In North America in 1760, river obstructions were used—unsuccessfully—by the French at Trois Riviéres, Ile Aux Noix, and Fort Carillon (later Ticonderoga) to slow Lord Jeffrey Amherst's march on Montreal. At the very beginning of the Revolution, George Washington detached New Hampshire General John Sullivan from the siege of Boston to maintain revolutionary order in America's Portsmouth—the narrow strategic port of New Hampshire—and protect it from British naval incursion.

Using whatever materials were at hand, Sullivan fabricated in only two days a massive chained boom running across the mouth of Portsmouth's short Piscatauqua River, between Pierce Island and Henderson's Point. Although it was immediately broken by "the rapidity of the tide," Sullivan reported to the Commander-in-chief on October 29, 1775, "we have again fixed it, so that I hope it may hold." To play safe, Sullivan also stationed several fire ships and rafts above the boom, with "a great quantity of combustible matter."

On November 2, Lieutenant Colonel Stephen Kemble, then commanding the First Battalion of His Majesty's 60th Foot in Boston, noted in his journal that "Lieut. Grant, who was there, says there is a Boom or strong Chain thrown across the Harbour of Portsmouth, which is raised or lowered by Windlasses on each side."

Two hundred miles to the southwest, the embattled revolutionaries in the Hudson Valley were preparing to stretch their own massive chained boom. It would cross the Hudson to block British warships from ascending the river during the eight or nine months each year that it was free of ice.

Their primitive practice of structural engineering could hardly answer the question: Would a fully-loaded 5th Rate warship such as *H.M.S. Phoenix,* displacing 1,456 tons and moving at 11 knots with

*Entrance to the Highlands on the Hudson River:* Anthony's Nose at right, Iona Island at left; Bear Mountain and Popolopen Creek mouth in background.

Location of first chain in the Hudson Highlands (at present Bear Mountain Bridge): *H* = Hudson River; *P* = Popolopen Creek; *FM* = *Fort Montgomery;* *FC* = Fort Clinton; *C* = Chain.

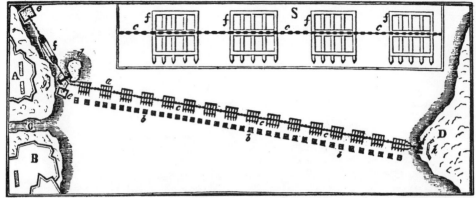

A   Fort Montgomery          B   Fort Clinton          C   Poplopin's Kill          D   Anthony's Nofe.
   *a*  Floats to Chain                    *b b b*  Booms in front of Chain,                  *c c c*  Chain
  *d* Rock at which the Chain was fecured with large Iron Roller.                  *e e* Cribs and Anchors.
  *f* Blocks and Purchafe for tightening Chain            *g h* Ground Batteries for defence of Chain.
        S Section fhowing Floats and Chain          *c c c* Chain          *f f f* Floats.

Sketch map of the chain (mistakenly indicating the never-installed boom)
from [A] Fort Montgomery to [D] Anthony's Nose.

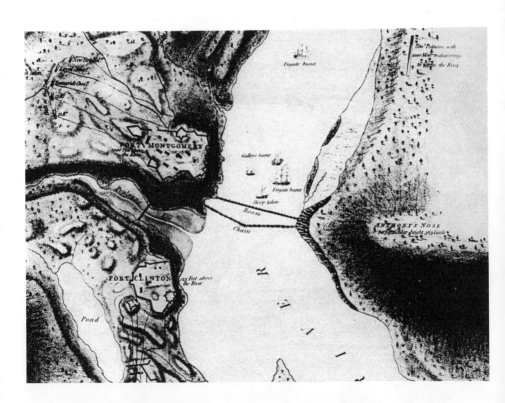

Detail: John Hills's *PLAN of the ATTACK on the FORTS CLINTON &*
*MONTGOMERY,* engraved by William Faden (London, 1784). Hills
incorrectly adds the never-installed boom *behind* the chain—a double error.

a favoring wind and tide, simply push through the protective boom and snap the 35-ton chain? The revolutionaries hoped the answer would always be "no."

*IN* 1775, completion of Fort Constitution on Martelaer's Rock was the major consideration in the defense of the Hudson Valley, but that project occupied everyone's attention only until the end of the year. On January 13, 1776, with Congress ready to dismiss Bernard Romans, activity on his fort was discontinued. Military activity shifted six miles down the Hudson to "Puplopes Point," the north bank of deeply-incised Popolopen Creek, opposite Anthony's Nose—the spot Lord Stirling had called "the most proper Place I have seen on the River to be made the Grand Post."

Stung by Romans's elaborate and costly upriver experiment, the Continental Congress offered conservative advice: "That the Battery at Pooplopen's kill be made of earth and fascines, and to mount a number of Guns not exceeding forty." Under Thomas Palmer's capable direction, the winter work went rapidly. Palmer even took advantage of the frozen Hudson to suggest sledding timbers for the fort down the river.

In April, the new fort was christened for General Richard Montgomery—killed in a New Year's Eve snowstorm while trying to battle his way through four-foot drifts into Quebec's Citadel, before his Continental troops' 1775 enlistments expired.

During Fort Montgomery's construction, to help implement James Clinton's concept of a chained boom across the river, General Philip Schuyler detached his aide-de-camp, 19-year-old Lieutenant Henry Brockholst Livingston (later an Associate Justice of the U.S. Supreme Court) to sound the Hudson River throughout the Highlands.

From Fort Constitution on May 21 Livingston forwarded the results of his survey direct to General Washington in New York City. He noted that "on the West side of the River is an Eminence [Con Hook, opposite present-day Manitou] that Commands a Long reach both up and down the River. If it should be thought necessary to Boom Across, I think it much more practicable there than in any other part of the Highlands, as the River at this place is no more than 500 Yards, its depth 18 fathoms, the tide not so rapid as at New-York, and a very bold shore." But Con Hook was judged too vulnerable to enemy attack, and was never fortified.

An unsettling increase in enemy naval activity along the lower

Hudson in July prompted establishment of the New York Convention's powerful Secret Committee. That group immediately began a plan to obstruct the river at Fort Montgomery. It took little imagination to convert the line of iron-shod *chevaux-de-frise* successfully stretched across the Delaware into some form of monolithic iron barrier for the Hudson.

But first the Committee disposed of a visionary scheme by John Jay, who wished to see "eight or ten thousand well-worked" Continental soldiers tumbling huge boulders off Anthony's Nose into the river, leaving it "so shallowed as to afford only depth sufficient for an Albany sloop." Jay was apparently unaware that the Hudson at Anthony's Nose was over 150 feet deep.

To many revolutionaries, the Committee's substitute proposal on July 19 may have appeared as absurd as Jay's: "That in order to prevent any of the Ships of the King of Great Britain coming up Hudson's River, it will be necessary to throw across the River at or near Fort Montgomery a Boom of Pine Logs not less than 50 feet long, placed ten feet apart, and framed together by three cross Pieces; that each Raft be placed 15 feet apart and Connected by strong Chains of 1-½ inch iron; that the Rafts be anchored with their Butts down the River; that the Butts be armed with Iron."

In front of that boom the Committee planned to float 40 additional shock-absorbing frames of timber attached to several downstream anchors, "the points or ends whereof to be shod with Iron so as to answer the double purpose of founding any Ships who may sail up to it, and if that should fail, to Lessen the Shocke of those Vessels when they come at the Boom." The Committee sketched such a frame, with "pointed Beams about the length of 16 foot, and to be made about 16 foot apart, with two Cross Beams worked in and Bolted."

DESPITE AN optimistic note in the July 18 *New York Packet* reporting the works at Fort Montgomery to be in good condition, the Secret Committee confided to Washington two days later that "notwithstanding their importance and advantageous situation, the Fortresses in the Highlands are by no means in a proper posture of Defence," and were in great need of artillery, as well as men to serve the guns.

"Even if the Enemy should be defeated at New-York," the Committee pleaded, "they might take such Posts here as we should find it impossible to dispossess them of. A few howitzers might be of singular use at this place. A skilful Engineer could be at no place more serviceable than here." Unbeknownst to the committee, the Commander-in-chief was already working on the problem of supplying such a skillful engineering officer.

The following day, the Committee urged the New York Convention to send all felled timber in the entire Hudson Valley to Poughkeepsie, for use on the river obstructions at Fort Montgomery. The members noted that since *Phoenix* and *Rose* were "already advanced as far as Haverstraw and only wait for a favourable Opportunity to pass the Fortifications, the Necessity of a Boom is rendered exceedingly pressing."

Two weeks before those two enemy warships ran upriver, George Clinton, a staunch whig sitting as one of New York's delegates in Philadelphia, was elected to the New York Provincial Congress. No sooner had Clinton arrived back in New York than he was also appointed a militia brigadier general, in command of the Highlands. He immediately set up headquarters at Fort Montgomery.

Before long, Philadelphia also named him a brigadier general of the Continental Line. The amazingly popular Clinton served as a pillar of patriotic strength throughout the Revolution. Elected as New York's first governor—and simultaneously as its lieutenant governor—he soon resigned the latter post in favor of the able runner-up, Pierre van Cortlandt. No other Revolutionary figure possessed Clinton's talent for combining the officer with the official (after the war he would follow Aaron Burr as Vice-President of the United States).

In July, General Clinton voiced anxiety to Washington from his new headquarters: "Should the Enemy ever attempt to gain Possession of this Fortress by Land, even with equal Numbers we are in a bad Situation to defend it—The Hill on the South side of Pouplopen's Kill & not above 1/7 of a Mile of it, overlooks our works, every Gun on our Battery lays in open view of it. It is accessible to the Enemy from a Landing that we cannot command without Batteries & a Road from thence to it that Field Pieces may be brought up.

"We must for the safety of our Works keep a Body of Men there," Clinton continued, "while it is fortified. A less Number will then hold the Ground, annoy the Enemy's Shipping, and render us safe from that Quarter. Indeed it is the spot where our first works should, in my poor judgment, have been." With Washington's approval, a new star-shaped fortification was soon opened on the south side of Popolopen Creek—predictably named *"Fort Clinton."*

By July 20 the Secret Committee learned with dismay that a supply of 50-foot or longer pine logs for their proposed defensive boom was unavailable anywhere along the Hudson south of Albany. They quickly pushed forward on the more ambitious concept—a chain of heavy iron links stretched completely across the narrowed river at Fort Montgomery. Like the obstructions at Forts Washington and Lee, this one was expected to halt or sufficiently impede the swift passage of enemy warships, while batteries of heavy cannon played on them from the shore.

DURING THE previous spring, under orders from foresighted General Charles Lee in New York City, bar forging for such iron chain links had actually begun, both at Mount Hope in northern New Jersey, and at the blast furnace operated by Colonel Robert Livingston, Jr., at Ancram, 40 miles northeast of Poughkeepsie. The Livingston family was politically powerful, long allied by marriage to the Albany Schuylers. Robert Jr. was a cousin of Continental Congressman and Secret Committee member Robert R. Livingston—who adopted that middle initial merely to distinguish himself from his ironworking relative.

Ancram, (dismantled in 1854), was New York's first ironworks, located at a small waterfall on Roeliff Jansen Kill at the easternmost edge of the Livingstons' 160,000 acre East Hudson manor. The cold-air furnace was erected in 1743 by Robert's father Philip, exactly one century after North America's first bog-iron works was built on the Saugus River in Massachusetts. The Livingston furnace produced true molten iron, replacing an earlier, less efficient bloomery—a large stone hearth where a waterpowered bellows blew air on charcoal, heating chunks of ore into a red hot spongy mass, which foundrymen hammered directly into wrought iron "blooms."

Most of Ancram's iron was smelted from unusually pure (up to 45 percent) concentrations of reddish brown hematite, imported by horse and muleback from "Ore Hill" and the rich Chatfield and Davis ore beds at Salisbury, 15 miles away across the Connecticut border. The wealthy Livingstons always maintained a substantial financial interest in those Salisbury mines, whose ore contained a high percentage of manganese that lent unusual strength to the completed forgings.

General Lee's plan was to work up Ancram bar iron into a long chain that the revolutionary forces could eventually stretch across

the Richelieu (or Sorel) River at Île aux Noix, near the town of
Sorel on the south bank of the St. Lawrence River. The chain
would keep any marauding Canadian war galleys from working up
the Richelieu into lake Champlain.

The Ancram links were hammered from 1½ ″-square wrought iron
bar ingots, both by foundry workers, and the blacksmiths at
Poughkeepsie's Kemble forge. The bars were heated cherry red,
triphammered, and doubled into shape. Like all wrought iron hot-
working, the hammering drove out impurities and refined the coarse
crystalline structure of the original casting, improving the strength of
the finished product.

On May 3 Washington dispatched $300,000 in currency to
General Philip Schuyler to pay Continental soldiers serving in
Canada—noting they "should not remain unpaid at this critical and
interesting period"—and added, "You will receive the Chain which
General Lee order'd, and which I think should be sent to and fix'd
at the Place it is designed for with all possible Expedition. It may
prove of great Service and Benefit."

On May 5 the Commander-in-chief advised John Hancock in
Philadelphia that he had shipped "the Chain for a Boom at the
Narrows of Richelieu, and have wrote General Schuyler to have the
Boom fixed as soon as possible." On the 10th Schuyler
acknowledged receiving the chain from Poughkeepsie, and
forwarded it north to General Arnold on the Richelieu.

But the revolutionary invasion of Canada, racked by smallpox and
defeat, was already faltering. Continental Army scout Justin Smith,
writing from Sorel in late May, noted that when the ice finally went
out on Lake Champlain, unusually high water on the Richelieu River
"prevented Arnold from sinking a *Chevaux-de-frise*, as he called it,
and as the flood still continued, the chain brought from New York
proved useless."

By June 14 General John Sullivan's rear guard was evacuating
Sorel. The peripatetic chain links, shipped south ahead of the
retreating army, were now destined for Fort Ticonderoga—to help
block the portage between Lakes Champlain and George. On that
news, the Secret Committee sent an express to Schuyler on July 20
noting that since the "chain intended to Obstruct the River Sorel
cannot now be applied to that use, the whole or such Parts of it as
may expeditiously be had" be returned to Poughkeepsie as quickly
as possible.

The Hudson River at Fort Montgomery was far wider than the

Richelieu; even if the chain was returned from Ticonderoga, more links would be needed. The Secret Committee asked the Northern Department commander how much chain would be returned, so they could start forging the necessary additions. They also asked for 150 trimmed pine logs that could eventually support the chain. "We flatter ourselves," the committee told Schuyler, "that your Attention and Influence will be extended to both these Objects."

The patrician Schuyler, still shaken over his narrow defeat by George Clinton for the new governorship of New York State, was far from encouraging. He forwarded the Committee's request to General Gates at Fort Ticonderoga, advising Chairman Yates "& the rest of the Gentlemen of the Secret Committee" that he would order the chain shipped to Poughkeepsie "in Charge of a Carefull Officer, *If it can be spared* [Schuyler's emphasis]. Before I left Tyconderoga," Schuyler explained, "we had it in Contemplation to Draw it across that part of Lake Champlain which Divides Tyconderoga from the Camp we occupy on the East shore opposite to it. I would not wish you, therefore, to make too great a Dependence upon Receiving it."

(When Burgoyne invested Ticonderoga a year later, he reported to Lord George Germain that his army did find at least one boom "made of very large pieces of round timber, fastened together by rivetted bolts and double chains, made of iron an inch and a half square." Recalling those specifications in his memoirs 32 years later, British Sergeant Roger Lamb—like Colonel John Peters before him—could not resist smiling over such an ineffectual result of "ten months of labour.")

"Whether the chain is sent or not," Schuyler advised Yates, "perhaps you will think it expedient to sink Cassoons [*chevaux-de-frise* caissons] or Sloops filled with Stone in the river from Tancanten-hook [Con Hook] to the Eastern Shore, to stop the Passage. Part of the Channel there is so Shallow that I was once on board of a Sloop so Deeply Laden it touched at low Water [Schuyler was mistaken—the channel at Con Hook is 90 feet deep], and that at any part where the Channel there is too Deep, Two Cassoons or Vessells one upon the other would answer the purpose. A Passage might be kept open in the shallowest part, and one or more Vessels ready for sinking kept at Hand.

"This place," Schuyler acknowledged, "is indeed above Fort Montgomery, but the Enemy would find it Extreamly Difficult to Force a Passage thro. the Highlands If a Body of Troops well

Intrenched were opposed to them. This may have occurred to you, and perhaps there are Difficulties with which I am unacquainted. My Motives will be a sufficient Apology for the Libery I have taken."

But Yates and the Secret Committee were far too preoccupied with their own plans to pay much attention to Schuyler's suggestions for double-decked *chevaux-de-frise*. On July 22 they appointed Jacobus Van Zandt, a member of both the Sons of Liberty and the politically influential New York City "Committee of 100"—together with Captains Augustin Lawrence and Samuel Tuder who had been supervising construction of *Congress* and *General Montgomery*—to oversee the Poughkeepsie blacksmiths in "making a chain to fix across Hudson's River at the most convenient place near Fort Montgomery, & fixing the same. And," the committee anticipated, "if it should be found Impracticable at or near the said Fort, then to fix the same at or near Fort Constitution."

The Secret Committee also ordered the busy Ancram ironworks to continue smelting and manufacturing—both from Salisbury raw materials and recently opened beds of local "Tauganick" ore—"a quantity of Bar-Iron of about 1-½ inches square to be sent from Time to Time to the Works at Poughkeepsie." On the margin of their order they scribbled: "For 600 yds. or 1,800 feet of Chain, you want 4,800 foot of Bar Iron in length," suggesting a link about 14 inches long.

That same week Gilbert Livingston and William Paulding reported to the Secret Committee: "We found the River considerably wider at Montgomery than at Constitution—and the Rocks on both shores much more difficult to fasten Chains to." Both urged that the finished chain be installed at Fort Constitution, for "several Considerations—of the Narrowness of the River—The Tides being less rapid—the Wind not blowing in so direct a Manner up the River."

Livingston and Paulding also believed a quantity of chain links still remained in New York City: "We intend this day to send off an Express to [Colonel Peter T.] Curtenius [a former hardware merchant and ironmonger serving as New York Commissary] to send them up." Under Charles Lee's original order, the Curtenius links were fabricated for Canadian use at the Mount Hope, New Jersey blast furnace, 40 miles west of New York. That furnace and foundry, working a rich local magnetite ore, had been established three years before the Revolution by ironmaster John Jacob Faesch.

(An ironworking facility still operates at Mount Hope.)

"Since the chain is made of Barrs not more than 1 & 2 Inch square," reported the committee members, "our Orders to Mr [Robert] Livingston Must be altered, for it will certainly be of no use to have one part thicker than another. Perhaps before you receive this," they advised Yates, "you will have an opportunity to Measure that part of the Chain which is now at Albany, that You may be certain as to the exact size of the Iron, as we did not actually measure that in N. York."

It was never an easy job to ship the chain, even in unassembled or disassembled sections. From Poughkeepsie, Livingston and Paulding wrote to Curtenius: "We understand that part of the Chain (you had made for Canada) is still in New York [City]. We have sent to Genl. Schuyler for that part sent to Albany, separately to be sent to this place. We wish you to send what is with you as soon as possible. If the River as far as Tarre Town or Croton River is passable, it would be more expeditious and cheaper to send it by water than by land to Peeks Kill, from thence by water to this place.

"If there should be any difficulty in obtaining leave to send the chain away," they continued, "please to apply to General Washington & let his Excellency know that the Secret Committee from the Convention of our State have applyed for it, Whereon we make not the least doubt you will have an Order to send it up."

Paulding and Livingston had been misinformed; all of Curtenius's chain links had been shipped north two months earlier. "The Chain I had made for Canada," Curtenius wrote back on July 26, "I have sent all to Mr. Vanrenssalaer of Albany in May last. If any remained here I would comply with your Request. The size of the Barrs that the Chain was made of, I think was two inches. If should any more chain be wanted, I make no doubt but Mr. Fasch would do it readily."

From Fort Montgomery, General George Clinton reported to the Commander-in-chief on July 23 that "Mssrs. Livingston, van Zandt and Lawrence arrived here, to consult on the most advisable way of fixing a chain across the river, and to view the shores." Although the ironworking at Poughkeepsie moved slowly, the log supply was improving. By August 1 the Secret Committee had finally amassed enough timber and materials to piece out a boom obstruction.

"As the Chain made for the river Sorel will in all probability be retained at Ticonderoga," the committee members noted, "the making one of sufficient length will occasion great delay. The [chained] rafts heretofore agreed upon by this Committee at a meeting held at Fort Montgomery & laid aside on acct. of the difficulty of procuring the necessary spars, will be the most effectual and speedy means of obstructing the navigation of the river.

"It appears to this Committee," the August 1 Poughkeepsie report continued, "that the Wood necessary for forming the rafts may be procured, a contract having been made for the same by Mr. Tappen with the approbation of Mr. Yates Esq. and Mr. Robt. Livingston." Major Tappen, by now relatively inactive on the Secret Committee, received its contract on July 26 to supply 160 more boom logs 50 feet long. Despite the urgent nature of his contract, several Convention members found Tappen's £1,000 bid excessive.

Straightforward specifications were given to Van Zandt and Lawrence for the rafts to be constructed from Tappen's logs: "Each to be formed of 5 logs of not less than 50 feet in length placed 12 feet apart & formed together by 3 cross pieces. Every raft to be placed 15 feet apart & connected by strong chains of 1-½ thick iron, & moored in line with their points down the river. Their points to be shod in iron." Each member of the Committee was additionally charged to "enquire for & purchase as many anchors and cables as they can procure & send word to this committee by the 7th day of this month of the number they can obtain."

At that same moment, General Gates authorized release of the Richelieu links still at Ticonderoga, and the alternate plan for a *chain* across the Hudson River at Fort Montgomery could proceed. Although the Secret Committee had been in existence for almost a month, its weight was finally being felt. On August 10 the members contracted with Ebenezer Young at 12 shillings a day to superintend installation of the chain.

As fast as ore could be smelted, the Ancram blast furnace cast pig iron, refining and triphammering it into anconies—dumbbell-shaped iron bars with large square ends. Before they were sliced off, the ends helped maneuver the work under the hammer, as the center was wrought to the required dimension.

On August 11 ironmaster Livingston requested a vessel be sent to his landing 30 miles north of Poughkeepsie: "I have now brought down to my Wharf two tuns of Iron, and there is now three tuns more drawn, ready to come down on Tuesday; and expect by Saturday to have five tuns more. All the Iron made since your last Orders is 2 inch, and the Bars as long as we could make them."

A sloop was dispatched upriver with orders from Paulding and

Gilbert Livingston "to fetch What Iron is ready for the Chain. We shall want no more iron drawn of the size of 1-½ Inch," the Committee advised the Ancram ironmaster, "save What is now finished. The Remainder contracted for shall be drawn of 2 Inches square. As soon as there is a quantity down at the River, should be glad to know it by a Line, that it May be sent for immediately." The sloop captain reported loading 185 iron bars; several days later Robert Livingston demanded a recount, claiming he had actually shipped 205 bars.

On the 13th the Committee met with Theophilus Anthony, Isaac van Dusen, James Odell and George Smart—four Poughkeepsie blacksmiths who earlier had helped forge the chain links sent to Canada. The four smiths offered to make up additional sections of chain at six pence a pound "rendered neat." After some haggling, they agreed to take a penny less per pound, with 32 shillings paid for each hundred pounds of bolts for the chain floats. Committee Chairman Robert Yates ordered the smiths "to Proceed to the making of it immediately."

"We are pleased to find the new fortification [Fort Clinton] opposite to Fort Montgomery going on with spirit," Yates advised General Washington. "We think it a most important Post, and are confident that if it be well fortified and defended, it will together with Fort Montgomery effectually secure that important Pass. The attention General Clinton has paid to that work merits approbation.

"The chain intended for the Sorel has now arrived from Albany," Yates informed the Commander-in-chief, "and will form a quarter part of the one designed for Hudson's River. The iron for the remainder is come to hand, and the smiths begin this day to Forge it. We have agreed to fix one end at Fort Montgomery, and the other at the foot of a mountain called Anthony's Nose. It will cross the river obliquely, and for that reason will be less exposed to the force of the tide, and less liable to injury from the Ships of the enemy. The length of the chain will, at least, be 2,100 feet."

While defensive measures in the Highlands were finally taking shape, fitting out the frigates *Congress* and *General Montgomery* had been agonizingly slow since their June christening on the ways at Shipyard Point. To speed things up, the Secret Committee wrote on August 21 to the Kingston Committee of Safety, urging them to dispatch an extra dozen carpenters with tools—"round Adzes, broad and Wood Axes, Gauges, Squares and Compasses" to the shipyard at Poughkeepsie. The committee also offered a very high rate of pay: "7s 6d, and half pint Rum per Day."

Response by the upriver carpenters was so quick and positive that the Committee at considerable cost had to order "two hhds. of Rum, marked *Congress*" out of its storehouse to be "sent by the Wagon herewith to the Ship Yards."

On August 30 New York Congressional delegate Philip Livingston wrote to Abraham Yates, President of the State Convention at Fishkill, enclosing Philadelphia's "resolve to employ the blacksmiths now engaged in building the Frigates, for the purpose of obstructg. the Navigation of Hudsons River. We wish much to hear from You," Livingston continued impatiently, "on what is done in that Affair & what more is proposed to be done."

Invoices for all this mounting activity poured in on the Secret Committee. On September 2 ironmaster Robert Livingston sent a £902 bill for Ancram iron shipped to date, including the disputed 17 bars. Eighty years before, New York Governor Benjamin Fletcher—a name synonymous with 17th century provincial corruption—wrote sneeringly of Livingston's Scots grandfather: "Robert Livingston has made a considerable fortune, never dispensing six pence but with the expectation of twelve pence. His beginning being a little Book keeper, he has screwed himself into one of the most considerable estates in the Province. He had rather be called knave Livingston than poor Livingston."

Although Fletcher's feelings were clearly a case of pot vs. kettle, Robert Livingston, Jr.'s economic outlook was as expedient as his grandfather's. In the midst of a continental war, while privately selling his 1¼″, 2″ and 2½″ iron "merchant bars" for £17 and £20 a ton, Livingston advised the New York Convention that he could no longer supply the State with bar iron for less than "£45 per tun [a figure the Convention considered exorbitant], as my Workmen cannot Work at the same Wages they have done, every Article they want to support their Famileys being double, and some Articles, such as Linens, more than double."

Livingston insisted that an unusual summer drought cost him extra money; he had to dig a new feeder sluice to maintain the level of his waterpower pond at Ancram. "You are pleased to say," he warned the Committee, "that as soon as you have the whole quantity of Iron you want, you will draw an Order on your Treasurer for the Payment. I hope that Gentleman does not live wide of Poughkeepsie, for if he does, I should not chuse in these difficult Times to go after him."

The revolutionary disaster on Long Island at the end of August cast a somber shadow over all this bustling Hudson River activity, and on September 9 the Committee was forced to confirm Robert Livingston, Jr.'s worst fears about being paid. Robert Yates wrote to the ironmaster: "We are sorry that after inspecting our Treasury, we find our Finances so low, that we cant possibly pay the full sum due you on the Iron that has been received." Whereupon Livingston, already battling the Committee over price, slowed his iron shipments. Tory William Smith, under house arrest at his relative Peter Livingston's, soon recorded how "several Tons of Iron Bars ordered for the intended Chain across the River in the High Lands, long since reported to have been constructed, still lay on a Wharf" in the Livingston Manor, 35 miles below Albany.

On September 11 Convention president Abraham Yates wrote nervously from Fishkill to Gilbert Livingston in Poughkeepsie: "It is conceived highly necessary that the Iron Chain should be immediately dispatched; pray send it down to the Fort without Delay. If it is not finished, let no Time be lost, and in the interim give us the earliest particular Account of its present State."

Three days later the Convention learned from Robert R. Livingston: "The Iron that the Committee first engaged (by the advice of the Smiths), on Working up we find vastly short of the Quantity wanted." He added: "I have been obliged to send an Express to the Forge for ten tun more; it is impossible for me to give the Time when the Work will be finished."

Livingston described how materials for the chain had practically exhausted the Secret Committee's treasury. He asked the Convention for an additional £2,000 or £3,000, before he departed for Fort Montgomery "to see that the Aparatus is got ready to fasten and stretch the Chain, that there may be no delay on that account."

Fearing an imminent enemy naval attack, the Secret Committee on September 27 "orderd and requested the blacksmiths employed in Continental Service in the Ship Yards at Poughkeepsie to proceed with all possible Expedition in making and completing the Chain ordered by this Committee," and requested they "severally desist from any other Business until they have completed the said Chain, as soon as furnished with iron."

A fortnight later on October 9, a worried Committee authorized working all 1½″ bar iron already delivered to Poughkeepsie into additional chain links. It also ordered a battery erected on Anthony's Nose, and resolved that a fort be started at West Point. In addition it attempted to requisition for chain construction all the various ship's carpenters on the Continental payroll at Poughkeepsie. This burst of defensive engineering required some source of fresh enthusiasm to pull it all together. At that critical moment such an individual appeared.

On October 14 Secret Committee members Gilbert Livingston and Robert Harpur, with Jacob Cuyler (Deputy Commissary General of Purchases), met with three Continental officers at Fort Constitution; the post was now serving as a general rallying point for Highlands area militia. The officers were General James Clinton, militia Colonel John Bailey (Chairman of the Poughkeepsie Committee of Safety)—and the recently-arrived *"Mr. Machin, Engineer."*

*"MR.* Machin" was 32-year-old Lieutenant Thomas Machin of the Continental Artillery—prototype of the "can-do" army engineer. Machin, son of an English mathematician, was born near Wolverhampton in Staffordshire on March 20, 1744. At fifteen years of age he entered military service as a cadet, fighting against the French in the bloody German battle of Minden during the Seven Years War.

Machin was still in his teens when he returned to England. He left the army for a job as assistant surveyor and paymaster for the brilliant but illiterate engineer James Brindley, then constructing the very first English barge canal. This revolutionary waterway spanned the Irwell and Mercer Rivers on the arches of two huge stone aqueducts, carrying the "Canal Duke" of Bridgewater's coal an unprecedented 40 miles by barge from the mines at Worsley direct to Liverpool.

By his early twenties, with those pioneering canal-building days behind him, Machin styled himself a mining consultant. Following a voyage to the East Indies, he sailed for America, where he had been asked to evaluate recently discovered copper deposits in northern New Jersey. By 1772 Machin moved to Boston, and was soon caught up in the fever of revolutionary politics. On the evening of December 16, 1773 he and 117 other Sons of Liberty "went out with the Tea Party." That loosely disguised group also included the adventurous 23-year-old Boston bookseller Henry Knox.

At the outbreak of war, Machin joined the troops besieging Boston, and was wounded at the Battle of Bunker Hill. By January 18, 1776 he had recovered sufficiently to accept a commission as

2nd Lieutenant in the new Continental Artillery, led by young Colonel Knox. Machin helped Knox emplace the cannon from Ticonderoga on Dorchester Heights, apparently impressing Washington with his engineering ability. When the army left for New York, the Massachusetts Provincial Congress requested the Commander-in-chief to leave Machin behind—to obstruct the channels in Boston harbor, and survey a canal route across the neck of Cape Cod, to provide greater safety for coastal shipping. The waterway was to be 14 feet deep with double locks at either end—a visionary project only completed (at sea level) 138 years later.

On June 10 Washington urgently requested James Bowdoin, president of the Massachusetts Congress, to forward the dependable engineer to New York: "I am hopeful that you have received all the assistance that Mr. Machin could give ere this in determining upon the practicability of cutting a canal between Barnstable and Buzzard's Bay. The great demand we have for engineers in this department has obliged me to order Mr. Machin hither in that branch of business."

Without waiting for a reply, the Commander's military secretary Robert H. Harrison issued an even stronger summons, ordering General Artemas Ward, commanding at Boston, "to send immediately to this place Lieutenant Machin of the train, provided he does not belong to either of the Artillery companies in Boston. If he does not, he will come with all possible dispatch." Which Machin did, leaving all his books and instruments behind at Sandwich with a physician friend.

Four days later Washington urged Governor George Clinton to "use every possible diligence in forwarding the works at Forts Montgomery and Constitution, as these are or may become Posts of infinite importance, expecially the lower one." On his arrival in New York, Lieutenant Machin was immediately assigned to Clinton's Fort Montgomery headquarters.

To a fresh plea from the Secret Committee for additional engineering assistance, Washington announced on June 21: "I will this day send Mr. Machin, a Lieut. of the [artillery] Train, who has just returned from overseeing the works at Boston. He is as proper a person as any I can send, being an ingenious faithful hand, and one that has considerable experience as an Engineer."

The Commander-in-chief ordered Machin upriver with a note to Colonel James Clinton: "The Bearer Lt. Machine [*sic*] I have sent to act as an Engineer in the Posts under your Command."

Washington's order to Machin himself read: "Sir: You are without delay to proceed for Fort Montgomery or Constitution in the High Lands on Hudson's River, and put yourself under Command of Colonel James Clinton or commanding Officer there—to act as Engineer in compleating such Works as are or may be laid out for the Defence of the River & adjacent defiles on each side the River, and such others as you, with the advice of Col. Clinton, may think necessary.

"Your being steady & giving close Attention to this Business is necessary," Washington continued. "'Tis therefore expected & required of you that you personally attend where you may be most wanted to forward the Works. In Case of an Attack from the Enemy, or in any Engagement with them, you are to join the Train of Artillery on that Station, & act according to your Office."

George Clinton quickly put the new engineer to work on the Popolopen fortifications. On August 2 the Governor advised the Commander-in-chief: "I have taken possession of the hill mentioned in my last, and the proper works are laid out there by Mr. Machin, which shall be executed with the greatest dispatch and economy."

On the 10th, anticipating the British landing on Long Island, Washington ordered the Governor down to New York with several regiments of new recruits to help defend the city. Before he departed, Clinton instructed Machin: "You will want many Necessaries for compleating the new works we have begun on the South Side of Poplopin's Kill, and the works to be erected for securing the Pass at Anthony's Nose. Use your best endeavours, applying to Colo. [James] Clinton from Time to Time for his aid and advice. The Artificers already employed & such others as may be wanted, are to be under your Direction."

Installed at Fort Montgomery, Machin immediately contacted Robert Erskine's Ringwood Furnace in northern New Jersey and ordered additional links needed to complete the first Hudson River chain. He also began work on a downstream boom—never emplaced. Using more than 200 1½ ″ and 2 ″ iron bars, the Ringwood blacksmiths, during nine weeks beginning August 21, manufactured more than £3,700 worth of links (276), clips (303) and bolts (197). All were hauled by a dozen teamsters, carrying up to half a ton of metal on wagons drawn by two yoke of oxen, along forest roads north to Brewster's Forge near New Windsor on the Hudson River. There Machin assembled the chain on log floats, before rafting it downriver to Fort Montgomery.

Following the October 14 military council meeting on Constitution Island, underlining the absence of any "Works erected at this Post that can properly defend the Chain proposed to be stretched across the River here [Fort Constitution], and the impracticability of executing any in Season for the above purpose, and believing that the River at Fort Montgomery in the narrowest place is but 1,600 feet wide, which exceeds the width of the river here but 100 feet," the Secret Committee members "Resolved, that Mr. Machin immediately prepare a place at each Side the River at Fort Montgomery, to fasten the Ends of the intended Chain to; that he place two or three Guns in a small Breast-work to be erected for that purpose on the Flat place just under the North end of the Grand Battery, where the Fire-Rafts now lay; and also, if Time permit, a small work near the Water Edge, on the South side of Poplopen's Kill."

The Committee carefully mapped the Fort Montgomery position on the back of a copy of its minutes, showing the proposed location for the chain and the heavy shore batteries that would pound an enemy warship sufficiently foolhardy to sail against it. Machin was also ordered to build another small fortification—dubbed *"Fort Independence"*—on Roa Hook, south of Anthony's Nose.

By October 22 as work on the Continental frigates *Congress* and *General Montgomery* neared completion at Shipyard Point in Poughkeepsie, the New York Committee of Safety ordered Gilbert Livingston and Henry Wisner down to Popolopen Creek with whatever sections of chain were already affixed to log floats, urging them to "carry this Measure into Execution in the most Expeditious Manner possible."

Within days, everything was ready. During slack water on a day in early November—so secret the only clue is a November 1 Ringwood Furnace billhead for the last shipment of 37 links to New Windsor—the assembled log rafts supporting the chain were connected, drawn across the Hudson beneath the ramparts of Fort Montgomery, and firmly anchored on both shores. In a sense it was only a test; winter was at hand, and in a few weeks ice would be drifting up and down with the tides. The chain would have to be unfastened and stored until spring; its construction made dropping it to the bed of the Hudson—like the Maltese chain in Birgu harbor—impossible.

At maximum ebb tide, more than 65 million gallons of water pour seaward each minute through the Hudson's 26-fathom channel off

Anthony's Nose. As the tide ran out that November day in 1776, enormous pressure began to build on the long curving obstruction. To everyone's dismay, the strain proved too great. One weak connector snapped, and the two separated chain float sections arced slowly downstream to fetch up against the rocky banks of the river.

There was no time to lose. With the next slack water, the eastern end of the chain was loosed from its anchorage below Anthony's Nose and laboriously towed back across the river. All the chain links were carefully examined, and the broken connector replaced. In still another tidal interval, the reunited chain was once more stretched across the Hudson.

To the anguish of the assembled revolutionaries, a second connector proved too weak.

*WRITING HALF* a century later, a British historian graphically described the failure: "The boom rafts, together with the chain itself, presented such obstructions to the descending current as to raise the water several feet, by which its force was increased and the chain broken."

A London newspaper reported (with some confusion): "The People of New-York, we are told, have in vain endeavoured to lay a Chain across the River, to prevent Vessels from coming up to that City; but the Tide runs so strong there, that no Buoy could float the Weight of Iron which a proper chain would require."

The unexpected end of this major American effort to block the Hudson passage seemed disastrous. A week passed while Machin reexamined the chain, and the New York Convention drafted and redrafted an embarassed report to Continental Congress President John Hancock. "In perfecting the obstruction between Anthony's Nose on the eastern shore and Fort Montgomery," the State Convention finally told Philadelphia, "the greath length of the Chain, being upwards of 1,800 feet; the Bulk of the Logs which was necessary to support it; and the immense weight of the Water which it accumulated; have baffled all our Efforts. It separated twice after holding only a few Hours.

"Mr. Mechin, the engineer at Fort Montgomery," the Convention continued, "is of opinion that with proper Alterations, it may still be of service in another part of the River, and we have directed him to make the Tryal. But we have too much reason to despair of its ever fully answering the important Purpose for which it was constructed. A like disappointment, we are informed, happened at Portsmouth."

During two years of war, the New Hampshire harbor chain had indeed proved impractical.

Days of acrimonious debate in Fishkill and Philadelphia about what the revolutionaries in the Highlands should do next were capped with additional military distress. "I have just Received the Disagreeable News of the Reduction of Fort Washington," General Heath, commanding at Peekskill, wrote to General James Clinton at Fort Montgomery on November 18. "The Enemy will now have Possession of the River below us, and it Behooves us to Exert every Power to render the River Impassable at the Highlands. I beg therefore that you would Endeavour to Compleat your works and the obstruction in the River as fast as possible."

The only support the Convention could offer during its November 23 session at Fishkill was the resolution: "That the Committee appointed to Obstruct the Navigation of Hudson's River, be instructed not to Pay the Blacksmiths who made the Chain which was lately drawn across said River, and broken by the Tide, until such Time as the sufficiency of their Work can be properly Examined."

The following day in Philadelphia, worried South Carolina Congressman Edward Rutledge wrote his friend and political ally John Jay urging "Steps be taken to place REAL obstructions in the North River"; and on November 28 General Heath chorused pessimistically to Washington: "The Chain extended across the River above this place has broke twice. I must confess that from my first hearing of the Intention, I expected no real advantage from it."

As the bitter month of November 1776 came to a close, the single bright light was the long-awaited Shipyard Point launching of *Congress* and *General Montgomery*. The frigates were swiftly secured for the winter in Rondout Creek, 15 miles above Poughkeepsie, the safest anchorage on the river.

On December 2, General Schuyler wrote critically from Saratoga to Pierre van Cortlandt, vice-president of the New York Convention, expressing his belief that "a Chain sufficiently long to reach across the River ought to have better supports than floating Logs." On December 9 a four-man military commission headed by General James Clinton and appointed to examine the workmanship of the chain, reported the first rupture was caused when "a Swivel broke, which came from Ticonderoga, which was not welded Sound," and "the second Time, a Clevis broke, which was made at Poughkeepsie." No other flaws were "to be seen in any Part of said

Chain," and three days later the blacksmiths were paid in full for their labors.

By then winter had arrived; the river was beginning to fill with ice. Schuyler offered a new suggestion to van Cortlandt: if and when the chain was restrung in the spring of 1777, it should be suspended just below the surface of the river on sunken "Cassoons from 30 to 40 feet square. If 25 such Cassoons were sunk at nearly equal distances," Schuyler insisted, "the intermediate space between each would be about 200 feet. The tops of the Cassoons might come up to within two feet of the surface of the Water at ebb Tide." Schuyler went on and on relating details of his scheme, which also included a huge triangular protective boom—"I cannot at present think of a better Plan," he said. In any event, the Hudson channel off Fort Montgomery was far too deep for any of Schuyler's proposed ideas.

Lieutenant Machin insisted that a chain supported on log rafts was still the best engineering approach, and reported that all the links appeared serviceable. After conferring with Machin, Robert R. Livingston told the New York Convention that he had "reason to believe that, with proper alterations, [the chain] might still be made very useful," and he "had taken the liberty to direct Mr. Machin to remove it to any situation where it can be more advantageously placed."

To that end Washington's Chief Engineer Colonel Rufus Putnam wrote Machin from Peekskill on December 13 to ask for some "sketch of the North River through the High Lands, with a geographical description of the country on the west side. I am going in a few days to wait on his Excellency with the best account of this part of the country, that without an actual survey, I am unable to give."

Machin quickly drafted a map for Putnam, urging that the chain project go forward as planned. Following Putnam's meeting with the Commander-in-chief, Machin was authorized to refix the chain at the same Fort Montgomery site the following spring. Before ice completely locked up the Hudson, Machin towed the logs supporting the chain into Popolopen Creek, where blacksmiths could replace any questionable links and carpenters could hew additional log supports.

On January 6, 1777—in the first week of the year whose last three digits hopefully symbolized to every American tory the royal gibbets from which all the revolutionary leaders would soon be dangling—the New York Committee of Safety in Fishkill "Resolved: that Capn. Machine be empowered, with the advice and under the direction of General George Clinton, to employ such and so many laborers and artificers as will be sufficient to perfect the Obstructions in Hudson's river, and to lay out and erect such works as will be necessary for the defense thereof.

"And whereas," the Committee continued, seeking construction help wherever it might be found, "it hath been suggested that a number of the Disaffected persons taken in this State may be usefully employed in the above work; Ordered that the Committee for Discovering and detecting conspiracies formed within this State be required to send 30 of those now at Fishkill, whom they shall deem least dangerous, under guard to New Windsor, and to put them under the Direction of Capn. Machine."

The following day, Machin received his provisional commission as an artillery Captain Lieutenant, although the slow-moving Board of War would withhold its final approval for another 15 months. On the 29th Machin was summoned to Washington's headquarters in Morristown, New Jersey to give the Commander-in-chief a firsthand report on progress with the chain.

After the meeting, Washington sent a personal letter to Brigadier General Henry Knox, commending Machin to his fellow Tea Party member's continued attention, adding: "I cannot help reminding you of him, as he appears from observation, and information, to be a person of merit. He has also mentioned something to me respecting his pay, which you will cause to be enquired into—he has received none, he says, since the month of May."

The new Captain's enthusiastic approach to the problems of repairing and strengthening the chain led Washington to privately deprecate to John Hancock all the earlier revolutionary attempts to block the lower Hudson. "In endeavoring to obstruct the Passage of the North River in some place between the Mouth and the Highlands, where the Channel is amazingly wide and deep," the Commander-in-chief wrote, "our labor and expense has been thrown away." He was clearly hoping for better results from the fortifications and obstruction at Fort Montgomery.

The frigid Highlands weather was soon taking its toll, causing Governor Clinton to complain to Machin on January 31 that "the artificers neither go out early enough in the morning, or continue late enough in the evening, at work. I was surprised this day to see many break off a little after three in the afternoon. It was said they had not been home for dinner, but from nine in the morning until three in the afternoon is not a day's work.

"If you think the hours are too long," Clinton said, "make any alteration you think right; but pray, whatever hours are fixed on, contrive to make them work." He enclosed a cautionary order for Machin to issue to all "the artificers and others employed in obstructing the navigation of Hudson's river," which read: "As high wages are given by the public at this season of the year when the days are short and the weather fickle, in order to have this most necessary work (upon which not only the safety of this State, but the whole continent, depends) compleated in due season: It is therefore expected that those who are employed and receive the public's money, will be faithful in the service and do the most they can.

"The monthly Pay rolls must be attested (if required)," Clinton's order continued, "by the master workmen, and an honest man can never return a man for a full day's pay who has not done a full day's work. This would be dishonest and punishable. The Engineer is to mark the defaulters (if any), that a proper deduction may be made from their wages."

With the Revolution far from over, such positive observations reflected the new democratic perspective slowly beginning to reorder the revolutionary struggle against King and Parliament. For their part, in addition to so many other duties, Secret Committee members John Jay and Robert R. Livingston, together with Gouverneur Morris, spent much of the long winter drafting what would soon be New York State's first constitution.

Already a few Englishmen of keen political vision were perceiving a different light at the end of the North American tunnel. In February one candid Londoner wrote: "The small scale of our maps deceived us; and, as the word '*America*' takes up no more room than the word '*Yorkshire*,' we seem to think the territories they represent are much of the same bigness; though Charleston is as far from Boston as London is from Venice.

"Braddock might tell the difficulties of this loose, rugged country," the anonymous critic continued, "Were he living, Amherst might still do it. Yet those officers found a willing people to help them, and General Howe finds nothing willing. We have undertaken a war against farmers and farmhouses, scattered through a wild waste of continent, and shall soon hear of our General being obliged to garrison woods, to scale mountains, to wait for boats and pontoons at rivers, and to have his convoys and escorts as large as armies.

"We have hitherto spent one campaign and some millions," the British Cassandra concluded bitterly, "losing one landing-place at Boston; and, at the charge of seven millions and a second campaign, we have replaced it with two other landing-places, at Rhode Island and New-York."

On March 14, with temperatures warming and the river ice slowly disappearing, Governor Clinton reported to Washington that he only awaited sufficient anchors and cables to restring "the Chain across the River; the logs for buoying it are completely fixed, and are this Day sent off in a Raft down the River." *Congress* and *General Montgomery* were ordered down from Rondout Creek to Shipyard Point to complete their fitting out. On March 23, Clinton wrote Washington from New Windsor: "A number of our hands went to Fort Montgomery yesterday to prepare for drawing the Chain."

Within the next two weeks—the record is again silent on the exact day—Captain Machin's repaired and reinforced chain, weighing about 35 tons and supported on hundreds of pine logs, was firmly emplaced (at a sharper angle) between Fort Montgomery and Anthony's Nose. The revised location not only better fought the tidal currents, but could also deflect enemy vessels directly towards the fort's cannon. The 1,650 feet of chain—approximately 850 links, representing an outlay of about £3,500 ($12,000)—finally held perfectly.

Governor Clinton proudly advised Washington on April 18, "As it is now fixed, the tide has not the least impression on it; it is greatly strengthened by a number of Anchors and cables. I am in hopes it will answer some good end." On April 20, a day of political celebration—in Kingston, the New York Convention was adopting the new state constitution—the Commander-in-chief promptly expressed his military pleasure from Morristown, New Jersey "that the Chain across the River" did indeed "promise to answer the end."

That same week three thousand miles away in England, at Coalbrookdale in Shropshire, ironmasters John Wilkinson and Abraham Darby III were celebrating an equally momentous engineering achievement of the new Iron Age. They had just completed their 140-foot bridge across the Severn, the first river crossing ever constructed solely from iron castings. It was a harbinger of the peaceful Industrial Revolution that would follow the end of the American war in both England and the United States.

On May 5 Brigadier General Alexander McDougall replaced Heath at Peekskill. Visiting the Highlands forts with the conviction that an enemy attack was imminent, he wrote at once to Washington: "I think the passage is now secured by the chain against ships, as long as we can benefit from the uncertainty of the winds where it is drawn across. But how long we shall hold the Fort against a respectable force is extreamly uncertain; I think it a very weak Post against a vigorous attack by land.

"Experience is the best guide in war, as in every other science of Human Conduct," McDougall continued. "General Montgomery passed St. John's [sailing down Canada's Richelieu River in September 1775] at night with his heavy cannon, although the passage was narrower than that at Fort Montgomery, besides the difficulty of rapids. And General Howe will pass this at night, with Tide at Flood, as sure as he attempts it—unless the north part of the passage is also guarded by armed vessels."

The general's letter crossed one of similar sentiment from Washington. The Commander-in-chief wrote McDougall: "The imperfect state of the fortifications of Fort Montgomery gives me great uneasiness, because I think from a concurrence of circumstances that it begins to look as if the enemy intended to turn their view towards the Hudson River, instead of the Delaware. I therefore desire that General George Clinton and yourself will call upon every measure to put the fortifications in such a state, that they may at least resist a sudden attack, and keep the enemy employed till reinforcements may arrive."

On May 16 McDougall wrote directly to the Continental Marine Committee in Philadelphia, requesting direct Congressional assistance in "fitting and arming" two new row galleys, *Lady Washington* and *Shark*. "The Hurry of Business," said the Highlands general, prevented Washington himself "from Attention to the Points mentioned. The Enemy, I fear, will be able to pass the Chain laid across the River at Fort Montgomery, in the Night." The general had obvious doubts—not yet shared by the British—on the ability of the new chain to resist snapping by a 44-gun enemy warship favored by tide and wind.

"For these Reasons," McDougall pleaded, "I intreat you to give all the Assistance in your Power to the Speedy Arming of the new vessels. The Season is far advanced, the Campaign must soon open, and it's far from being improbable but the Enemy may direct their

Movement up this River. If they do, the want of the use of those Gallies may be extremely injurious to our bleeding Country."

The following day, McDougall persuaded three other brigadiers and a major general—Knox, Wayne, Clinton and Greene—to add their endorsements to his original report to the Commander-in-chief. The five generals also stressed the importance of adding anchors and a boom to the obstruction at Fort Montgomery, "to break the force of the shipping before they come up to it."

The generals' round-robin report continued: "The two Continental ships [*Congress* and *General Montgomery*] should be immediately man'd and fix'd [no cannon had yet been mounted on *Montgomery*]; and the Two Row-Gallies [*Lady Washington* and *Shark*] be stationed just above the obstructions, which will form a front fire equal to what the Enemy can bring against them. The fire from the Ships and Gallies in front, and the Batteries upon the flank, will render it impossible for the Shipping to operate there if the obstructions in the river bring them up; which, with the additional strength proposed, we have great reason to expect." Clearly stated, this was the basic strategy of the Hudson River chains.

The generals again emphasized the military importance of the Highlands barrier: "The communication between the Eastern and Western States is so essential to the Continent, & the advantages we shall have over the Enemy by the communication, and by having the Command of the River, warrant every expence to secure an object of such great magnitude.

"We are very confident," the joint letter to Washington concluded, "that if the obstructions in the River can be rendered effectual, the Enemy would not attempt to operate by Land, the passes through the Highlands are so exceedingly difficult."

General George Clinton's obligations in the capital at Kingston as new governor of New York State placed extra military responsibility on Israel Putnam, headquartered at Peekskill. Washington wrote Hancock: "I have instructed General Putnam to use every possible means in his power for expediting the Works and obstructions. Fearing that the cables [heavy ropes] might not be procured in time, I have directed his particular and immediate attention to fixing the Boom."

While he searched everywhere for long cables for the boom, Captain Machin also ordered required iron forgings from Erskine's Ringwood Furnace; the ironmaster himself was off serving in the Continental Army as Washington's Surveyor General. Before long many additional tons of iron boom hardware were being slowly carted through the woods of northern New Jersey up towards New Windsor and the foundrymen at Brewster's Forge

"In the Opinion of the Officers," Washington told Hancock (with his usual scrupulous attention to detail), "cables will render the boom more secure and extremely serviceable. If they are to be had in Philadelphia, I would advise Congress to order them to be purchased and forwarded without loss of time; they cannot be got elsewhere. They must be proportioned to the width of the River which is Five hundred and forty yards, and as they will be of most use if diagonally laid, the Gentlemen think they should be not less than Four hundred and fifty fathoms long, and of the largest size that can be had. Unless they are large and substantial, they will answer no purpose, and will not sustain their weight when stretched."

A month later on June 30 from his headquarters at Middle Brook, New Jersey, Washington again spurred Putnam: "Do push matters and let no pains be spared to complete the Booms. We may not, or may, have occasion for 'em. But we should be prepared at all points, and the sooner the better for our security." Putnam immediately passed the word to Governor Clinton, who queried Machin wishing to reassure Washington that the engineer was not encountering any unforeseen difficulties.

In the absence of adequate cabling, Machin was finally forced to improvise, and drew upon the two partially-rigged frigates at Poughkeepsie. On July 11 Clinton was able to advise the Commander-in-chief that Machin had stretched "the *Montgomery* cables ['spliced and fix't for the purpose'] across the River in Front of the Chain, which appears as if it would answer a good Purpose, & hope in a Day or two to have those of the *Congress* across likewise." The temporary expendient became permanent; a more formal boom arrangement was never completed.

As the war went on, a grudging British respect was developing for the exceptional organizational abilities of the American Commander-in-chief. On July 13 a British traveler in New York, who spent time in the Southern Colonies and visited Mount Vernon, wrote mockingly in his journal: "That a Negro-driver should, with a ragged Banditti of undisciplined people, the scum and refuse of all nations on earth, so long keep a British General at bay, nay, even oblige him—with as fine an army of Veteran Soldiers as ever England had on the American Continent—to retreat, is astonishing.

It is too much. By Heavens, there must be double-dealing somewhere!

"Considering the little military knowledge and experience [Washington] had before he was made a general, he has performed wonders. General Howe," the diarist scoffed, "a man brought up to War from his youth, to be puzzled and plagued for two years together with a Virginia Tobacco planter. O! Britain, how thy laurels tarnish in the hands of such a lubber!" Sir William Howe, the writer concluded, was "a Chucklehead."

Meanwhile, a tory espionage agent reported to Howe: "On the west side of ye River at the mouth of Pooplopen's Kill, opposite to Anthony's nose, a Battery on each side of ye kill, ye largest Battery on the upper side. The Rebells have in both six 32 pounders, 20 or 30 small Cannon from 4's to 12's." Interlined in the spy's report was the afterthought: *"A Chain across ye river at this place."*

The spy also brought the British general up to date on any threat that might be offered by Fort Constitution: "This fort stands on a place called Martlers Rock on the East side of the River, but may properly be called an Island, as a large Meadow runs round ye East side & is overflooded at High Water. Stands in a low situation & is commanded by hills on both sides of ye river. Has a Block house & 4 different Batterys, few grand, & no heavy ones."

Modestly apologizing that "diffidence of my own judgement in military operations leads me to inform your Excellency of every little step we have taken," Governor Clinton advised Washington July 23 of preparations to counter a possible enemy surprise in the dark against Fort Montgomery: "I keep out an advance guard every night," he told the Commander-in-chief, "on the extreme point in view [Dunderberg Mountain] about two and half miles below our works, properly prepared to kindle up a large fire upon the enemy's shipping heaving in sight.

"I have also on the shore opposite the battery, for a considerable distance up and down the river," Clinton noted, "put large piles of dry Brushwood mixed with leaves and the best combustible matter I can procure, with proper persons to set them on fire upon the signals being given from the first point; so that by having the Enemy between us and those lights, we will be able to play upon them with great advantage, while our shore will be thereby darkened to them."

At that moment 300 miles to the north, a colorful military ceremony at the mouth of the Richelieu River in Canada heralded the beginning of the enemy's long feared full-scale invasion of New

York State and the Hudson Valley. Under orders from the War Office to pass Lake Champlain and move expeditiously on Albany—an effort Washington feared would be attended by "the most fatal consequences"—General John Burgoyne with 7,173 men embarked on the lake and also marched along its shores. He was trusting on British forces in New York City to simultaneously thrust north up the Hudson, joining him at Albany to successfully split the Revolution in two.

Even though Burgoyne's hopes went glimmering, within three months every revolutionary plan for defense of the Highlands also went up in smoke.

ON THE foggy morning of October 6, 1777 after countless British alarums and excursions along the lower river, a combined enemy force of four thousand infantry (including three German mercenary regiments) commanded by Generals Henry Clinton (a distant relative of Governor George Clinton), William Tryon and naval Captain James Wallace—all supposedly carrying out London's master stroke to link with Burgoyne's Canadian invasion at Albany—were ferried ashore from transports near Stony Point, seven miles downriver from Fort Montgomery.

Clinton, bolstered by reinforcements from England, correctly surmised that Howe's campaigns around Philadelphia had effectively stripped General Putnam's Highlands defenses, with large numbers of Continental soldiers ordered south to assist Washington. From Peekskill a week earlier, Putnam carefully warned Governor Clinton: "Unless a greater force is supplied, you must be sensible I cannot be answerable for the Defence of the post."

In the event Burgoyne's force might prove incapable of dealing with General Gates's Northern regulars and militia, Sir Henry Clinton's upriver foray would only be temporary, lest the 4,000-man British expedition suddenly find itself trapped between a victorious Gates (with 17,000 men) and a swiftly-reinforced Putnam.

But up the river Clinton came, avoiding a frontal naval assault on the first Hudson River chain. Instead, the British commander moved to outflank the two Highlands forts by land. Following informer Brom Spingster along forest tracks and through rugged mountain defiles—also assisted by tory Colonel Beverley Robinson's intimate knowledge of Highlands geography—the enemy slipped over Dunderberg and marched three abreast in a pincers movement around Bear Mountain, pouring down the high banks of Popolopen

Creek, to attack Forts Montgomery and Clinton from the rear.

Most of Governor Clinton's Highlands regulars were not at the forts, but with the Continental Army around Philadelphia; many local militia replacements had also slipped back to their farms to harvest grain for the winter. In addition, the British thoroughly confused General Israel Putnam with a feint against his 1,200 regulars held in reserve across the Hudson at Peekskill.

As autumn shadows lengthened on the afternoon of October 6, Captain Machin joined Colonel William S. Livingston for a brief and unsuccessful parley outside Fort Montgomery with British Lieutenant Colonel Mungo Campbell, who was bearing a flag of truce "to prevent the effusion of blood."

The enemy's final "desperate attack" was resisted, reported Governor Clinton, "with great spirit by Continentals as well as militia." Machin helped serve a heavy cannon until a musket ball nicked his right shoulder—his second wound of the Revolution. As the undermanned forts were overwhelmed, many revolutionary defenders, including the crippled engineer, managed to stumble off into the gathering darkness. Two hundred and sixty-three Americans—including 26 officers—were killed, wounded or captured, with the loss of 67 irreplaceable cannon.

Daniel Taylor, dressed in civilian clothes, was dispatched by an exultant Sir Henry Clinton to convey greetings to Burgoyne's Canadian invasion force, now a little more than 100 miles away. Taylor's message was hidden in a hollowed silver bullet. Captured by the revolutionaries on October 9 and sentenced to hang, the spy confessed on the gallows: "I was to inform General Burgoyne that we had now the Key of America—the passes thro' the Highlands of Hudson's River."

"The forebearance and humanity shown by all the troops to the rebels after they became their conquerors, was astonishing," publisher Hugh Gaine reported five days later in his reestablished *New-York Gazette: and the Weekly Mercury.* "It savored," said Gaine, "of that benign temper which ever characterizes the army of Great Britain." (A few months earlier the *Pennsylvania Journal* asked rhetorically about the reborn tory—"*Who is the greatest liar upon Earth?*" The answer: "*Hugh Gaine, of New-York, printer.*")

Major Abraham Leggett was carried as a prisoner from Fort Montgomery to New York. He wrote in his journal: "After we was Shut in Gard House the Keeper Came In and Search'd and Took Everything we had about us not leaving a pen knife and on

Wednesday they Threw in through the Hole in the Door Some Raw salt Beef and a little Damaged sea bread—as soon as the bread fell on the floor it Took legs and Ran in all Directions—so full of life."

ON THAT terrible day of October 6, directly above the Hudson chain barrier, frigate captains Thomas Grenell aboard *Congress* and William Mercier aboard *General Montgomery* stood duty, guarding the river with small and inexperienced crews. It was their first—and only—engagement; it rapidly became an appalling disaster. Along with the galleys *Shark* and *Camden*, the two brand-new frigates slipped their cables and hoisted sail to escape upriver, only to be trapped by foul winds and an ebb tide. Before long *Congress* was aground near Fort Constitution; the revolutionaries' only resource was to set all the ships afire.

"Flames suddenly broke forth," reported a British army officer turned historian, "and as every sail was set, the vessels soon became magnificent pyramids of fire. The reflection on the steep face of the mountain opposite [Anthony's Nose], and the long train of ruddy light that shone upon the water for a prodigious distance, had a wonderful effect." As the fire reached the ships' guns and magazines, "the whole was sublimely terminated by explosions, which again left all to darkness." It was a bitter end to a year and a half of Poughkeepsie shipbuilding.

James Clinton, wounded in the thigh during the final British assult on Fort Clinton, somehow managed to limp down and up the steep slopes of Popolopen Creek, into the works at Fort Montgomery. He and his brother George then slid separately down the western cliffs of the river; James is even reported to have somehow hobbled across the chain rafts to the trackless eastern Hudson shore.

A 19th century American historian relates how once James crossed the river, he "reached the woods, and wandered through the night, enduring extreme torture. In the morning he caught a horse and rode 16 miles before he came to a house, the inmates of which were startled by the frightful spectacle he presented, his regimentals covered with blood, his cheeks flushed with fever and his voice hollow and husky." Colorful; but the spot where James Clinton reportedly limped ashore was only four miles from a well-organized revolutionary hospital at Beverley Robinson's commandeereed farmstead.

An aide helping the crippled Machin to escape was killed by a British bullet; his body fell across the Captain's. Attempting to extricate himself, Machin called for help to a retreating Continental soldier. Many years later he recalled the fleeing man's reply: "It is a damned good fellow who can help *himself* now."

Others, however, quickly came to the Captain's rescue. They bore him to a skiff, rowing ten miles upstream, eventually leaving Machin to recover near Blooming Hope, the Orange County home of Governor Clinton and his family.

ON October 15 in the midst of very heavy fighting around Philadelphia, Washington consoled Governor Clinton. He noted that without the timely help of Clinton's regulars drawn from the Highlands, "we should scarcely have been able to have kept the Field against General Howe. You have the satisfaction," the Commander-in-chief reassured Clinton, "of knowing that every thing was done that possibly could be, by a handful against a far superior force." Washington temporarily ignored General Putnam's failure to support Clinton during the enemy attack.

Several months later, when London's *Annual Register* reported the capture of the two forts in the Highlands, its editor exulted that "a large chain, the making of which was supposed to have cost £70,000 [$175,000], and the construction of which was considered an extraordinary proof of American labour, industry and skill, was in part destroyed and in part carried away." London's *The Remembrancer* for 1777 quickly picked up that considerablly exaggerated expense figure: "The boom and chain which ran across the River from Fort Montgomery to St. Anthony's Nose is Supposed to have cost the rebels £70,000."

With the two forts reduced, the enemy fleet, which until then had lain concealed behind Dunderberg mountain, moved up to the chain. A link was filed through to open the Hudson passage, and the next morning a flag of truce was dispatched upriver, demanding the immediate surrender of whatever remained of Fort Constitution. The fort's inadequate garrison fired cavalierly at the British emissaries. Once darkness fell, however, instead of mounting some sort of passionate resistance—like the legendary defense of Baltimore's Fort McHenry against the British 37 years later—the revolutionary commander demonstrated his belief in the post's actual strength by setting fire to everything that would burn, and abandoned the fort, unfortunately leaving all of its 77 guns unspiked.

Early next morning General William Tryon, in one of his last acts as royal governor of New York, sailed up the river from the captured posts on Popolopen Creek "to correct the insult to his flag of truce." Finding Fort Constitution evacuated, Tryon's advance party clambered ashore with powder, axe and crowbar; the works soon joined the other despoiled revolutionary fortifications in the Highlands—installations that had cost the young nation so much toil, argument, armament, and hundreds of thousands of dollars.

Back at Fort Montgomery, British Commodore Sir William Hotham reported to Admiral Howe: "I have directed such part of the Chain and Boom as cannot be saved to be destroyed: the construction of both give strong Proofs of Labour, Industry and Skill." Seven years later Sir Henry Clinton took confusing credit in his memoirs for also snapping a "smaller"—but non-existent—chain at West Point, during the same expedition.

Plundering and burning on both sides of the Hudson, a ten-warship British invasion fleet under Captain Wallace, including *Cerberus*, *Tartar*, *Preston*, and *Thomas*, plus two brigs, three galleys, and a sloop—along with transports, tenders and horse ships—carried General John Vaughan and 1,600 British troops 35 miles farther upriver to Esopus landing and Kingston, the seat of New York State's revolutionary government. That area, according to General Vaughan, was "a nursery for almost every villain in the Colony."

On October 16, after receiving scattered fire from a few small defensive redoubts and blockhouses—fortifications erected by Machin himself several months earlier—Vaughan and Wallace burnt Kingston to the ground, "laying everything in ashes."

Through such "wantoness of Power," deplored a Fishkill newspaper, "the third Town in New York for size, elegance, and wealth, is reduced to a heap of Rubbish. The once happy Inhabitants, are now obliged to solicit for shelter among Strangers; and those who lately possessed elegant and convenient Dwellings, obliged to take up with such Huts as they can find to defend themselves from the cold blasts of approaching Winter. Britain, how art thou fallen; ages to come will not be able to wipe away the horrid Guilt!"

One of Vaughan's officers eventually expressed an unsympathetic view of the general: "Without abilities, he was ill-tempered and capricious, ever censuring the conduct of others; particularly his senior officers." As for Captain Wallace, a brief biographical note, also by one of his countrymen, refers to his willingness to conduct "desultory Operations calculated to produce the greatest possible Irritation with the least possible advantage." The sack of Kingston was one such gesture—of no benefit to the outnumbered Burgoyne. Bogged down 25 miles north of Albany, that general was preparing to surrender one-quarter of the King's soldiers in North America to Gates's revolutionary army.

*WHEN* General Vaughan learned of Burgoyne's impending Saratoga capitulation, he sent word to Clinton that any further attempt to assist that northern invasion force was unrealistic. One hundred and fifty miles away from his base in New York City, Vaughan was now half that distance from Gates's huge army. He re-embarked his "Burgoyne relief force" at Esopus, scooped up all the temporary British river garrisons (one Popolopen fort had already been renamed *"Vaughan"*), destroyed the installations, and sailed back to New York.

Later Sir Henry Clinton complained: "I had flattered myself with hopes that, as soon as [Lord Howe] found I had opened the important door of the Hudson, he would have strained every nerve to keep it so and prevent the rebels from ever shutting it again— even though he had been obliged to place the back of his whole army against it. And I hope I shall be pardoned if I presume to suggest that, had this been done, it would have most probably finished the war." Howe, of course, had always intended to spend the winter in Philadelphia, not along the Hudson River.

The stunning news of Burgoyne's surrender led to an understandable improvement in the treatment of revolutionary prisoners taken in the Highlands. Major Leggett records: "The way the news was Convaid to the Prison was in a Large Loaf of Bread— the statement was on Paper, Placed in a loaf and Baked. As soon as that was Read in the Congress Room, the whole Prizen Resounded with three Cheers—the Keeper was alarm'd with Such an uproar as he Call'd it—Hasten'd to the second floor—then He was Inform'd— he denide it and Said it was a D____d Rebel lie."

By early November the upper Hudson Valley was again sufficiently secure to permit the retiring President of Congress, John Hancock, to cross the river on his way home to Boston from Lancaster, Pennsylvania, escorted by only a dozen Continental dragoons. In the Highlands, General Putnam was slowly picking up the pieces, while Washington maneuvered against Howe outside Philadelphia.

Putnam discussed the future of the ruined works at Popolopen Creek with Governor Clinton. From Fishkill, on November 7 he suggested an important strategic change to the Commander-in-chief: "Governor Clinton and myself have been down to view the Forts. We are both of the opinion that a Boom thrown across the River at Constitution with a Battery on each side would answer a much better purpose than at Fort Montgomery. The Governor would be reinforced by Militia with more expedition, and the Ground much more Defenceable. All these circumstances considered, we have concluded to Obstruct the Navigation at that Place, and shall go about it immediately."

The aging Connecticut general was attempting to put a brave and busy face on what had become a very difficult HIghlands situation. In addition to his other problems, living quarters for Continental troops stationed at Fishkill during the forthcoming months (this was the winter of Valley Forge) were, in the words of one observer, "miserable shelters . . . made with uneven stones, and the intervals filled up with wood and straw, a few planks forming the roof."

Before long, Putnam reported to Washington: "I am sorry to inform you that for the want of Pay, Genl. Poor's Brigade of [New Hampshire] Contl. Troops [fresh from Saratoga and ordered down to join the main army at winter quarters at Valley Forge] have Refused to cross the River. The Troops mutinied, the Officers endeavouring to suppress them, and they so determined to go home that a Capt. in the Execution of his Duty Run a Soldier thro' the Body, who soon expired, but not before he shot the Capt. thro', who is now dead. About 20 of them have made their escape and gone home; I have sent off some Light Horse and Officers of the Brigade to bring them back."

Colonel Philip van Cortlandt, commanding the 2nd New York Continentals, witnessed that unfortunate incident at Fishkill's Lower Barracks: "Coming within sight, I met several soldiers Bearing in a Blanket Capt. Beal. On Enquiry I found he had attempted to stop the Troops who had mutinied and was on the march, headed by a Serjeant whom the Capt. ran through the Body with his Sword, and the Serjeant as he fell fired and shot the Capt., so they both died."

Van Cortlandt attempted to restore order among the rebellious New Hamsphire soldiers "by alluring them first back to their parade by the Barracks which was near, and then in a long harangue or Preachment, pointing out the impropriety of their conduct, with promise of Pardon when the Genl. should arrive."

Meanwhile, "to make peace, and Reinforce you as soon as possible," Putnam advised his Commander-in-chief, "I am endeavouring to borrow about £1,000 or £1,500 to give them a Month's Pay. This I acknowledge is a bad precedent, but it is a worse one to keep Troops ten months without pay."

Despite the inspiring revolutionary victory at Saratoga, such mutinous rumblings were only one of many problems confronting Washington. Outwardly unperturbable, he wrote privately to his favorite Major General—the 20-year-old Marie Joseph Paul Roch Yves Gilbert de Motier, Marquis de Lafayette—from the worst depths of the Valley Forge winter, counseling the Marquis: "We must not, in so great a contest, expect to meet with nothing but sunshine."

Despite the Commander-in-chief's burdens, one positive fact remained. When the Royal Navy ascended the Hudson, its warships deliberately avoided any direct confrontation with Captain Machin's handiwork. As Governor Clinton reminded Washington five days before Christmas: "The enemy chose to risk every thing for the reduction of Fort Montgomery, rather than to attempt passing it with their shipping." The basic strategy of obstructing the river still appeared sound. "A new chain should be procured," said Clinton, "and with the boom, which is nearly completed, thrown across the river." The early spring of 1778 offered sufficient time to construct such a stronger chain—with a heavy boom for additional protection.

Reliable Captain Machin took exactly 85 days to recover from his wound, for which he later carefully billed the United States eight shillings a day for "Board and Nurse at Mr. Bornses"—plus £10 for "The Doctor's Bill." It was well into January before Washington could once again count on his talented and hardworking engineering officer to help create the new barriers.

BURNING THE SHIPS.

CHAPTER VI

# Pollepel Island's
# *Chevaux-de-Frise*
# (1776–1777)

*In which General Schuyler urges construction of additional underwater defenses farther up the Hudson—and after a little revolutionary infighting, a new line of* chevaux-de-frise *is built and sunk*

*DESPITE THE* obvious and distressing failure of the *chevaux-de-frise* in the Hudson off Fort Washington, there was strong high-level pressure for continued use of that defensive weapon.

Two weeks before the British ground forces overran Fort Washington, Albany's influential Major General Philip Schuyler learned from Governor Clinton that the new chain being installed across the river at Fort Montgomery had snapped twice. At least temporarily, chains, too, were proving undependable.

To fill the gap, Schuyler urged the New York State Convention at Fishkill to sink a new line of *chevaux-de-frise* further upriver in the Highlands. Schuyler's recommendation caused some stir in the Convention—the place proposed was 40 miles outside the Albany general's Northern Department jurisdiction.

With Washington's troops completely occupied by Howe's superior British and German ground forces in Westchester County,

Schuyler insisted the new river obstructions should be built by civilians. Although the revolutionaries had been sounding and surveying the river for more than a year, Schuyler also suggested that the Convention, "taking the earliest opportunity afforded, order the Depth & Breadth of Hudson's river to be carefully taken at such places as they conceive would be the most effective to obstruct the Navigation—Ver Plank's Point or Jan Kanten Hook may be proper places, perhaps the latter the most eligible of any."

The Albany general's inclusion of Jan Kanten Hook—today's Con Hook, in the narrowest part of the middle Highlands where the Hudson is only 1,400 feet wide—displayed a lack of knowledge of the river and its 21-fathom depth off that rocky promontory. Nevertheless, the Convention's Committee of Safety, sitting in Fishkill, forwarded Schuyler's suggestion to Secret Committee members Henry Wisner and Gilbert Livingston at Fort Montgomery, with orders to take a whaleboat crew and discover the shallowest areas for a brand-new line of Hudson River *chevaux-de-frise*.

In less than two weeks, Wisner and Livingston sounded almost 20 miles of Highlands channel from Stony Point on the south, to Pollepel Island at the north. On November 20, 1776 they reported to the Safety Committee on an absence of any options; nowhere did they find "less than eighty feet in the Main Channel, till within a short Distance of [Pollepel] Island."

Pollepel Island, lying south of present-day Beacon, New York, is a tiny dipper-shaped bump of wooded rock flanked by shallow mud flats. It is less than 250 yards off the east bank of the Hudson, and just beyond the northern gate of the Highlands. Its name, like so many others along the river, comes from the Dutch; it means *ladle*—the kind of drinking scoop that hung in old wellhouses.

About a mile northwest of the island, across the Hudson, lies New Windsor's Plum Point—not far from the mouth of Murderer's Creek—where Thomas Machin drew up plans for a shore battery with 14 cannon, to serve as the western anchor for the new line of obstructions to be stretched across the river.

"The Channel at the Middle of the River at that Place," reported Wisner and Livingston, "is about eight Chains [528 feet] broad, and fifty feet deep. From the Island to the western Shore, we found by measurement the Distance to be fifty-three Chains [3/5 mile—an underestimate]. From the Channel, the water Shoals gradually on both sides to the Flats. This above described Place is the only One

Looking north from Anthony's Nose through the central Hudson Highlands, Con [Jan Kanten] Hook in the middle distance (1985).

Northern gate of the Highlands, looking south towards Pollepel Island (1985).

Pollepel Island (upper left), over the shoulder of Storm King Mountain (1985).

Pollepel Island from the northwest (1985).

in our opinion that it is possible for an Obstruction to be made by docking [sinking *chevaux-de-frise*], effectually to impede the Navigation of Hudson's river." But the extensive line of obstacles would take a long time to build, in water not as uniformly shallow as Wisner and Livingston believed; it averages a full six fathoms for a distance of more than 4,000 feet.

As noted, Pollepel Island was far south of Schuyler's command. Nevertheless the Committee of Safety relayed Wisner and Livingston's findings to the general in Albany, requesting his advice. It also ordered the two Secret Committee members to suggest ways "not only to impede the Navigation, but likewise to prevent the landing of troops below such obstruction."

At the New York Convention's next meeting November 26, Robert R. Livingston moved the resolution "That: The navigation of Hudson's River be obstructed at the northern Entrance of the Highlands, and that the Convention of this State will exert every measure necessary for that purpose." The resolution also began an attempt to shift responsibility for constructing the new *chevaux-de-frise* at Pollepel Island to Schuyler, "whose well-known abilities and activity, knowledge of the country and military command, will give him great advantages in the execution thereof. We request him to take on himself the superintendence and direction of such works as he may think necessary, either there or elsewhere, for the security of Hudson's river." Livingston also sent a copy of the Convention resolution to Washington.

*AT THIS* tumultuous moment, Livingston—like many well-to-do revolutionaries—had little difficulty reconciling his public leadership with private investment as usual. To many wealthy patriots, the Revolution often promised material rewards far exceeding the spiritual; the business of liberty could often be good business indeed. John Adams was a critical observer; in the spring of the year he had written, "The Spirit of Commerce corrupts the morals of families. It is much to be feared, as incompatible with that purity of Heart and Greatness of Soul which is necessary for a happy Republic." Adams always viewed private greed masquerading as public good with disdain.

The most money in 1776 was certainly made in commercial privateering, that absolutely essential legalized piracy that would slowly throw the Royal Navy in the Atlantic off balance. In the first three years of the war—the House of Lords openly acknowledged—

revolutionary privateers were able to capture or destroy 733 British ships with ten million dollars worth of cargo. The unsettling success of this naval guerrilla warfare soon suggested to many powerful British shipowners and merchants that the struggle to contain the North American rebellion could very well be a losing battle. The Yorktown surrender in 1781 generated growing concern among commercial interests that any Parliamentary attempts to replace Cornwallis's lost army in America would simply be throwing good money after bad.

Robert R. Livingston's younger brother John was a Revolutionary speculator in scarce sugar, rum, cotton, and coffee. From Providence, Rhode Island, he wrote to Robert: "The many ship Captures that are daily made convinces me that it is best to lay out our money in Privateers. I wish you, Mr Duer and Mr Jay would be concerned in one, a small Sloop now laying at Hartford." The suggestion to enroll John Jay was hardly inappropriate; on March 15—long before he became a Secret Committee member—the New York Congressman helped draft the formal Philadelphia resolution authorizing privateering.

"I wish you and Mr Duer would endeavour to buy up all the 6 and 4 pounders you possibly can," young Livingston went on, "If you can buy the Cannon, endeavour to buy muskets likewise. I find I can't exchange any of my Tea here, as the merchants are afraid of engaging in that Article. They are a set of Vagabonds that shall never have the honor of my company Among them again."

RESPONSIBILITY FOR constructing the new line of obstacles at Pollepel's Island—reflecting state vs. national, and civilian vs. military concerns—was taking on overtones of a mild Convention vendetta against Schuyler. The general—austere, somewhat arrogant, somewhat meddlesome—was an old-Dutch patrician who had been automatically chosen by the Continental Congress to command its Northern Department (within a year he would be relieved and court-martialed over the loss of Fort Ticonderoga to Burgoyne).

Asperity mounted when the New York Safety Committee, communicating Wisner and Gilbert Livingston's river soundings to Philadelphia, noted that "the distance and depth of water at the north entrance [Pollepel Island] is found, on the experiment, to be the fittest place for the obstruction of the navigation with cassoons," and added, "We wish the direction of this work be committed to Major-General Schuyler, who we believe to be every way qualified to ensure its success." The Albany general refused to accept the responsibility, undoubtedly angered by the Convention's wry observation to Congress regarding the failed invasion of Canada— "the termination of the northern Campaign hath probably given General Schuyler leisure to attend to other objects of publick use and importance."

In the end, calculated protocol yielded to strategic impatience. On November 30 Robert R. Livingston told the Convention he was ignoring Schuyler and meeting with Generals Heath and George Clinton. Their discussion centered on mass production of more than 100 *chevaux-de-frise* to obstruct the Hudson at Pollepel Island, "at which Conference Mr Machin assisted." Despite failure of the device in the lower river, the group still agreed the project seemed "extremely Practicable."

"Both Generals," Livingston added, "seemed strongly impressed with a Sense of the Importance of the Work, and determined to give every Assistance in their Power to perfect the same, or rather to take it upon themselves, which His Excellency Gen. Washington's orders on that Head happily enabled them to do." By that time, the Commander-in-chief's soldiers were retreating through the snows of New Jersey towards the Delaware, leaving General Heath and 4,000 troops behind at Peekskill to fortify and protect the Highlands.

Heath immediately put two regiments of his Continental regulars under direct command of Governor Clinton, with orders to cross the ice and rally at Fort Constitution Sunday morning, December 1, 1776. Construction on Constitution Island had long been abandoned; the half-finished barracks were empty and most of the militia guard had been sent home. Livingston promised Clinton that the State government would provide the regulars with 300 axes for felling *chevaux-de-frise* timber—"all other Tools to be furnished by Continental stores."

The Convention issued an order requisitioning necessary axes from any local resident who possessed more than one; the response was disappointing. Clinton angrily complained to the Convention about the "Scandalous Manner in which some of the Militia left this Place, without returning the Public Stores they had been furnished with"; that Sunday the general found only ten axes left at the fort for his 500 men.

From New Windsor on December 10 an increasingly impatient Clinton unburdened himself to Convention Secretary John McKesson at Fishkill. It was a cheerless communication. "On my arival here with two Regiments of my Brigade to be imployed in obstructing the Navigation of Hudson's River," Clinton wrote, "I applied by Letter to the Honorable, the Convention for sundry Articles which were absolutely necessary for carrying on that Business, and which could not be furnished by the Quarter Master Genl's Deputy at Peek's Kill. Among these were scows, Cables, & Light Anchors, Takles, & Ropes for Draggs &c., and without which nothing to any Purpose can be effected.

"The 3rd Instant," Clinton continued, "I was Favoured with a Letter from a Committee of your House, promising me an immediate supply of these Articles, notwithstanding I am sorry to say I have not yet been furnished with one of them; except a Number of sloops, most of them without Hands or scows; a Parcel of axes if such they can be called, not fit for Use; & a Quantity of Iron. Without the others, these are only idly creating Expence.

"The sloops cant be loaded or unladed without scows," said Clinton, "& Timber cant be rafted without Ropes; the Blocks [*chevaux-de-frise*] cant be set up without Takles, nor sunk without Cables & Anchors. Indeed it is a mode of carrying on Business that cant fail to bring those concerned in it to Disgrace.

"As I have not yet learned the art of making Brick without straw," Clinton concluded, "I am determined, tho with the utmost Reluctance, to quit; & order my Regiments now here, back to the Forts & Peeks Kill, where perhaps it may be in their Power to render the public some small service; their tarrying here without Materials to work with can be none but the Contrary. Of this I thought it my Duty to give you Notice."

Bricks—with or without straw—for the blacksmiths' forges at New Windsor, as well as axes, remained in short supply, but the Convention members responded to the uncharacteristically harsh tone of Clinton's letter, and cooperation between the army and civilian authorities slowly began to improve. Three agents were immediately named to requisition boats, scows and other craft to sink opposite Pollepel Island. "The advanced season of the year," the Convention's letter of appointment stated, "requires that your preparations should be made with the utmost vigour, fidelity, despatch and cheerfulness."

Shipping along the river was ordered to collect *chevaux-de-frise* stone ballast for delivery to Machin; timber being gathered at Poughkeepsie was rafted to New Windsor. The Convention allotted Gilbert Livingston £400 to obtain "three tons of Iron an inch and a half and an inch and three quarters thick, or such other sizes as Gen. Clinton may direct," to be delivered downriver for *chevaux-de-frise* construction.

Not all such supply problems were so easily surmounted. On December 12 General Clinton wrote Livingston from the construction site at New Windsor that "Last Night Mr Ebenezer Young arrived here with a Raft of Timber said to contain 74 Logs of thirty Feet long and upwards, and 67 of about 13 or 14 Feet. A great Part of it so Short that it cannot be of any Use to us in making Blocks to obstruct the Navigation of the River, having got a Sufficiency of that Length before it arrived."

The inevitable speculators were also busy. "I am informed," Governor Clinton complained, "that most if not all of the Timber have been procured at such an extravagant price that I can't, without particular Directions from the Honorable Convention, think of using the longer Logs at the immoderate Price of five or six Pounds a Piece, which I have been informed they cost you. Perhaps it may be applied to some other Purpose that will better justify the Use of such high priced Timber [eventually many of the logs were used to support the West Point Chain]. The iron you sent—except for the quantity and Size I applied for," the governor chided, "I don't imagine we shall be able to use."

As ice slowly formed in the Hudson, construction activities ashore under the supervision of Captain William Bedlow, who earlier had served as one of the Commissioners for Fortifications in the Highlands, moved ahead. On January 6, 1777, at Clinton's recommendation, the Convention "empowered Capt. Machin to employ such and so many Laborers and Artificers as will be sufficient to perfect the Obstructions in Hudson's river, and to lay out and erect such Works as will be necessary for the Defence thereof."

But common laborers were now so scarce in the Highlands area that the New York State Committee on Conspiracies met in a Fishkill tavern the following day to implement a Committee of Safety order that several of "the least dangerous of the disaffected persons taken within the State be sent under guard to New Windsor and employed in the works, and that Captain Machin be requested to keep a watchful Eye on them and use his utmost Endeavours that none escape."

In midwinter, axemen and carpenters were in very short supply—and with good reason. On the 29th of January a dozen of the workers stationed on Constitution Island "most Humbly" petitioned the New York Convention regarding "the Distresses We at present Lye under Concerning Provision for this labourious undertaking of obstructing the Navigation of Hudsons River. Men so fully Devouted to Try their utmost to Carry sd. works into Execution, Cannot with Soldiers allowances Live at these Unprovided Barracks."

The war was entering its third year and the revolutionary economy was beginning to unravel. Only a day after the men at Fort Constitution sent their petition, a "body of Mechanicks" at the Poughkeepsie shipyard took up the cry—"with the greatest Reluctance Immaginable"—complaining to the Convention that "Every Idea of want & Misery most Impertinately stare us in the face, occasion'd By the Curtailing of our wages and the great Rise of every Necessary of Life."

As inflation spiralled, formal contracts with workers became a necessity: "We the subscribers do severally promise & engage to work as Carpenters in the Business of Obstructing the Navigation of Hudson's River near Polopen's Island under the direction of General George Clinton until the first of May next, unless sooner dismissed. On being engaged, the following Wages & Allowances to wit, Eight shillings [$1] p'r Day for our Foreman and five shillings a Day [63¢] for each other Man; a Ration & a half, and half Pint of Rum for each Man p'r Day."

A tory spy reported to Lord Howe: "The Rebells are now endeavouring to stop the Channel of the river by sinking Blocks of Frames & old Vessells, but whether they can effect it or not is uncertain, the Channel is upwards of a mile wide & ye greatest part 8-½ fathom water."

By the middle of February, Erskine's Ringwood ironworks was forging 40 points a day for the *chevaux-de-frise* picks. By the beginning of March, a construction subcommittee was able to carry to the Convention Governor Clinton's news that "the Obstruction of Navigation is in great forwardness; a number of Frames and Blocks are ready for sinking." The Convention immediately appropriated an additional £2,000 for the work.

Frames for the Pollepel Island *chevaux-de-frise*, stretching from Plum Point to the island, were being sunk 15 feet apart. "Every frame consists of a floor of Logs 40 foot by 45 foot," another British spy carefully reported, "with sides so high as to hold stones enough to sink it. They were made on the shore, and carried off by Scow to

Idealized drawing of *cheval-de-frise* off Pollepel Island (1860).

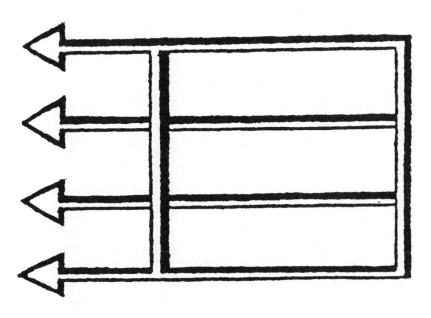

19th century misrepresentation of the Faden *cheval-de-frise* as a boom section (1860).

Relic of Pollepel Island *cheval-de-frise*, Washington's Headquarters, Newburgh.

Now fitting for a

# Privateer,

In the Harbour of *BEVERLY*,

The BRIGANTINE

# Wafhington,

A ftrong, good veffel for that purpofe and a prime failer.

Any Seamen or Landmen that have an inclination to

## Make their Fortunes in a few Months,

May have an Opportunity, by applying to

# JOHN DYSON.

*Beverly, September* 17th. 1776.

Privateer recruitment handbill, Fall 1776.

the place where they were loaded and let down. On the side looking south, there are two upright posts close together and one at each end. Their weight is suited to the depth of the water. They support long standing Beams with Iron Beaks, projecting beyond the uprights and rising to about eight feet of the surface of the River at full Tides.

"The frames are not sunk exactly in a line across the River. The place left open and buoyed off for the passage of [revolutionary] sloops is near the Western shore a little below New Windsor. There are no frames in the [very shallow] sloop-channel to the east of Pollopel's Island."

HALF A year later, when news of Sir Henry Clinton's unexpected Highlands invasion reached Congress in York, Pennsylvania, delegate Charles Carroll of Carrollton noted how much he was depending on the Pollepel Island *chevaux-de-frise* to slow it down: "If the Enemy finds them impossible to remove, they must land their troops & march by land upwards of 100 miles before they can possess themselves of Albany." But again, to everyone's dismay, General Vaughan and Captain Wallace worked their way through the still incomplete revolutionary obstructions and sailed an additional thirty miles upriver to Kingston.

At 5:00 p.m. on October 12, 1777 one British galley, *Dependence*, logged its passage, "in Comp his majesty Brig *Diligent, Spitfire*, and *Crane* Galley and transports, through the *Chivaux-de-frise* Polepens Island," and sailing downstream three days later: "At 9 A.M. weighed per signal in Compy as before, at ½ past Passed the *Chiveaux-de-frize*."

Two days afterwards, at Saratoga, Burgoyne surrendered his entire army to General Gates, who was now free to dispatch units in Sir Henry Clinton's direction. The remainder of Wallace's fleet realistically abandoned the upper Hudson, and without difficulty sailed south through the revolutionary obstructions.

DESPITE THE repeated failure of these unusual Hudson River obstacles, Governor Clinton obsessively relied on them to frustrate any further enemy depredation in the northern half of the state. Timber was again the real problem. On December 21 John Nicoll wrote to Clinton from New Windsor: "As youre Excellency is No Stranger to the Destruction made in this Neighborhood, By taking all the Best of the Timber for the obstruction of the River, &c. for which not one farthing hass ever Been Paid, Neither Hass the Timber ever Been [ap]Prised, Beg youre Excellency to appoint such Honest men for that Business as are Proper judges & freeholders in oure Country, & have had No Timber cut of theire Lands."

Ingoring the obvious lack of materials, the Governor continued to call for full completion of the obstructions at Pollopel Island: "I am highly sensible that the Security of the North River is a Matter of the utmost Importance to the United States in the present war," he wrote Washington at Valley Forge five days before Christmas 1777, "& that the safety of this State in a more particular manner depends upon it. It gives me great concern, therefore, that so little has yet been done to effect it.

"Works had ought to be begun," Clinton insisted, "to defend the *Chevause De Frize*, & something done towards finishing and sinking such of them as were not compleated when the Enemy came up the River." On January 17 Clinton repeated his request that the *chevaux-de-frise* "be completed, under the direction of Capt. Machin, who has hitherto had the Management of that Business. He knows," insisted the governor, "how many are yet wanted, and where to be sunk, so as to perfect the Obstruction."

On March 16 from "Camp West Point"—where Machin was now spending much of his time preparing river chain anchorages—General Samuel Parsons advised Washington that "a sufficient number of *Chiveaux de Frize* to fill those parts left open last Year are ready to sink, as soon as the Weather and the state of the River will admit it to be done. For it we have borrow'd and beg'd and hir'd Money." Parsons noted, "I have several Times advanced my last Shilling towards purchasing materials, etc., & I believe this has been the case with almost every Officer here."

Parsons's selfless comment went almost unnoticed; the need for *chevaux-de-frise* above the Highlands—or anywhere else in the Hudson—was quickly passing into American military history. In the incredibly short time of six weeks, Captain Machin forged and assembled a heavy new iron chain. Everyone was waiting to see it stretched across the river at "Camp West Point."

# CHAPTER VII

# Machin's West Point Chain

# (1778–1782)

*In which "General Washington's Watch Chain" is stretched across the Hudson in the Spring of 1778 to forestall any further attempts by the Royal Navy to ascend the river and split the states, creating a fresh feeling of revolutionary security*

SIXTY-YEAR-OLD General Israel Putnam was a legendary veteran of the colonial wars against the French. Commander of the American center during the siege of Boston, he was highly regarded by the New England troops in the Continental Army, and had been in charge of the strategic Highlands Department for half a year before his striking paralysis during Sir Henry Clinton's October 1777 surprise.

Two weeks after that attack, Putnam was still floundering. From "Three miles above Fishkill" he wrote to Governor Clinton at Kingston. He had received news, he said, of the enemy's capitulation at Saratoga, and "desirous of doing everything to subserve our important cause, and bring our struggles to a happy and speedy issue, I should be glad of your opinion—whether I shall proceed to Albany, remain to watch the motions of the enemy on the river, or move immediately down to attack King's Bridge."

The ordinarily calm and rational Clinton could not contain himself. From a mocking "Seven miles from Kingston," he answered Putnam the next day: "I am sorry to inform you, by a letter from General Gates of the 15th, the enemy had not surrendered. You do me the honor to ask my opinion regarding your future movements. It is needless and impossible for me to advise; because having once settled our Plan and your afterward deviating from it, concerting any future measures might be productive of ruin to one of us, if deprived of those Succours and that support which form a part of the general operation.

"My opinion of your attack at King's Bridge," Clinton continued, "is that it will be utterly inefficacious. Two prisoners tell me that Albany is the ultimate object. For the rest, I can only inform you of facts. Kingston was burnt yesterday afternoon, because I had not Troops to defend it. If I advance much farther northward, it will be in the power of the Enemy to ruin my little corps, by landing above and below me, as I shall then have the Catskill Mountains to the west, and Hudson's River to the east."

The Governor concluded ruefully, "I expect every instant to hear that Rhinebeck is in flames," and signed himself—

*"Your most obedient and humble servant,*
GEORGE CLINTON

New York's militiamen suffered most in the bloody Highlands action and were growing increasingly vocal over what they considered Putnam's support failure. The New Yorkers also demonstrated a common military problem—allied soldiers from one region deprecating the worth and bravery of those from another. "Whole colonies," wrote a young Continental captain Alexander Graydon, "are traduced and vilified as cheats, knaves, cowards, poltroons, hypocrites, and every term of reproach, for no other reason but because they are situated east of New-York."

In General Orders 15 months earlier, the Commander-in-chief himself had addressed the problem, cautioning all his "troops from the different Provinces that the honor and success of the Army, and the safety of your bleeding country, depend on your harmony and good agreement with each other, with all distinction sunk in the name of *An American.*"

On November 5, the axe began to fall on aging General Putnam, who—according to New England military myth—dropped his plow reins in the field at Pomfret, Connecticut to dash off to Bunker Hill.

Congress's new president Henry Laurens ordered Putnam to pay a flying visit to headquarters in Pennsylvania "for discussions."

At that moment, Alexander Hamilton was leaving Gates, who had turned a characteristic deaf ear to any attempts to detach additional Continentals to meet Howe's attacks around Philadelphia. Five days later from New Windsor, Hamilton wrote bluntly to Washington: "I am pained beyond expression to find every thing here has been neglected and deranged by General Putnam, and sacrificed to his hobby-horse, the whim of taking New-York.

"I fear," Hamilton went on, blasting the failing Connecticut general three times his age, "that unless you interpose, the works here will go on so feebly that they will not be completed in time, whereas it appears to me of the greatest importance they should be pursued with the utmost vigour. I wish General Putnam was recalled from the command of this post and Governor Clinton would accept it. The blunders and caprices of the former are endless."

Two days later, Hamilton repeated his complaints, telling Washington that Putnam's "conduct gives general disgust." The fiery young aide-de-camp even confessed to deliberately opening "a letter from you to General Putnam, that fell just now into my hands, as it might possibly contain something useful to me." There is no record of Washington's reaction to this indiscretion, but Putnam's Highlands command was temporarily transferred to the new hero of Saratoga, General Horatio Gates. A captured Hessian officer who encountered Putnam near Valley Forge on New Year's Day, confided to his diary that while the "old greybeard may be a good, honest man, nobody but the rebels would have made him a general."

*IN SHARP* contrast to Putnam's inertia in the weeks that followed the loss of Forts Montgomery and Clinton, the general's junior officers busied themselves along the Hudson River, "viewing the River, Bluffs, Points, &c., in order to erect some further obstructions." On November 24 General James Clinton wrote from New Windsor to Gates—then ready to leave for York, Pennsylvania and his Congressional appointment as president of the new Board of War: "A Chain or boom at a part of the river called the West Point, where it is quite narrow and the wind, owing to the crookedness of the River, very uncertain, with proper works on the shore to defend it and water-batteries calculated to annoy Shipping, would, in my opinion, perfectly obstruct the navigation."

Few recalled the similar suggestion 16 months earlier from
Jacobus van Zandt, the tough Poughkeepsie blacksmith and militia
officer. Van Zandt had insisted that the chain being forged for Fort
Montgomery would be better intalled at West Point: "I have
obtained from Coll. [James] Clinton the distance from fort
Constitution to the West Point, to be ab't 23 Chains [1,518 feet],
and on Examing the Shore on Each side of the river have found
Rocks Sufficient to Secure the ends of Chain.

"The Cityvation of the forts," van Zandt counseled, "and Cross
running of the tides, with the Bafiling winds generaly here, and with
the assistance of what Cannon already mounted, we can defend the
Chain much better here than at fort Montgomerie; and what will add
grate Strength to us, by placeing Number of men on the hills at
West Point with Musquetry, we can annoy the Ships in Such
manner that no man will be able to Stand her decks.

"You may perhaps object fixing the Chain here," continued van
Zandt, "on acct' of not heaving Cannon. I can assure you that we
Shall have plenty of Six pounders Mounted before the Chain is
ready; these in my opinion will be Sufficiant to do the needful, If
they are well Sypply'd. Coll. Clinton I hope in the Course of one
Week, will have addition to his forts of 18 Six pounders, and if Mr.
Jay Succeeds at Salsburry, I am also in hopes to have the 12
pounders ready to annoy our Enemies, if they should attempt to
come up long before the Chain is ready.

"So that on Whole," van Zandt concluded, "I am fully Convinced
that fort Constitution will far Exceed the fixing of Chain Cross
River, than at fort Montgomerie. I Could wish you would Examing
both places well, and Consider ware the chain can be best
Defended. I hope you'l Excuse this Scrol, having no time to fair
Copy."

No one had heeded van Zandt's reasoned suggestion. A similar
proposal was put forth at the same time by George Clinton—who
wrote to Washington in July 1776 concerning a chain of fire ships to
be strung across the river at Fort Constitution: "I have dispatched
Expresses to owners of sloops and boats 20 miles up the west side
of the river," Clinton advised the Commander-in-chief, "ordering
them down to Fort Constitution, as I believe by drawing a chain of
them across the narrowest part of the river and fixing them properly,
should the enemy shipping attempt passing by, they would answer a
most valuable purpose."

*TWO WEEKS* before taking up his legendary winter quarters at Valley Forge, Washington ordered construction in the Highlands to continue throughout the coming months. "The Facts are familiar to all; they are familiar to you," the Commander-in-chief had exhorted the yet-undisciplined General Putnam. "I therefore request, in the most urgent Terms, that you turn your most serious and active Attention to this infinitely important object. Seize the present opportunity, and employ your whole Force and all the Means in your Power for erecting and completing, as far as it shall be possible, such Works and Obstructions as may be necessary to defend and secure the River against any further attempts of the Enemy.

"You will consult Governor Clinton, General Parsons and Colonel Radière upon the occasion," Washington continued. Louis Deshaix de la Radière was a Continental Army engineering officer recruited in France in the spring of 1777 by Benjamin Franklin and Silas Deane. He would figure prominently in the earliest history of West Point.

"By gaining the Passage," the Commander-in-chief went on, "you know the Enemy have already laid waste and destroyed all the Houses, Mills and Towns accessible to them. Unless proper Measures are taken to prevent it, they will renew their Ravages in the Spring or as soon as the Season will admit. Perhaps Albany, the only Town in the State of any importance remaining in our Hands, may undergo a like Fate, and a general Havoc and Destruction take place.

"To prevent these Evils," Washington urged Putnam, "I shall expect that you will exert every Nerve, and employ your whole Force in Future, while and wherever practicable, in constructing and forwarding the proper Works and Means of Defence."

The Commander-in-chief refused to let matters rest there. On the same day, in a further effort to prod into action the Connecticut general who was 14 years his senior, Washington sent similar letters to Governor Clinton and General Gates. Gates made no reply, but the New York governor suggested a strong work be built on the West Point opposite Fort Constitution: "This I propose as the most defensible Ground, because the Navigation here is difficult & uncertain, and the River something narrower as it was at the Lower Place [Popolopen Creek]."

His letter echoed the May 14, 1776 proposal of Lieutenant Colonel Henry B. Livingston, who had reported to the Commander-in-chief from Fort Constitution: "A few improvements will render the Fortifications here impregnable—and impassable if a Boom was thrown across the River opposite them; which I think very practicable, as the River at this Place is no more than 500 yards, its depth 18 fathoms, the Tide not so rapid as at New York, and a very Bold Shore."

The letter from Clinton repeated earlier suggestions that "Iron chains should be procured (if possible) and with the Boom, which is nearly compleated, stretched across the River. This, with a Floating Battery or two, & some Gun Boats, I am perswaded would answer the purpose effectively, and in that opinion I am confirmed by the Enemy Choosing to risque every Thing for the Reduction of Fort Montgomery, rather than to attempt passing it with their shipping. If the West Point should be the place fixed upon," Clinton concluded, "it might be a great advantage to erect several strong Works on the high Point on the opposite shore, a little above Fort Constitution."

But to give other possible strategic Highlands locations their due, Clinton commissioned his rapidly recovering artillery officer Captain Thomas Machin to prepare a new military map of a 23-mile stretch of the Hudson River between Stony Point and Newburgh. Finishing the survey in only a week, Machin dedicated his carefully drawn and decorative chart to "George Clinton Esqr."

The map indicates landmark homes (a few mislocated), important roads and ferries, revolutionary fortifications—proposed, existing, or destroyed by Sir Henry Clinton in 1777 (including the ruins of "C.[ontinental] *Village*")—and Machin's own still unfinished "Chavo de Freais" stretching from "Polapls. I." across the Hudson to Plum Point.

Three months after its destruction by the enemy, Machin also depicts a forlorn-looking broken chain dangling downriver from either shore at Fort Montgomery.

Lightly pencilled hatchings indicate two new potential locations for installing the shortest possible new chain/boom; they may even have been added by some military hand. One spot is at the southernmost part of the Highlands, stretching across the Hudson from a planned fort on "Salbys [Salisbury/Iona] Is." to Anthony's Nose. While this low-lying area might appear from a sketch map to be a reasonable chain site, its land batteries would have been easily outflanked by the same enemy strategy that swallowed up Forts Montgomery and Clinton.

Another hatching, also with the suggestion of supportive fortifications, indicates what eventually became the final chain

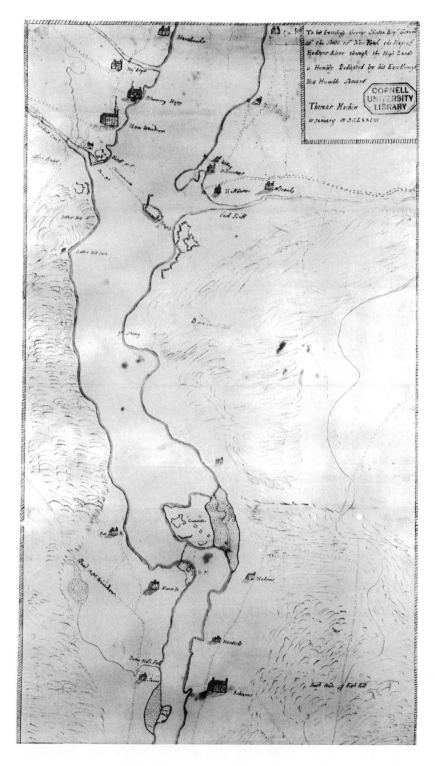

Captain Thomas Machin's January 4, 1778 military map of *Hudson's River through the High Lands* [Cornell University Library].

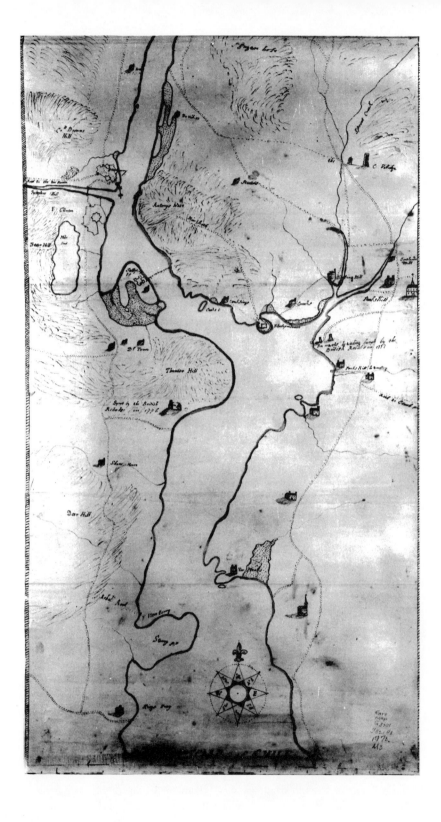

location—the Hudson River gut between Constitution Island and the "West Point."

ON January 8, 1778 with Washington continuing to call for action from Valley Forge, 125 miles away, "Old Put"—temporarily returned to his Highlands command—cautiously asked the New York Convention to name someone who could decide with him, Brigadier General James Clinton, and Colonel de la Radière the proper location for the defensive works to be erected in the Highlands.

It would have to be a major construction project, requiring close cooperation and joint economic support between the Continental Army and the New York State legislature. To minimize individual disagreements, the legislature reestablished a new group of five Fortifications Commissioners, headquartered in Poughkeepsie. These included John Sloss Hobart, Jr., one of the 1765 Sons of Liberty and now a Justice of the New York State Supreme Court; Robert R. Livingston, now—in addition to all his other duties—Chancellor of the state; Zephaniah Platt, a militia captain and chairman of the Poughkeepsie Committee of Safety; Henry Wisner, gunpowder manufacturer and former member of the Secret Committee; and active New York militia colonel John Hathorn.

Within one week the new commissioners issued a lengthy report. It first reviewed all the strategic disadvantages of the Popolopen Creek installations, so cruelly overrun by the enemy three months earlier. It noted how the area was "so intersected with long deep Hollows that the Enemy might again approach, without any Annoyance from the Garrison within the Fort, to within a few Yards of the Walls, unless a Redoubt should be raised to clear the Hollows next to the Fort.

"That must be built," the commissioners noted accurately, "at such Distance from the Fort that it could not be supported from thence; in case of an Assault the Enemy might make themselves Masters of the Redoubt the first Dark Night after their landing; it would be a good Work, ready to their Hand for annoying the Fort and facilitating operations against it. Together with the Eminences and broken Ground within a short Distance of the Fort, it would render it impossible for the Garrison to resist a General Assault.

"Another objection that appeared to the Committee," the Commissioners continued, "was the want of Earth on the Spot, which reduces the Engineer to the necessity of erecting his Works entirely of Timber, which must be brought to Pooploop's Kill in

Rafts, and from thence drawn up a steep and difficult Road to the top of the Hill. These Rafts cannot be made until the Water is Warm enough for Men to Work in, by which time it is probable that a Fort cannot be erected before the Ships of the Enemy will come up the River."

As for reinstalling the chain at Fort Montgomery: "At this Place, the Chain must be laid across the River so that it will receive the whole Force of the Ships coming with all the strength of Tide and Wind, on a line of three of four miles. Add to these, if the Enemy should be able to possess themselves of the Passes in the Mountains, through which they moved to the Attacks of Forts Clinton and Montgomery, it would be extremely difficult, if not impossible, for the Militia of the Country to raise the Siege."

But the commissioners weighed the alternate chain site at West Point with equal candor: "The Committee found that there were several places at which the Enemy might land and proceed immediately to some high Grounds that would command a Fort erected at West Point, at a distance of six or seven hundred yards; from which they might carry on their approaches through a light Gravelly Soil, so that it would be impossible for the Fort to Stand a long Siege.

"But to balance that disadvantage," they continued, "in this Place there is plenty of Earth. The Timber may be brought to the Spot by good Roads from the high Grounds at the distance of one to three miles. There are so many Passes across the Mountains that it will be almost impossible for the Enemy to prevent the Militia from coming to the relief of the Garrison."

The commissioners noted another factor: "Three hundred feet less of Chain will be requisite at this Place than at Fort Clinton. It will be laid across in a place where Vessels going up the River most usually lose their Headway. Water Batteries may be built on both sides of the River, for protecting the Chain and annoying the Ships coming up the River, which will be completely commanded from the Walls of the Fort.

"From these considerations," the commissioners concluded, "the most Proper place to obstruct the Navigation of the River is at the West Point." They cautioned, however, "that no obstructions on the banks of the River can effectually secure the Country, unless a Body of light Troops, to consist of at least two thousand effective Men, be constantly stationed in the Mountains while Navigation of the River is practicable, to Obstruct the Enemy in their approach by Land."

Sterling Iron Furnace (restored), Sterling Forest, New York (1985).

Morris Town Jan: 29th 1777

Dear Sir,

I have no doubt but that in the new appointment of artillery officers, you thought of Mr. Machin in the manner he deserves — however, as he is not here, and has heard nothing from you on this subject, I cannot help reminding you of him, as he appears from observation, and information, to be a person of merit. —

He has also mentiond something to me respecting his pay, which you will cause to be enquired into — he has receiv'd none, he says, since the month of May; I am D Sir Yr Most obt

G: Washington

Washington's note commending Captain Machin to General Knox.

The civilian committee met with the military, and the next day Colonel de la Radière wrote directly to Washington: "The council that was called for fixing the place to be fortified on Hudson's River decided last night that West Point is the best place to bar the river with a chain." General Putnam observed to Governor Clinton that de la Radière and another committee member opposed that decision "with considerable vehemence," and Clinton soon complained to General Gates at the Board of War that the temperamental French volunteer appeared to be "deficient in point of practical Knowledge; without which, altho possessed of ever so much scientific, I need not mention to you Sir, how unfit he must be for the present Task, the Chief Direction & Management of which requires a Man of Business and Authority."

The fortifications commissioners insisted that "the chain should be immediately made of the very best iron the Country afforded; that the diameter of the chain should be double of that used at Fort Montgomery." The New York State Senate and Assembly in turn resolved: "That if a Chain or Boom is to make a Part of the Water Obstruction, all the Iron Works in the Country which have proper Metal and Conveniences for the Purpose should be immediately employed at making different Parts of it; and that all the necessary Cables, Cordage and Anchors ought to be collected without delay."

Captain Machin was requested to draw up appropriate specifications. Fired by the inevitable excitement of creating a pioneering, large-scale mechanical design, and working closely with 2nd Deputy Continental Army Quartermaster General Hugh Hughes, former New York schoolmaster and founding member of the city's Sons of Liberty, Machin made an obvious choice from among several local blast furnaces in the nearby Ramapo Mountains, a range of high hills straddling the New Jersey/New York border.

It was a big, critical order. The furnace had to be capable of hurriedly smelting and forging a massive chain at least twice as strong as the one that finally withstood the Hudson tides at Fort Montgomery. With supporting floats and hardware, the new links had to be tough enough to arrest the movement of a 44-gun enemy warship favored by wind and tide. At the same time, they had to be light enough to permit seasonal manhandling in and out of the river.

Machin and Hughes's selection of a furnace and foundry—the well-known Sterling Iron Works—came quickly. Unfortunately, the government already owed that facility a large amount of money; during 1776 Sterling had produced "for Continental service" 16 tons of heavy anchors, 18 tons of bar iron, and five tons of steel, with more in 1777.

Two years of war in the northeast had almost emptied the military treasury. On January 22 the Deputy Quartermaster General wrote Governor Clinton from Poughkeepsie: "I find it impracticable to engage the Sterling Iron-works for the public service, unless Arrearages are discharg'd, which it is not in my Power to do, as the office is entirely out of Cash.

"If the Legislature of this State would advance about £5,000," Hughes urged, "I think there will be little or no Difficulty in getting all the Iron that is necessary for the Obstruction of the River. But without this small Loan, the Business of the Chain for the Security of the River must be retarded." Hughes added, "P.S. This Sum shall be punctually repaid out of the first public monies rec'd."

Clinton endorsed Hughes's request to the New York legislature, and also appealed to General Gates and the Board of War: "Colo. Hughes meets with Insuperable Difficulties for want of Cash in his Department; his Credit as a public officer is Impaired by his Inability to pay off the many old debts which he has Necessarily Contracted, & unless he is speedily supplied with that indispensably Necessary article, his utmost Efforts will in future be fruitless."

Without waiting for any reply, Machin and Hughes set off through deepening snows for Chester, New York. There they spent three days negotiating specifications and delivery with Sterling's proprietor Peter Townsend, discussing an item no American furnace had ever been asked to produce—a 750-link chain of two-inch bar iron, with eight swivels and 80 clevises.

Townsend, a hardheaded but patriotic businessman, had taken the Revolutionary Association oath at Goshen, New York in June 1775. He ran Noble, Townsend & Company's Sterling ironworking complex, located at the "Long Mine," a thick vein of black magnetite ore of 60 percent to 70 percent purity, discovered in the Ramapos more than 40 years before. This ore was easily broken into chunks sufficiently pure to bypass customary and time-consuming 18th century washing and drying procedures.

The original facility was a bloomery erected in 1751 near the rocky outlet of Sterling Pond. It hammered large red-hot lumps of local ore directly into wrought iron bolts, edges for wooden tools, axe-heads, crude firebacks, grates, wagon tires, plowshares and other essential colonial iron items too heavy or too costly to continue to import from Great Britain. A sluice from the pond above the bloomery supplied necessary water power to work the air bellows of the stone hearth, as well as other simple machinery.

The bloomery output was severely limited, and the following year a true smelting furnace was established on the site by father and son William and Abel Noble. By 1753 the Nobles' ironworkers were pouring large quantities of molten metal directly into sandcast molds, and into "sows" and "pigs" for further refining. Much of the iron then forged from Sterling's reheated "pigs" became "merchant bars." The remainder was hammered into wrought iron trade articles such as "Cart, Waggon, Chair and Sleigh Tire-Mill Spindles; Wrines, Clanks, and Axle trees," plus "Cast Mill Rounds and Gudgeons"— according to ads placed regularly in the *New-York Gazetteer and Post-Boy* and *The New-York Mercury*. Sterling also cast teakettles, skillets, pots, and even small ship anchors.

In 1758 the Nobles took in William Hawxhurst as partner; within three years the enlarged firm erected an improved forge, with a water-powered tilt hammer capable of working half-ton anchors. In 1768 Peter Townsend married Hawxhurst's daughter Hannah, and eventually inherited the entire Sterling ironworking operation. That year also saw Sterling's first shipment of substantial quantities of bar iron to England for tools and building materials, at a time when much of Great Britain's iron imports were coming from high-quality European sources, expecially Sweden and Russia. North American bar iron, the British counsul at Rotterdam reported at the time, "is found equal if not superior to Swedish Iron."

BUT IT also was a time of trouble for the English and Welsh iron industry (most of the furnaces in Ireland stood as ruined targets of 17th century risings). Industrial expansion was rapidly depleting Great Britain's ancestral wood supplies. The need for charcoal had not only swallowed up trees required for heating and cooking fuel, but was also fast destroying the raw material for ships' timbers so essential to British trade and defense. Out of necessity, Abraham Darby was beginning his initial Coalbrookdale experiments with coking coal as a substitute for wood charcoal.

With no such fuel problems, the American colonists had established their first successful cold (air) blast furnace at Braintree in 1644, using a gabbro flux to smelt chunks of limonite ore dredged from Massachusetts bogs. They could draw upon an apparently inexhaustible wood-charcoal supply. Two years later, an even more elaborate ironworks, Hammersmith, was erected 17 miles to the north on the Saugus River near Lynn. The British Parliament soon found itself whipsawed between encouraging or limiting the infant American iron industry, which was then able to sell merchant bars domestically at the highly competitive price of £20 a ton.

Traditional mercantilist dogma held that vast raw material shipments of charcoal from North America could still save Britain's vanishing forests, while American iron ingot ballast would make a perfect return cargo for vessels that had carried finished English goods, including many made from iron, to the colonies. The eventual Parliamentary response, after several abortive attempts, was the Iron Act of 1750.

That statute removed duties on all pig and bar iron exported to Great Britain from North America, but it also prohibited further construction of such colonial iron finishing facilities as slitting and rolling mills, plating forges equipped with tilt hammers, and small blister steel furnaces.

This repressive and vastly unpopular legislation was immediately interpreted in America as only applying to *new* construction; flagrant enlargement of existing installations was considered permissible. By the time of the Revolution, 72 colonial cold blast furnaces, as well as numerous forges and small scale slitting, rolling, and plating mills, were producing more iron than England and Wales combined. As fewer and fewer British iron articles found a ready market in the now almost self-sufficient colonies, the mother country came to consider further expansion of North American ironworking "a common nuisance that must be abated."

The repressive attitude that followed inevitably resulted in four colonial ironmasters becoming signers of the Declaration of Independence, while two dozen others served as important Continental Army officers.

In the midst of the Revolution, the infant United States was already producing 14 percent—30,000 tons—of the world's iron. While English blast furnaces were being forced to relocate in areas where resources of iron ore, coal, limestone, and comparatively inefficient low-head hydraulic power geographically overlapped, comparable North American installations continued to require far less critical locations. With the continent's limitless forest reserves, a good-sized smelting and forging complex could be established anywhere near a substantial ore body and a steady-flowing watercourse.

With obvious pride, "A New-Englandman" asserted in the

*Providence Gazette* shortly before the Revolution that "Of all the other countries of the world, Nature has best fitted the Northern Colonies for the iron manufacture."

FOR ORE purity, quality of workmanship, and location, the Sterling complex in the Ramapos had been Captain Machin's first choice to forge the new chain. It was also the largest, most productive, and most successful of the various ironworks in the area. DQMG Hughes had high praise for the qualities of iron smelted from Sterling's magnetite ore, noting General Knox's expressed preference that he "purchase no other for use of the [artillery]."

At the same time, Machin began seeking hundreds of heavy timbers for his chain rafts, recruiting 12 companies of artificers, with blacksmiths and carpenters to assemble everything at New Windsor on the river. The carpenters received 94 cents a day; the artificers and blacksmiths earned up to $1.50 a day, a very fair wage for the period.

IN THE weeks that followed de la Radière's report to Valley Forge, Washington's impatience mounted: "As the majority of the council were for erecting new works upon West Point in preference to the place upon which Fort Clinton was built," he wrote the French engineer, "I desire that they may be carried on with all dispatch. If we remain much longer disputing about the proper place, we shall lose the Winter, which is the only time that we have to make preparation for the reception of the Enemy."

On the same day, the Commander-in-chief wrote Putnam: "I begin to be very apprehensive that the Season will entirely pass away before anything material is done for the defence of Hudson's River." Congress was beginning to clamor for further investigation of all the general officers involved in the disaster at Forts Montgomery and Clinton; Washington suspected he would soon be forced to replace Putnam.

It was with great relief that the Commander-in-chief saw the new project to block the Hudson River now firmly in the hands of Machin, Hughes, and Townsend, and moving forward with uncharacteristic speed. Meeting again at Chester, Machin and Townsend agreed to final chain specifications. On behalf of the United States, Hughes drew up a relatively simple three-page contract to cover accelerated production of the required length of chain and its associated hardware.

Hughes's copy of that contract, carrying Peter Townsend's witnessed signature, is part of the manuscript collection at the New-York Historical Society [*Appendix A*]. Townsend's copy no longer exists; at one time among the Clinton Papers, it was reduced to ashes in the disastrous March 29, 1911 fire that destroyed Albany's New York State Library.

The agreement lists Machin's physical specifications for use of "the best Sterling Iron" in a 750-link chain. With payment set at £440 a ton—about 17 or 18 links to a (British 2,240 pound) ton—the total cost of the chain, not including anchors, came to almost £19,000—or, allowing for that spring's 31 percent depreciation in the Continental dollar, $92,000.

This substantial sum also reflected galloping wartime inflation; a charge of 4 shillings per finished pound of chain was several times what Robert Livingston and the Poughkeepsie blacksmiths had been willing to accept for their work on the Fort Montgomery obstruction.

Viewed another way, the chain would cost the United States government more than four times as much as Bernard Romans had demanded two years earlier to erect all of Fort Constitution.

A special clause in the agreement required Noble, Townsend & Company to reduce all its charges about 9 percent if Congress enacted its debated price controls—the "General Regulations on Trade, Provisions, &c."—before June 2, 1778.

Payments by the government would be staged to match the foundry's progress on the links and anchors. The initial failures of the Fort Montgomery chain—and the subsequent controversy with the blacksmiths—inspired both parties to establish an improved system of quality control. They set up an independent group of "not less than three, nor More than five Competent Judges, unconnected with the Proprietors, or the Works." Any material or workmanship found wanting, "whether at the Works, or River, or in extending it across," must be replaced at Sterling's expense.

For North America in 1778, the entire undertaking represented some very heavy industry. Sterling's major responsibility was to guarantee the continuous availability of a large work force of miners, quarriers, ore pounders, and teamsmen—as well as firemen and assistants, stock takers, carpenters, keepers, fillers, guttermen, turners, founders, molders, blacksmiths, wheelwrights, clerks, overseers, and a host of colliers. Almost half the Sterling crew did nothing but fell trees and cut them into lap-wood and billets for

Deputy Quartermaster General Hugh Hughes's copy of the February 2, 1778 *Articles of Agreement* covering manufacture of the West Point Chain (New-York Historical Society) [*Appendix A*]. Peter Townsend's copy, part of the Clinton Papers, was destroyed in the 1911 New York State Library fire.

the Date of this, In which case the Price is to be only Three Hundred Pounds $\dots$ for the said Chains & Anchors. — The Payments if _____ to be made in such Proportions as the Work shall be ready to be delivered, which shall be determined in ten days after requisition made by a number of competent Judges not less than three, nor more than ____ unconnected with the Proprietors, or the Works, and if _____ to be Compleated at the Expense of the said Company, who are also to repair, as agreed, all failures of their Works whenever happening, whether at the Works, or ____ or in extending it

across.                            the said Hugh Hughes also engages to procure of the Governor of this State, for the said Noble, Townsend & Company an exemption for Nine Months from the date hereof from Military Duty for sixty Artificers, that are _____ to be employed at the said Chains & Anchors, _____ that agreeable to the said Exemption, the said Company _____ with the Terms thereof; providing also that _____ _____ give the said Hugh Hughes, or his Successor in Office, the refusal by Letter, of all the Bar Iron, Anchors &c. made at the said Works in the said Term of Nine Months, at the present Prices, unless what is necessary to Exchange for Clothing and other Articles for the use of the Works.

                            It is also agreed by the said Parties, that if the Teams of the said Company shall Transport the said Chains, or Anchors, or any Part of them, to any ____ Post, they shall receive for such Service the same Pay, as shall be given by the United States for the like. — The Teams of said Company being exempted from Impress, by any of the Quartermasters Department during the Space of Nine Months from the date hereof.

Lastly the said Company engage to use their Utmost Endeavours to keep given Tires, at Forging and Item at Wellburg, if [Afsisted] with such Hands as are necessary, & can be spared from the Army, in case of their not being able to procure them, the said Company making Deduction for their Labour —

In Witness whereof the Parties have Interchangeably subscribed their Names, this [____] Day of February, One Thousand, Seven Hundred, & Seventy Eight, and in the Second Year of American Independency —

Present

Peter Townsend

in behalf of

[Winghart]

Sterling Iron Furnace throat, Sterling Forest NY (1985).

charcoal-making; each day's furnace operation consumed an acre of forest.

The passage of *Phoenix* and *Rose* up the Hudson in 1776 had raised the local militia on both shores of the river. On August 8—only a few days before the fire ship attack on those two enemy warships—Abel Noble and Peter Townsend complained to the New York Convention that "workmen and Labourers are being taken from our works" while the furnace was still in blast, and on the 22nd they requested exemptions for 134 itemized Sterling workers.

On April 12 of the following year the firm again petitioned the New York Convention for specific exemption from further militia service for a group that included 42 furnacemen and 87 forgemen. In their petition the owners caustically observed that many of Sterling's workers "have absconded, owing chiefly as we suppose to the weakness of their minds in not believing it is Reasonable that men of so low fortunes as the most of them are, should be Called away with the militia so frequently to Defend, as they Imagine, the Rich people of the Country. Upon such weak principles," the owners concluded, "a great part of them last fawl, winter and this present spring, have left the said works."

It was now a year later, and as part of their contract, Noble, Townsend pressured DQMG Hughes to obtain from Governor Clinton formal military exemption for 60 Sterling ironworkers for nine months—obviously far longer than required to complete work on the chain. In the absence of any alternative, the DQMG agreed.

Together with the final copy of the signed agreement, sent to Clinton in Poughkeepsie on February 3, Hughes wrote: "I wish that it was better on the part of the States. I did the best I could, and hope that it will meet with your Excellency's Candour, as well as that of the Legislature. The first Exemption [executed for Hughes by Clinton on February 1] was given them, which I transcribed and inclose a Copy, recollecting that there was no transcript kept by your Excellency."

That undertaking read: "I Consent that sixty Persons such as shall be employed by the Masters of the Sterling Iron-Works in making the Chain to stretch across Hudson's River, be Exempted from Military Duty for the Space of nine Months from the Date hereof, providing such Persons shall be steadily employed in the Business of Iron-Making, & Working at the said Works, during that Term. The said Masters returning to the Governor A List of such Persons Names with their Descriptions." A caveat excluded exemptions in any situation in which "the whole Militia of the Country are called out."

"There was no such thing as concluding the agreement," Hughes continued apologetically to Clinton, "without exempting their Teams [carters] for the same Time. Nay, they had the assurance to demand Exemption for all they should hire, which I positively refus'd, telling them that might enable them to sell Exemptions by giving Certificates that Teams were in their Service, when otherwise; which they affected to resent."

As partial *quid pro quo*, Hughes did negotiate first refusal for the United States at the going rate of all of the firm's iron output for the next nine months. To guarantee the swiftest possible chain delivery, Noble, Townsend agreed to keep seven forging and ten welding fires in operation at all times, with the United States deducting the additional labor costs should this extra effort prove impractical.

A final clause established the rate of pay—30 shillings a day—with additional military exemption for the Sterling teamsters. These were the men who would haul the chain and anchors on oxcarts through Central Valley to Brewster's Forge near the banks of the Hudson at New Windsor, where everything would finally be assembled by Captain Machin's artificers.

Putting the furnace in blast, Townsend's now-exempt workers began their historic labor, thus making the Sterling foundry a potential enemy objective. Former Secret Committee member Henry Wisner wrote anxiously to Governor Clinton from West Point on February 19 regarding one neighbor of questionable political sympathy who had applied for permission to go to New York City. Don't let him go, urged Wisner, lest "Mr. St. John advise the Burning of Sterling works in order to prevent our giting the Chain Done."

As they sought proper timber for chain floats, Machin's axemen and carpenters were encountering serious civilian problems. In the middle of February, Clinton advised the engineer: "I have directed that no more Timber should be cut on Mr. Ellison's land until a proportionate share of timber was also got on lands lying equally near the River. He is willing you should take such long Walnut pieces as you want and can't get as conveniently elsewhere; other kind of timber we certainly can. I am surprised to hear that a company of carpenters are in his Woods cutting away timber of every kind."

Machin's tart reply, routed through the New Windsor Committee of Safety, reminded those involved with the new river obstructions that time was rapidly passing and not much was being accomplished. The Captain urged everyone to *"remember Kingston,"* and noted that although he did not "think it consistent with my duty to distress any individual by cutting all the Timber off one man's land and thereby render a good Farm of little value, I cannot always be with the Men in the woods.

"I should be glad," Machin groused, "if the Honorable Committee would appoint a Wood Ranger to oversee the business."

*AT* Valley Forge, Washington received an optimistic February 17 progress report from Putnam, advising that the contracted chain would be completed around April 1. "Parts of the [Ringwood] Boom intended to have been used at Fort Montgomery, and sufficient for this place," Putnam wrote, "are remaining. Some of the Iron is exceeding bad." [In hindsight, one 19th century ironmaster criticized the Fort Montgomery links as "cold short Iron of a small diameter, and as regards strength, very feeble"].

"This," advised Putnam, "I hope to have replaced with good Iron soon. The Batteries near the water & the Fort to cover them are laid out. Barracks for the artificers & Huts for about three hundred Men are compleated, and barracks for about the same number are nearly covered. A Road to the River has been made, with great difficulty." West Point was well on its way to becoming a permanent American bastion.

But for the old veteran of Bunker Hill, it was just too little too late. Regional feelings were running high; New York's militiamen still refused to forgive Putnam's vacillation during the bloody British strike up the Hudson. Rumors had even spread that the general, warned of the enemy movement, was too deeply involved in a Peekskill game of chess with an attractive tory lady to leave the board.

There were even uglier rumors—impugning Putnam's loyalty. Under a flag of truce prior to Sir Henry Clinton's attack, Beverley Robinson was permitted to visit his occupied Highlands farmstead "Beverley"—ostensibly to see how his fine home was faring both as a hospital and Putnam's headquarters. Putnam was away, and Robinson was said to have assured the general's ailing wife that Putnam could always honorably return his allegiance to "legal government."

George Washington easily masked his emotions, but had certainly been offended by a dismissive letter from Putnam from Fishkill two days after the Highlands debacle: "I have repeatedly informed your Excellency of the enemy's design against this post; but from some motive or other, you always differed with me in opinion. This conjecture of mine has for once proved right." Besides, continued Putnam, "Our loss does not exceed 250 killed, wounded, and taken prisoners. This evening I intend writing you again, but am now very busy."

In a letter the next day to Horatio Gates—in the middle of the Saratoga action—Putnam continued this unjustifiable optimism: "The loss of Fort Montgomery, instead of depressing the spirits of the country, has animated them." During that same week, Putnam learned that his wife, "after a long and tedious illness," had died.

On March 16 Washington ordered McDougall to relieve "Old Put," and allow him to prepare for a court of inquiry into the events of the previous October. Four days earlier the Commander-in-chief in Valley Forge was both apologetic and bitter in a reply to a January letter from Robert R. Livingston, which had said in part: "I sincerely lament that [General Putnam's] patriotism will not suffer him to take that repose to which his advanced age and past service justly entitled him."

Washington apologized for his delayed response, based on hopes for a change in the Highlands situation, and added: "It has not been an easy matter to find a just pretence for removing an Officer from his command, where his misconduct appears to result from Want of Capacity. It is to be lamented that General P_____ cannot see his own defects, and make an honorable retreat from a station in which he only exposes his own weakness. It is more than probable that the issue of the inquiry will afford just grounds for the removal of General P_____. Whether it does or not, he must, in all events, be prevented from returning."

Writing to Putnam himself on the 16th, Washington was courteous but direct: "General McDougall is to take command of the posts in the Highlands. My reason for making this Change is owing to the prejudice of the people, which, whether well or ill grounded, must be indulged. I should think myself wanting in justice to the public or candour towards you, were I to continue you in a command after I have been almost in direct terms informed that the people of the State of New York will not render their necessary support and assistance while you remain at the Head of that Department."

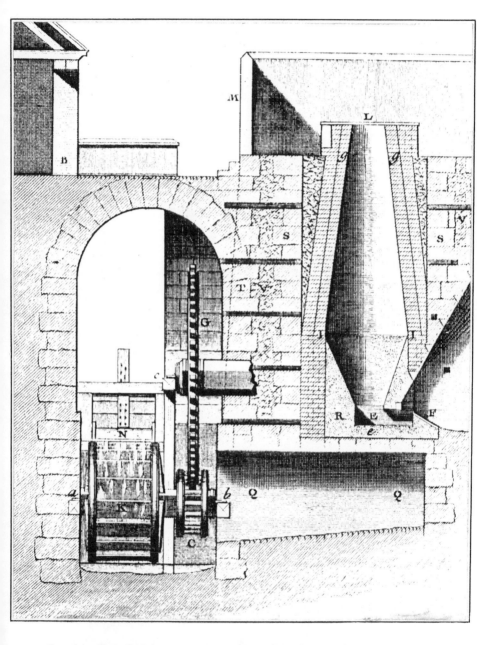

Cross section of 18th century (cold) blast furnace, showing overshot water wheel and smelting stack—bellows/tuyere inferred [detail, Diderot's *L'encyclopédie*, 1770].

18th century foundryman using waterpowered triphammer to shape ancony into iron bar [detail, Diderot's *L'encyclopédie*] (1770).

He dictated two additional sentences to his fellow Mason: "Your own experience must have convinced you that when once the people have imbibed strong prejudices, it is impossible to remove them. As we cannot enforce their Services, we must indulge them in order to obtain their assistance"—but when his military secretary Tench Tilghman read them back, Washington struck them out.

Once the official spring inquiry was over—Washington advised Putnam—he could return to Connecticut and "Superintend forwarding-on the new Levies with the greatest expedition." Distinct from regular army soldiers in the Continental Line, the emergency levies included men—mainly militia—who could be drafted without time limit for service anywhere in the United States. For three months, until Congress restored Putnam's military honor by resolving that the Highlands forts "were lost solely through the want of an adequate force to maintain and defend them," the old Connecticut general became little more than an army recruiter.

*DURING MUCH* of this smoldering controversy over who would command in the Highlands, the ironworkers at Noble, Townsend & Company—one with the highly appropriate name of Francis Welding—continued to smelt, tap, pour, and pound at what had always been (and still is) the dirty and dangerous business of making iron.

Sterling was a typical colonial blast furnace, a huge square structure more than 35 feet high, constructed of rough-faced fieldstone boulders. The bellows were cranked by a water wheel, which was in turn powered by a long sluice from Sterling Lake. The bellows generated a steady flow of air at pressures of about one pound per square inch through a pipe tipped with a copper *tuyere* (nozzle) that extended directly to the furnace hearth. A gate on the sluice controlled the speed of the turning wheel—and the amount of air flow.

Once this "cold" furnace was fired up (in later more efficient furnaces, the blast would be pre-heated), its brick-lined stack and "bosh" were continually charged with charcoal previously smoldered from four-foot billets of forest hardwoods (preferably chestnut), chunks of iron ore pried from the thick local veins of magnetite, and lime flux—in that order. Unlike the compact masses of sedimentary hematite ($Fe_2O_3$) in the ore bodies found at Salisbury and Ancram, Sterling's igneous magnetite ($Fe_3O_4$) was purer, and from a far earlier geologic era.

With the furnace in blast, a flow of ore and charcoal was continuously trundled out in low-slung handcarts along a wooden bridgeway and dumped down the open top of the stack into the egg-shaped interior. From time to time, quantities of lime flux—often ground-up clamshells—were also shoveled down the stack. The intense heat of the furnace, generated by the air blast, soon reduced the iron ore to molecules of ferrous and ferric oxide, while the force-fed oxygen allowed some of the charcoal's carbon to combine with the iron. The waste products were slag impurities, carbon monoxide, carbon dioxide, hydrogen, methane, and smoke.

In this complicated chemical reaction, molten iron was freed in an almost pure state. The basic principles of the process were known throughout the ages; since primitive times, iron has been the most important metal of our civilization. Scaled up, the design of the Sterling blast furnace evolved into Pittsburgh's behemoths.

The lime flux not only served as catalyst for the reaction, but also combined with the sand, silica, sulfur, phosphorus, manganese, and other minor impurities in the Ramapo magnetite ore to create a slag that floated atop the molten iron. In the arch at the base of the furnace, a stone crucible, temporarily blocked by a clay plug, caught the dripping metal. Slag floating atop the crucible was periodically skimmed off through a "cinder notch" above the plug. The plug was broken twice a day; the molten iron flowed out through "sow" channels cut or pressed into the sandy earth near the furnace hearth. The sows ended in a series of branching narrow shallow pits that resembled suckling "pigs."

Sterling ingots (pig iron) ranged from three to 10 feet in length, four or five inches in width and thickness, and weighed from 35 to 100 pounds. Cooled ingots were reheated red hot in "finery" fires, and then wrought through repeated hammering at the "chafery" hearths into various simple but very tough forms.

Despite one of the cruelest winters of the century—"about seven days of the time we could do absolutely nothing," said General Samuel Parsons, the new commander at "Camp West Point"—the same manufacturing processes used at Ancram and Poughkeepsie for the earlier, lighter Fort Montgomery links turned out the new chain.

Protected by what in warmer weather would have been almost unbearable heat, foundrymen pounded 750 of the thick red-hot bars taken from finery hearths, under the huge Sterling tilt hammer. This was a triumph of wooden machinery design. One end of a pivoted long beam was alternately lifted and dropped by cams affixed to a waterpowered rotating shaft. The cams caused the heavy cast iron beam head (helve) to continuously rise, slip loose, and fall back on the anvil. It took skill, giant tongs, and a good deal of muscle to hold the forging in place, amid squirts of hot metal.

Once hammered into proper shape, the bars were heated again, and their ends scarfed (flattened). They were then bent into links around a giant mandrel, with each pair of scarfed ends welded together to create nine-link chain sections. This required heating the center of the weld to the proper temperature without overheating the surface. The button-nosed swivels and heavy pinned clevises were more difficult to form.

With a dozen Sterling hearths showering sparks, various-sized water wheels groaning away, their bellows wheezing, and the great hammer pounding relentlessly on the anvil day and night, this unusual project allowed no time for fancy metalworking touches; most of the West Point Chain links ended up with a considerable twist. Production was primitive, but it was effective; it would be another three quarters of a century before America developed heavy iron and steel bar rolling equipment.

BY March 16 General Parsons was able to write elatedly to Washington at Valley Forge: "If the Chain is compleated, we shall be ready to stretch it across the River next week. If no other Difficulties appear than at present offer themselves, an attempt may be made within Eight Days." Then Parsons turned to a sensitive subject. Colonel de la Radière now found himself in serious argument with a fellow volunteer, the 31-year-old Polish military engineer Thaddeus Kosciuszko. The latter's work on the Delaware forts below Philadelphia in 1776 had earned him a colonel's commission. In the fall of 1777 his impromptu fortifications on Bemis Heights helped General Gates achieve victory at Saratoga. In contrast to de la Radière, Kosciusczko had been praised to Parsons by Governor Clinton as an officer "disposed to do everything he can in a most agreeable Manner."

The quarrel between the two foreign engineering officers was typical of the many petty conflicts that plagued the early Revolutionary years. In a style not unreminiscent of Bernard Romans, the impatient and petulant de la Radière was attempting to operate on a scale that displayed his ingenuity but strained Continental Army resources. Over the Polish engineer's objections, de la Radière was laying out unnecessary curtains, banquettes and terreplains at West Point all over the eastern and northern edges of the Hudson shore.

Kosciuczko pressed for a much deeper chain of strongpoints and redoubts, each commanding several others, with a major fort [Putnam] covering the whole. Their argument climaxed when de la Radière requested—and General Parsons granted—permission to ride off through deep New Jersey snows all the way down to Washington at Valley Forge, to personally resign his colonelcy. Early the previous year when Congress asked Washington to raise its new corps of engineers, the Commander-in-chief was specifically empowered to appoint or dismiss any officer below the rank of brigadier general.

In de la Radière's absence Parsons immediately summoned Machin from six miles upriver, where he was both hammering together the new chain sections, and keeping busy "in persute of Deserters." "As Col. Labradier has left us," wrote Parsons, "I wish if you can be absent from New Windsor for a Day, to come tomorrow or the Day after, to advise about the proper Method of fortifying this Place." Machin spent March 15 and 16 with Parsons and Kosciuszko, sorting out construction at West Point and designing a huge Constitution Island capstan to winch his new chain across the river.

Washington took de la Radière's negative report at face value. On March 17 he wrote from Valley Forge to Congress at York, Pennsylvania: "From the information I have from Colo. Radiere, who has just come from thence, I find that the intended defences [at West Point] are far less advanced than I had any idea of, tho' I have repeatedly and constantly urged the prosecution of them with all possible industry."

The Commander-in-chief persuaded de la Radière to return to the Highlands, and noted to Congress President Henry Laurens the French engineer's complaint that Putnam and Kosciuszko had impugned his "honour and the Public Interest." Laurens, in turn, urged Major General Lafayette, who was leaving on a New York state military tour, to let him know what this teapot tempest in the Hudson Valley was all about.

On March 20 General McDougall, finally replacing Putnam, arrived at West Point. Washington acted with great certainty, urging Congress to also give McDougall command of all Continental troops in the State of New York, with authority to concentrate the entire force in the Highlands "until such Time as the Fortifications and

Obstructions should be out of Danger of any sudden Attempt from the Enemy."

A month later on April 22, Washington finally resolved the ongoing engineering dispute at the Point by instructing McDougall: "As Colo. Radiere and Colo. Kosiusko will never agree, I think it will be best to order La Radiere to return [to Valley Forge], especially as you say Kosiusko is better adapted to the genius and temper of the People." After that decision, things moved rapidly; the Polish colonel perfected the land fortifications while Captain Machin busied himself with the chain emplacements on both sides of the river.

Although 25 miles of rough mountain trails connected Sterling Furnace directly with West Point, a longer but far easier route angled northeastward from the Ramapo ironworks through Central Valley directly to New Windsor. Relays of sledges drawn by pairs of oxen, guided by well-paid teamsters earning 30 shillings a day, slowly hauled the heavy sections of chain through mountain snows from the furnace and forge at Sterling Pond to Samuel Brewster's small foundry on the south shore of Murderer's Creek; a mile from the Hudson and just downhill from the farmhouse where Generals Knox and Greene eventually established headquarters. There the cumbersome chain and boom sections were finally assembled and connected for rafting down the river. Each sledge load, weighing slightly more than half a ton, consisted of nine links, plus a huge joining clevis and pin.

At Brewster's Forge, Machin's artificers tapped the clevis pins home to join the sections, stapling the completed chain onto huge white pine log rafts that lay awash in the creek. Even those floats did not escape Machin's careful attention: "The yellow sort of white-wood is much the best," he advised, "it being six pounds less specific gravity than the white sort."

Throughout February and March, the Sterling ironworks operated 24 hours a day, reddening the dark winter skies with periodic showers of sparks each time the great stone stack was recharged. An attendant necklace of charcoal-making tumuli smoldered all over the surrounding Ramapo hills. Less than 100 trips of the link-laden ox sledges completed the furnace and foundry's responsibility. Within the severe limitations of the period, manufacture of the great chain in a matter of weeks was a triumph of early American mass production with interchangeable parts, a truly remarkable industrial achievement.

On April 7 and again on April 16, rafts of pitch-covered logs supporting the chain—with swivels inserted every hundred feet to prevent twisting and binding—were floated down to West Point from New Windsor. On April 18 Colonel Robert Troup enthusiastically reported from Fishkill to General Gates and the Board of War: "If the enemy let us alone two weeks longer, we shall have reason to rejoice at their moving this way."

Two days later Machin told General McDougall: "Seventeen hundred feet of the Great Chain, which is more than equal to the breadth of the river at the place last fixed upon, is now ready for use. The capson [capstan] and docks are set up in the lower place; the mud blocks [rock cribs] are launched and only wait for good weather to carry them down. If the weather should be favorable, I am in hopes to take the Chain down all fixed in about six days."

On the slack tide of April 30, 1778 the chain—made fast to a huge rock crib in Chain Cove between Horn Point and Love Rock on the west bank—was slowly winched across the 25-fathom-deep Hudson to a similar structure on the east bank by exuberant teams of soldiers straining at the Constitution Island capstan.

The Hudson Valley, greening in the spring, was again blocked to British warships. Nevertheless, from New York City north to Peekskill, the Royal Navy could still operate at will—and for the next five years the enemy continued to mount sproradic amphibious raids along the lower river, punctuated by the desperate exchanges at Stony Point in June and July of 1779. A year later, with relative impunity, *H.M.S. Vulture* could convey John André to Haverstraw Bay—and immediately thereafter rescue Benedict Arnold.

But the British War Office's dream of another invasion force sailing north to Albany was permanently shattered.

*TWO WEEKS* before the West Point chain was finally winched into place, a peace commission headed by young Frederick Howard, fifth Earl of Carlisle, sailed from England for Philadelphia. The group was empowered to offer the embattled revolutionaries the most magnanimous terms; the extended olive branch even included recognition of *de facto* independence, provided the colonies would once again acknowledge the overall sovereignty of the mother country. But the heady experience of two years of political freedom was not so easily contained; the scornful response by the military, Congress—and the people of the United States—to the British Ministry's foolish proposals (with accompanying bribes of money and

Chain Battery Cove (looking towards Constitution Island, 1985).

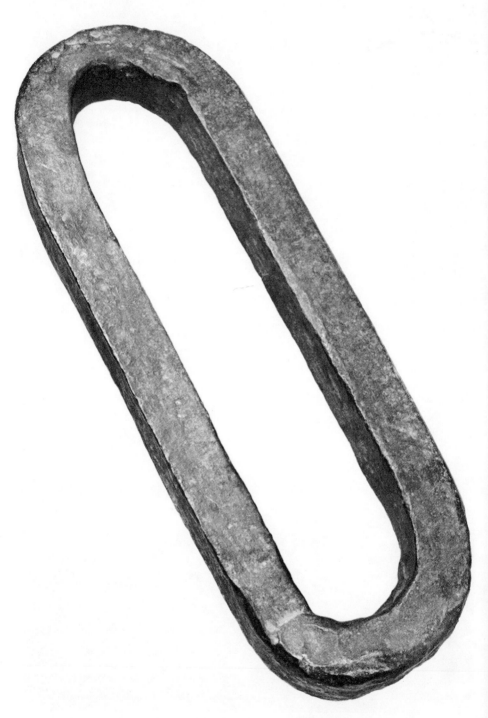

West Point Chain link, Connecticut Historical Society (1986) [R.J. Bitondi].

East bank anchorage plaque (Constitution Island), West Point Chain.

West bank anchorage plaque (Chain Battery Cove), West Point Chain.

Contemporary conception of West Point Chain and boom installation,
looking north over a slack river.

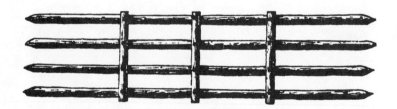

1864 visualization (after Thacher) of a chain float.

*Portion of the Boom at West Point*
*During the Revolutionary War*

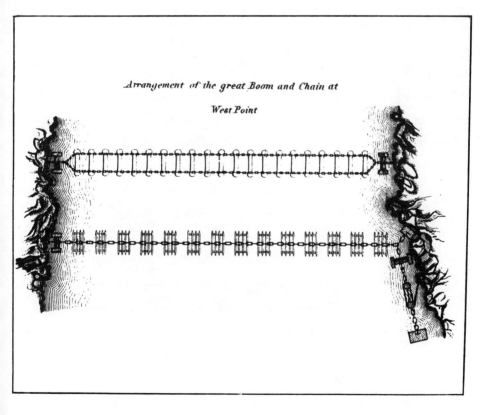

*Arrangement of the great Boom and Chain at*

*West Point*

Representation of West Point boom and chain (1864).

Salvaged West Point boom timbers with chain connector, Washington's
Headquarters, Newburgh (1985).

titles; Washington was actually promised a dukedom) proved as unyielding as Machin's new chain.

In his journal, Dr. James Thacher, a Continental Army surgeon stationed at West Point, described the revolutionary barrier "at the short bend in the river, under the fire of batteries on both sides. The Links are about 12 inches wide and 18 long, the Bars about two inches square. It is buoyed up by very large Logs about 16 feet long, pointed at the ends to lessen their opposition to the Force of the Current at flood and ebb Tide. The Logs are placed at short distances from each other, the Chain carried over them and made fast by Staples. There are also a number of Anchors dropped at proper distances, with cables made fast to the Chain to give it greater stability."

With studied casualness, General McDougall proudly concluded his May 6 report to Washington: "The Chain was stretched across the 30th ultimo. I have the Honor to be your very Humble Servant—Alxr. MDougall."

Three years after Congress's first request, the Hudson was finally blocked—with a chain far heavier than the one lost with the fall of Fort Montgomery. But for the next 31 months, the question persisted. Could the expensive new obstruction and its protective boom halt the upriver progress of an 850-ton British warship? No one was able to say.

On May 3 from Poughkeepsie, Governor Clinton sent Machin warm congratulations. "I am happy to learn that the Chain is across the river," he wrote, "and that you had the good fortune to accomplish it so expeditiously." Meanwhile Machin's New Windsor blacksmiths continued furious work on the boom. The versatile Captain was detached to Kingston, where in less than three weeks he was able to raise the *Lady Washington*, scuttled in Esopus Creek during Vaughan's raid the previous year.

The West Point boom was designed to float slightly downstream from the chain to help absorb the shock of an approaching enemy warship; Machin thought a single boom would be sufficient protection. Confirmed by the relic at Newburgh, the boom was designed of logs about a foot in diameter, 15 feet long, and spaced four feet apart. It was connected by 15 tons of iron bolts (184), clips (142), chain links (58), swivels (21), bands (8), and clevises (7). The original hardware invoices show the government paid £5,945/6s/1d (about $24,000), in addition to what was already spent on salvageable Fort Montgomery boom materials.

Boom logs were held in place by smaller chain links attached to clips bolted to their ends. At their middles, the logs were adzed into octagonal shape to assist anyone who had to cross the boom on foot. A July 1779 entry in the diary of Quartermaster Sergeant Benjamin Gilbert of the 5th Massachusetts Regiment records how he frantically "crost the River on the Chain" to escape a "very hard shower of Rain and Extream hard thunder" that "struck one man Dead on the spot and seven more Rendered unfit for duty." Whenever wind and the Hudson cooperated, loosely laid planks could temporarily convert the boom into a reasonably secure footbridge.

*IN ALL* his correspondence during the summer and early fall of 1778, Washington maintained discreet silence about the chain, referring to it only as one of "several works for the defence of the river"—as if the less said about this new defensive weapon the better. Inevitably, an anonymous tory spy reported to British headquarters in New York City: "The Chain rests on Logs anchored at both Ends on the north part of West Point. The extremities of the Chain are fixed to wooden Crates filled with stone, set up by the strand and conjectured to be 8 feet in breadth and the height 10."

What new and unpredictable defensive device had the revolutionaries actually developed? Rumors continued to vex lugubrious Lord George Germain, Secretary of State for the Colonies, who by the end of August expressed his frustration that the Americans were "not, as they have been represented, a respectably body of yeomanry, fighting *pro aris et focis* [for their altars and firesides]; but a contemptible body of vagrants, deserters and thieves."

By October, with major military activity in Pennsylvania and New Jersey behind him, Washington was finally able to pay a visit to West Point to view Kosciuszko's and Machin's work firsthand. For the Commander-in-chief, it was a pleasant respite from endless supply problems with Congress, whose own president, Henry Laurens, had accused it of "venality, peculation, and fraud."

After a congratulatory meeting with Machin, Washington wrote Governor Clinton from Fishkill: "Capt. Machin has been employed since the year 1776 in the engineering Branch without coming to any regular settlement for his Services. He does not chuse to fix any price himself, and as I am really ignorant of what is just and proper, the sum therefore to be determined is what he is entitled to above his pay of an Officer of Artillery and an allowance for extra

1780 French military map of West Point, indicating *Chain with Iron links* (and Romans's *Old Barracks* at *B*).

West Point, as seen in the fall of 1778.

Constitution Island [at left], the chain and *West Point, as seen in the fall of 1778* (1845).

1778 Chain Battery memorial boulder (1985).

1778 Chain Battery, West Point, looking SE (1985).

expences."

Clinton agreed that Machin's efforts on the river chains and *chevaux-de-frise* were of enormous value to the revolutionary cause, pointing out to Washington that the engineer had "frequently endangered his Health by working in the Water when it was floating with Ice." Heavy and destructive ice can form on the Hudson as early as November, shifting continually up and down with the tides. Since that ice often remains through March, each winter it was necessary to detach the boom and chain from their Constitution Island anchorage and haul them up on the western shore.

On October 28, before that first wintry maneuver, Washington anxiously advised Deputy Commissioner of Purchases Royal Flint: "Genl. Schuyler, who is well acquainted with the River, informs me that it is no uncommon thing to have it froze over by the middle of November."

From that moment on, almost without exception, the officers commanding at West Point deferred to Washington on the proper moment to lift—and restore—the chain. On November 6 Colonel William Malcom wrote from the Point's almost-completed Fort Arnold: "With respect to the Chain & Boom, I have asked the Engineer about them and he agrees with me that in a short time both ought to be taken on shore lest the Ice carry them away. Does your Excellency choose to have it done ere the Winter sets in severe?"

"You may, if you think it proper," Washington replied, "put all things in readiness to take up the Chain and the Boom. I do not think there is any danger of a Visit from the Enemy this Fall, but still there is no need of running any Risque by taking it up before there is a necessity for it."

Whereupon Malcom hesitated, and a sudden freeze required the entire West Point garrison to fall to and rescue the chain before it was swept away in the grinding ice. With block and tackle, the shivering soldiers hauled the floats up into a huge pile on the river bank—at the spot where the United States Military Academy's 19th century steamboat dock would eventually be located.

In December much of Burgoyne's 4,991-man "Convention Army"—after 15 months of unparoled captivity in the Boston area— was ferried across the Hudson near Fishkill on its way to a more secure military quarantine at Charlottesville, Virginia. Prisoner Lieutenant Thomas Anburey took the opportunity to remark on the fortification of West Point: "It is not at present completed, but when it is, will be impregnable, and effectively prevent any fleets passing; it being a point of land that projects and makes a winding in the river and at the same time narrows it, so as to have the whole command at that place.

"It is by this important post," Anburey wrote, "that the Americans are able to keep possession of the North River, and a communication between the Northern and Southern Provinces, and I do once more assert, not only upon my own opinion but of the Americans themselves, that had *we* kept possession of the north River, the war would have been over by this time."

Military construction at West Point resumed in the spring of 1779, and the Commander-in-chief wrote early in March from headquarters at Middlebrook, New Jersey to General McDougall: "If there is no longer danger to be apprehended from the Frost, the chain I conceive should be fixed." Excepting for occasional raids in force and several exasperating British naval feints up the Hudson, enemy military activity in the northern states was winding down. But McDougall was always cautious. From Peekskill on April 22, he sent Governor Clinton news of a refugee from New York City, "a sensible Negro, who waited on Colonel Emerick [Hessian Lieutenant Colonel Andreas Emmerich], and who informs me he heard a Conversation pass at Dinner between him and Governor Tryon and other Officers, to cut the chain."

The strategic problem posed by the year-old chain was now a topic of more than passing interest in British military circles. On June 6 Major General James Pattison wrote home to George Viscount Townshend, son of the Cabinet finance minister who pressed the infamous and restrictive 1767 Acts on the colonies: "A deserter reports that the chain which runs across the River to Fort Constitution is much stronger than that which was at Fort Montgomery, each link weighing about 70 Pounds." The actual weight of the links was almost double Pattison's estimate.

As major military operations shifted to the south, the revolutionary holding pattern along the Hudson River became more important than ever. On June 22 Washington even moved his warm weather headquarters to New Windsor to be "more contiguous to the forts."

But during that summer, could a British man-of-war sailing upriver under favorable circumstances of wind and tide have snapped the West Point boom and chain? The new Chief Engineer of the Continental Army, 36-year-old French volunteer Major General

Louis le Beque de Presle du Portail, graduate of the government military engineering school at Mezières (and one day to become France's Minister of War), could only speculate. Like Louis Radière, du Portail had also been recruited in France in the spring of 1777 by Franklin and Deane, and had been kept busy at various engineering assignments for the army. On August 20, 1779 he wrote down his opinions in the first of two detailed studies of the new defenses of West Point.

Du Portail began by once again reviewing the "fatal consequences" that loss of control of the Hudson River would bring to the revolutionary cause: "In all the lands to the east of the river, there is no flour. In the lands to the west there is no meat. As to the other things necessary to an army—foodstuffs, munitions, horses, tents—the two parts of the continent have an absolute need for each other. If one supposes their communications broken, each will be able to maintain an army in the field for only three months."

The dedicated Chief Engineer—who once privately asserted: "There is a hundred times more enthusiasm for the American Revolution in one coffee house at Paris than in all the Thirteen Provinces united"—outlined five possible enemy routes and strategies against West Point. His first consideration dealt directly with the strength of the chain: "Since all that has been accomplished was aimed at barring the river and preventing the enemy from coming upstream with his warships, the chain is the principal element; the fortifications are only to back it up. The enemy's first idea, therefore, must be to act against the chain itself.

"Would not a large ship," du Portail wondered, "well loaded, and armed at the prow, if you wish, with a vertical piece of iron (to render the shock more direct), striking the chain at full sail, break it? It is difficult to determine. One often sees the anchor rings of ships broken which undergo no other force than the movement the sea makes against the vessel in a small space. The anchor ring of even a 600-ton vessel is already larger than our chain. What is more, it must be noted that it would require only one defect somewhere in the chain, to break it. If there be none on such a great length, it would be a phenomenon."

"To give the chain better resistance," du Portail continued, "I do not propose making a larger one, but rather winding one end around a cylinder so that it could give way to a certain point at the shock of a vessel. The extreme importance of this makes me almost want to have two chains. One would be suspended about two feet beneath the surface of the water, and the other eight feet. The timbers supporting them would be linked by strong cross bars; before being able to reach the chain, a vessel would also have to break the cross bar protecting it.

"The enemy can make another kind of attempt against the chain," du Portail's analysis went on, "During a dark night, armed boats could come up to it and attach bombs in different spots, or better still, set off devices filled with powder and designed to be crammed inside a chain link. Although such an operation might be difficult with the chain two feet under water, it is not impractical.

"We can counter this," argued du Portail, "with armed ships, galleys and other vessels. We also have Batteries which can bring 20 heavy cannon to bear on any individuals attempting to cut the chain, which assuredly would not permit them to complete their work; enemy vessels must be fired on only if no enemy is working on the chain. From the moment any person appears to attempt something against the chain, all fire must be brought against them.

"In the event of a night attack," du Portail concluded, "we will have a pile of wood on each bank ready to fire, to light up the river. Furthermore, we will have on hand an amount of cable and chain in order to repair the chain should it be broken in one spot; and even in two, if the broken parts are not too large." Duportail was ready for everything, even for a disaster that fortunately never took place.

*IN THE* fall, Washington shifted his headquarters back to Morristown. On November 6 General McDougall queried him about what had now become a semi-annual West Point ritual. "It will soon be Time to draw in the Chain," McDougall observed, "lest we run the Hazard of losing it, which was the Case last year from the lateness of the Season, besides employing the Garrison in the Ice during the severe weather to get it out."

"The Chain might be taken up whenever you thought the appearance of the Weather required it," the Commander-in-chief replied a week later. "I only wished it might remain as long as possible consistent with its safety." Within days, spurred by the previous year's experience, the chain was expeditiously removed from the river—under the supervision of erstwhile row galley commander Colonel Benjamin Tupper—and safely stored ashore.

The "Hard Winter" of 1779–80 that followed ranks as one of the most severe in the history of northeastern United States. Eight inches of snow fell November 26, eight more December 5, and 17 more December 18—followed by three severe northeast storms within a ten-day period. On January 1 the resultant "cabin fever" at West Point, aggravated by currency depreciation and inadequate supplies of food and clothing, led more than 100 three-year Continentals of the Massachusetts Line to mutiny. They discharged themselves, even though most had only enlisted late in the spring and summer of 1777. The deserters were eventually surrounded by troops from other states and returned to their encampment; the ringleaders were severely punished. Meanwhile, New York City remained under four feet of snow, with below-zero temperatures during six of the last seven days of January, when several British sentries actually froze to death in their guardhouses.

New York Harbor and the Hudson River were solidly iced over during the first two months of the new year. The enemy, accepting immobilization—as they did each North American winter—in their headquarters city, pursued, among other diversions, such amateur/ professional theatricals as *The Beaux' Strategem* and *Richard III* in the sold-out John Street theater. But the unusual thickness of the winter ice gave Washington fresh concern for the safety of West Point.

From winter quarters at Morristown on February 2 he warned General Heath: "The Ice from the City of New-York to the Highlands may tempt the enemy to carry their men up in sleighs, of which they have lately collected a large parcel. We ought to take every precaution against a surprise, which is the only mode in which the Enemy can operate at this season." Eight days later, Heath confirmed—via the reports of two British deserters—that 150 sleighs were indeed in use at Fort Knyphausen, but he reassured the Commander-in-chief that they were only being used to gather wood.

Once that terrible winter had passed, artilleryman Machin was detached for special service in central New York State against Britain's native allies, the Iroquois. Brigadier General James Clinton undoubtedly drew upon Machin's firsthand experience in ponding English canals when he dammed Lake Otsego, eventually releasing a head of water down the Susquehanna River sufficient to float a train of 250 supply boats southwest to join Major General John Sullivan at the Pennsylvania border.

On March 16 Washington received a detailed letter from a fresh commander at West Point, Major General Robert Howe. Howe, replacing General Parsons, was an able but querulous North Carolina officer who had been court-martialed from southern field command after losing Savannah to the British in the closing days of 1778.

Through various ups and downs Howe maintained a long view of history; long before abandoning the Georgia seaport, the general exhorted his troops to perform as "actors upon that glorious stage where every incident is to become an historical fact." Howe began his new assignment at West Point by offering Washington several suggestions on strengthening the chain.

Within the week, the Commander-in-chief wrote back: "Your ideas respecting the Chain have not escaped me, but although I have thought of its insufficiency and looked towards its improvement, yet I could not conceive much reasonable hope of any considerable alteration. With so much to do in our circumstances, it was impossible to do all. What in my opinion will augment the strength of the chain are extra cables and anchors that have been proposed." Washington suggested that Howe contact Lieutenant Colonel Udny Hay, his hard working Deputy Quartermaster General, if he needed any materials.

On April 3 Howe advised the Commander: "I hope to put the Chain down tomorrow. It has for many days past engaged the principal attention of Colo. Cosciasco. The river is now just fit to receive it."

Robert Howe's tenure at West Point remained uneasy; many influential northerners begrudged him the post. Typical among them was Robert R. Livingston, who wrote to Washington from Trenton on the 22nd of June: "What principally induces me to trouble your Excellency at this time is an apprehension which I, in common with many other gentlemen, entertain of the propriety of having the command at West Point in the hands of General Howe. The gentlemen from the south by no means speak so favorably of him as I could wish."

In reality, the influential Livingston was logrolling his own candidate—a distant relative through marriage—for the West Point command: "If I might presume so far, I should beg leave to submit to your Excellency whether this post might not be most safely confided to General Arnold?"

Before long, Arnold replaced Howe—who only four months earlier, in a Philadelphia court martial, voted to acquit Arnold of a charge of financial misconduct. Howe was soon guiding his new replacement around the position, pointing out several weak spots in its defenses and complaining that the garrison possessed only ten day's provisions.

Arnold quickly sent a coded letter from Fishkill to Sir Henry

Clinton, using intermediaries that included a tory clergyman and an aide to Hessian General Knyphausen. Based mainly on Howe's guided tour, the traitor's secret letter described West Point as "wretchedly planned" and "totally neglected."

Arnold also fed what must have been a growing British desire to make a naval assault on the chain: "I am convinced the Boom or chain thrown across the River to stop the Shipping cannot be depended on. A single Ship large and heavy-loaded with a strong wind and tide would break the Chain."

Early in June, Washington received a letter from General Putnam. The old veteran was recovering from a stroke suffered at his home in Pomfret, Connecticut the previous December—a stroke that left his right side partially paralyzed. "Although I should not be able to resume a command in the army," Putnam dictated, "I propose to myself the happiness of making a visit, and seeing my friends at camp." His amanuensis added a touching P.S.: "I am making a great effort to use my hand to make the initials of my name for the first time," after which Putnam painstakingly scrawled: *"I.P."* The old veteran survived for another decade.

Taking command at West Point on August 5, Arnold secretly requested an interview with a representative from Sir Henry Clinton to consummate his carefully planned treason, while he began to compile key military information the British required for an attempt on West Point's defenses.

Clinton chose his adjutant Major John André as courier. On the 8th, Arnold wrote Washington from headquarters at Beverley Robinson's confiscated home across the river from West Point: "I wish your Excellency, would be kind enough to order Mr. Erskine to send me a map of the Country from this place to New York, particularly on the east side of the river, which would be very useful to me."

On August 21 Arnold asked aide Major David Salisbury Franks to reply to a letter he had just received from Major Jean-Louis-Ambroise de Genton, Chevalier de Villefranche, another volunteer engineer assisting at West Point. Villefranche, a former French lieutenant of dragoons before joining the Continental Army in 1777, complained to Arnold about the condition of the chain floats: "I went to look at the chain today. It is absolutely essential to put in new logs to keep it afloat; the work should be done as soon as possible. If not, in a short time the chain will sink and then it will be a enormous job to float it again. I cannot get the logs to repair it until I have timber. Please talk to the General about it."

Franks responded in his best Philadelphia French: "Regarding the chain, I agree with you that it is necessary to move quickly to put it in order. In addition, the General [Arnold] has written to His Excellency [Washington] regarding some new timber, and received the answer that we already have all we can hope for, and that we should use it to our best advantage."

In 1851, the popular American historian Benson John Lossing gave new life to the fanciful myth that Arnold, under the pretext of making necessary repairs to the chain, was somehow able to remove one link. The story originated in the 1816 memoirs of Marquis François de Barbé-Marbois; for six years, beginning in 1779, the Marquis served as secretary of the French legation in the United States.

Barbé-Marbois wrote: "Arnold informed André that the chain was no longer an impediment in the way. He had detatched a link, ostensibly in order to have it mended; the smiths would not return it for some days, and the two ends of the chain were held together by a fastening too weak to bear even a slight concussion." But such an obvious attempt on the chain's integrity would have quickly betrayed Arnold, not West Point.

Twelve years later, in his *Encyclopedia Americana*, Francis Lieber picked up the Marbois story, with minor amplification. In 1844, J.H. Colton repeated Lieber's reconstruction in his *Guide to West Point and Vicinity*, booting the tale farther downhill.

Lossing may also have been influenced by Horatio Hubbell's romantic five-act neo-Shakespearian tragedy, *Arnold, or the Treason of West Point*, privately printed in Philadelphia four years before the historian published his massive two-volume *Pictorial Field-Book of the Revolution*. In Hubbell's histrionic *Act IV*, we find Arnold surreptitiously advising Major André:

> *Thou know'st the massive*
> *Chain, that now athwart the Hudson hung, clogs,*
> *For defence, its navigable stream; I*
> *Have from this detached a link, on pretence*
> *Of repair; a fragile rope its place supplies;*
> *Its rupture easy on the slightest shock;*
> *Thus, as your craft are mounting with the flood,*
> *This late obstruction will no hindrance give.*

In actuality, America's arch-traitor was far more ingenuous than

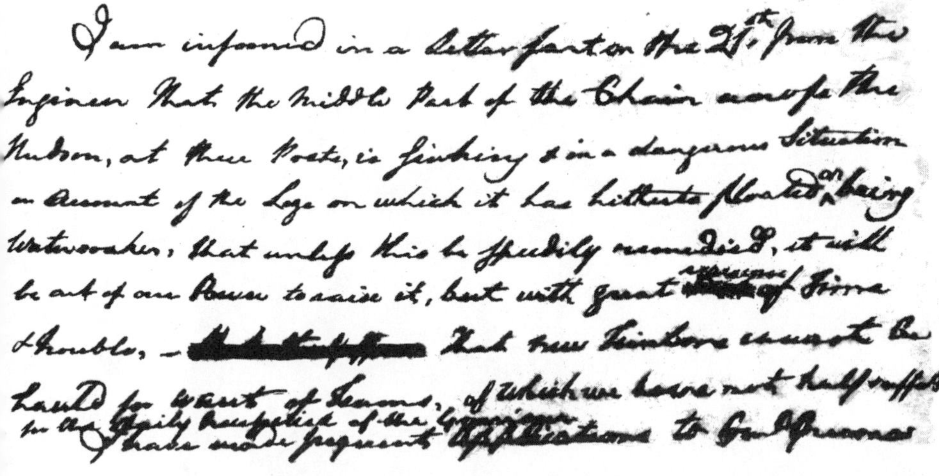

*[handwritten note, partially legible]*

I am informed in a letter sent on the 21st from the Engineer that the middle part of the Chain across the Hudson, at these Posts, is sinking & in a dangerous Situation on Account of the Logs on which it has hitherto floated on being Waterlogged; that unless this be speedily remedied, it will be out of our Power to raise it, but with great [crossed out] of Time & trouble, — [crossed out] That new Timbers cannot be hauled for want of teams, of which we have not half enough [crossed out]

Benedict Arnold's August 23, 1780 note to Quartermaster General
Pickering recommending lifting the West Point Chain for repairs.

1781 French intelligence map of West Point, executed by Rochambeau's
staff cartographers (*north* at bottom).

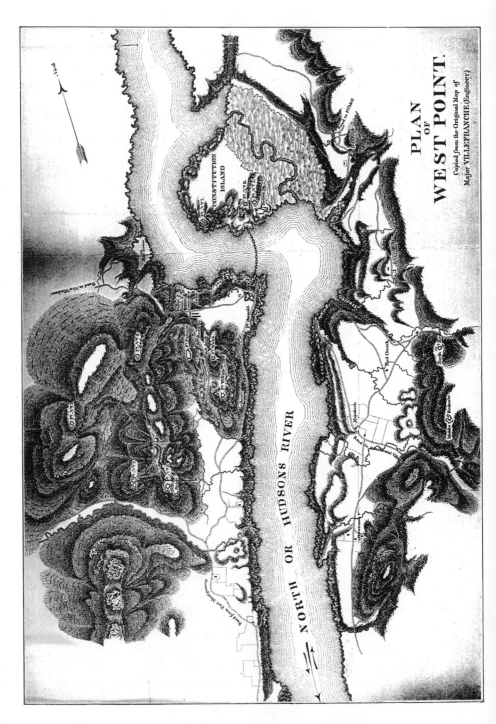

West Point and the Chain, based on a 1780 map by French engineer Jean
Louis Ambroise de Genton, Chevalier de Villefranche (1860).

that. On August 22, Arnold took further advantage of Villefranche's disturbing report to write Governor Clinton: "In a letter of Yesterday's Date from Major Villefranche, Engineer at these posts, I am informed that the Middle Part of the Chain is sinking in a very dangerous Situation. That unless it be soon raised and secured, it will not be in our power to do it but at a Great Expence of Labour & time, etc."

The next day Arnold sent a similar message to Washington's testy New England troubleshooter and new Quartermaster General, Colonel Timothy Pickering: "I am informed in a letter of the 21st from the Engineer that the Middle Part of the Chain across the Hudson at these Posts is sinking & in a dangerous Situation, on account of the Logs which it has hitherto floated on being Watersoaken, that unless this be speedily remedied, it will be out of our Power to raise it but with great expense of Time & Trouble."

But even the hero-turning-traitor had to admit: "New timber cannot be hauled for want of teams, of which we have not sufficient for the daily necessities of the Garrison." So nothing could be done about that particular problem until the chain would be once more lifted for the winter.

Meanwhile, Arnold felt it necessary to explain an unusual number of trips up and down the river in an open boat, advising the Commander-in-chief he was trying to "establish Signals as near the Enemy's lines as possible, by which I might receive Information of any Movements of a fleet or Troops up the Hudson."

At noon on September 25, 1780, Washington, returning to the Highlands from an important military conference with French General Rochambeau at Hartford, discovered with horror that his West Point commander was a turncoat. The plot unraveled when three Westchester militiamen almost accidentally apprehended Major André at Tarrytown, as he rode towards the British lines with Arnold's West Point information concealed in his boot.

It was the luckiest of strokes, and averted what might have become a revolutionary disaster; Sir Henry Clinton's forces were already poised to move against the chain and West Point. In a report to Lord Germain, now Prime Minister, the enemy general noted, "There were vessels properly manned and of a particular draft of water to have improved the design stroke to the utmost."

Washington's General Orders from Orangetown, New York on September 26 directed the attention of the Continental Army to this "Treason of the Blackest Dye," and the "providential Traine of

Circumstances which led to its timely Discovery, Affording the most convincing proof that the Liberties of America is the Object of Divine protection." The following day's military countersign *"Fortune favors America"* genteelly masked the enormous revolutionary rage and revulsion at Arnold's attempt to betray a key position everyone had so zealously guarded. When the British refused to countenance American hints of an exchange of André for Arnold, the spy was hanged.

In the first comprehensive history of the infant United States—published in four volumes in London only eight years after Arnold's plot—the expatriate New Englander Reverend William Gordon speculated on the possible military and political impact if Arnold's treachery had gone undiscovered: "Had the design succeeded, the consequences must have been ruinous in the highest degree. The plan for delivering up the post seems to have been that of engaging in a sham defence at the defiles, while a large body of the enemy took a circuit and possessed themselves of the fort [and the West Point Chain]."

"Arnold on the 8th of August," Gordon recounted, "had written to gen. Washington—'Would it not be better to continue a part or whole of the New York brigade, at West Point, where officers can be depended upon and the troops have in general bad arms and few bayonets? The Massachusetts or Hampshire troops will be better in the field, from this circumstance in their arms.' In conversation with one of the officers under him, Arnold asked which he thought would be the best mode of defence in case of attack; whether to defend the works, or to go and fight the enemy in the defiles as they advanced? The officer said, to defend the works; Arnold declared for the other. These things were recollected and supposed to have a particular meaning, when Arnold's main project was discovered.

"Had the execution of that been completed," Gordon continued, "the forces under his command must probably have either laid down their arms or have been cut to pieces. Their loss and the immediate possession of West Point, and all its neighboring dependencies, must have so exposed the remainder of Washington's army to the joint exertion of the British army by land and water, that nothing but final ruin could have been the result with respect to the Americans.

"Such a stroke," Gordon concluded, "could scarcely have been recovered. Independent of the loss of artillery and stores, such a destruction of their disciplined force, and many of their best officers, must have been fatal. The British might have also turned their whole force against the French fleet and troops at Rhode Island, for they had received a considerable naval reinforcement by the arrival of adm. Rodney with several ships of the line from the West Indies. Whether his coming to New York was in the least under the influence of flattering prospects upon West Point being delivered into the hands of the British, will be a matter of conjecture among many."

BY THE late fall of 1780, with the dust of treason slowly settling, General Heath was again posted to the Highlands command. On October 31 while Major Daniel Carthy, Assistant Deputy Quartermaster at West Point, was endeavoring to support the chain with emergency hogsheads, Heath reminded Washington—almost echoing Arnold: "This season is now nearly arrived when it will be necessary to take up and secure the Chain. Many of the buoys are become so watersoaken as to be on the point of sinking, and will grow more so every day as the cold increases. I think it ought to be taken up at farthest by the middle of next month; it may easier be done sooner." Heath requested that Colonel Tupper again supervise the difficult operation.

Washington's reply on November 5 repeated his concerns of 1778 and 1779: "I am of the opinion that [the chain] ought neither to be taken up too soon, nor suffered to remain too late. I could wish you had everything in readiness." On the 13th, Heath decided he could wait no longer—"the Chain having begun to sink, and part of it got upwards of 20 feet under water, a number of men and boats are required to be constantly with it to prevent the whole from sinking." He took up the chain and floats the following day, piling them on the beach near the "Red House"—the former Moore home on the west bank flats above the Point.

From Albany, Hugh Hughes congratulated ADQM Carthy: "I give you joy on the Resurrection of the Chain; it afforded a pretty clever piece of Business, I imagine. Let new logs be got ready without Delay—if you don't take old Father Time by the Foretop (for he is bald behind, remember) you will be calling on Hercules like the wagonner in the Fable, and he'll make you a similar reply."

On December 12, looking anxiously towards spring, Washington ordered Captain Daniel Niven of the Engineer Corps to seek out new timber floats, noting that "the Logs which supported the Chain at West Point are so water soaken that they will not do to lay down another summer." By February 2 in the new year, Niven reported to the Commander-in-chief that his men, working in deep snow, had "cut down the number wanting of large Logs, back of Newbrought [Newburgh], and brought them within five miles of the river."

Niven criticized Quartermaster General Pickering, who was pleading lack of teams and funds, for not immediately hauling the logs the rest of the way. "It will be very late in the Season," Niven complained, "before the rafts are ready to be put in the water, unless the Timber are transported to the river without a moments loss of time."

Although Washington ordered aide Lieutenant Colonel David Humphreys (later ambassador to Spain) to urge Pickering (later Secretary of State) to pay particular attention to the problem, on February 24 General Heath confessed to Washington "that the Logs for the Chain are not in so great forwardness as we could wish, occasioned by embarrassment in the QMG's department on account of forage and money."

In the end, Pickering came through. On the 27th, Heath was able to report: "The Logs for the Chain, at a Landing about two miles above Newburgh on this side of the River, are in tolerable forwardness." The new floats were fashioned during March as the snow melted, and on the 30th, General Orders detailed "a Sub[altern], Serjeant and 20 watermen to be sent immediately to Newburgh to assist Capt. Nivens in floating the rafts to, and stretching the chain at Westpoint."

On April 10, two hundred of Heath's men "began laying the Chain across the river. It was hauled from off the beach near the Red House, towed down to the blocks and fastened on one side, but night came on before we could secure the other and it will be effected today [the 11th] if the wind is not too fresh." On the 12th the general reported with satisfaction to Washington that the great chain was again strung across the Hudson "with dexterity and without the least accident or damage of boats, or otherwise."

*FIFTY MILES* to the south, Sir Henry Clinton, also stirring from winter quarters, maintained a watchful eye on the Highlands. With sly disappointment over Arnold's failure to deliver West Point to the British, Clinton wrote to Lord Germain on April 5: "Your Lordship does but justice to my zeal in supposing that I shall not let slip any favorable opportunity of rendering His Majesty and my country so essential a service as the securing, even by a regular attack, the important post of West Point, whenever the attempt can be made with propriety."

Clinton always claimed personal familiarity with the West Point area, which his troops held for three weeks in 1777. His letter to the Prime Minister continued: "As to Brigadier General Arnold's opinions, whatever he may have represented to Your Lordship, nothing he has as yet communicated to me has convinced me that the rebel forts can be reduced by a few days' regular attack."

Seventeen eighty-one was also the year of Yorktown, and the southern entrapment of Cornwallis. Without any grand strategic design, that British general had been uneasily "marching about the country in quest of adventures." As Comte de Rochambeau moved swiftly with the French army from Newport, Rhode Island to Head of Elk in Maryland, he employed skilled military staff cartographers to record the entire 300-mile march for future reference, assembling as much geographic intelligence relating to the countryside of the northeastern states as allied courtesy would permit. Along that march, accompanied by his aide Baron de Cromot du Bourg, Rochambeau made a detour—while his army was crossing the Hudson at Verplanck—to examine the fortifications at West Point. The Baron studied the Chain with great interest; on August 23 he wrote confidently in his diary: "Any vessel endeavoring to break it will be utterly destroyed."

The ubiquitous Captain Machin also marched and sailed to Virginia, where he participated in laying out the lines around Yorktown, firing one of the first siege guns. General John Sullivan characterized Machin's cannoneering as "elegant," and recounted how, "agreeable to the orders of Genl. Knox, he sent a shell into the magazine of a small British vessel lying in the river, blowing it to atoms. Genl. Knox is said to have remarked with evident satisfaction, 'See the d____d rascals go up!'" Cornwallis finally surrendered on October 19.

Four hundred miles north, along the Hudson, the chain was taken up the following month without application to General Washington, who remained in Virginia, visiting Mount Vernon for the first time in five years. By the spring of 1782, the Commander-in-chief was back at Newburgh headquarters, and again resumed responsibility for the chain. On May 1, unusually late in the year—perhaps with some scent of final victory floating on the soft spring air—General Heath wrote to Washington that "the chain is now ready to be stretched across the river, but the logs are every day proving dryer and lighter while out of the water, and will consequently swim longer in the

Fall. The chain will be laid down whenever your Excellency thinks it proper to direct."

Lieutenant Humphreys conveyed Washington's almost casual response to Heath: "The laying down of the Chain may be deferred a few Days longer." That fall, when Heath took up the chain once more, he did it without bothering the Commander-in-chief.

By spring of the following year, the indestructible Private Joseph Plumb Martin found himself stationed at West Point. A certain level of predictability and order was beginning to replace wartime chaos and uncertainty in the Hudson Valley. Martin noted how "the Great Chain that barred the river had been regularly taken up every autumn and put down every spring since it had been in use (that chain which the soldiers used to denominate General Washington's watch chain, every four Links of which weighed a ton)." (British troops had their own derisive nickname for the West Point Chain—they called it the *"Yankee Pumpkin Vine."*)

"But," continued Martin, suspecting correctly that the war was winding down, "we heard nothing of its being put down this spring, although some idle Fellow would report that it was going to be put down immediately. Those simple stories would keep the men in agitation, often for days together (for putting down or keeping up the Chain was the criterion by which we were to judge war or peace). Time thus passed on to the nineteenth of April [1783], when we had General Orders read, which satisfied the most skeptical that the war was over and the Prize won for which we had been contending for eight tedious years."

Six days earlier with ice long gone from the river, the schooner *Cottle* out of Nantucket with a load of fish oil and rum for Newburgh became the first revolutionary vessel to sail up the Hudson from its mouth since the enemy capture of Manhattan Island in 1776. With the loss of Britain's southern army, the war was guttering out. Only political formalities remained. The chain—still untested by any enemy warship—was never again replaced in the waterway.

ON August 29, 1783 with American troops ready to re-enter New York City on the heels of the evacuating British, Colonel Pickering, always the tough businessman, wrote from Newburgh to Washington in Rocky Hill, New Jersey: "The chain at West Point has already suffered considerably by the rust, and will be daily growing worse. If it is to be kept for future use, it cannot too soon be housed; and in this case it is said it may be preserved from rust by painting.

"If it is not necessary to keep it," the Quartermaster General continued, "the sooner it is sold the better. It would probably fetch about two thirds the price of bar iron; the Chain contains from fifty to sixty tons. I hope to be favored with your Excellency's orders concerning it."

Pickering neglected to advise the Commander-in-chief that he had been investigating possible disposal of the chain for the past three months. On May 22 he wrote from Newburgh to the Philadelphia merchant Samuel Hogden: "The Great Chain at West Point contains upward of 60 tons of excellent Sterling iron. The links, you may recollect, are about 30 inches long, made of bars about 2 inches square. If it be sold here, I am doubtful it will fetch much more than half the price of bar iron. Pray enquire if it will answer to send it to Philadelphia, and inform me of all these matters as early as possible."

To which Hogden replied on the 28th: "The chain at West Point I suppose, equals in value to new bar iron, but it should be sold in parts, perhaps one ton each. The links in their present form may be made to answer in Shipwork or with very little working, and in quantities abovementioned, the merchants concerned in trade will gladly purchase. Whether it will sell best in Philadelphia or New York, I am not able to determine; I will make particular inquiry concerning it, and will inform you in my next."

Like Pickering, Washington had no difficulty distinguishing practicality from historical romance. On September 3 he wrote the QMG from Rocky Hill: "If it is well ascertained that the chain can be preserved in perfect Order for future use, I should advise it to be housed in the manner you mention. But," he added, "if the fact is otherwise or even very doubtful, I would recommend that it be sold without delay."

Five days later, Pickering contacted Major General Henry Knox, summarizing the Commander-in-chief's reaction and adding, "Major Boyd was here this morning, and I asked his opinion of the loss the chain would sustain by rust if it were housed and not painted: he replied—not much in seven years; painted it would doubtless lose little or nothing.

"Nevertheless," Pickering continued realistically, "I would be of opinion that it should be sold, because the probability is that it will never be wanted again. Money is at the present moment in the highest demand for public uses: the chain would doubtless sell for a thousand or twelve hundred pounds, which sum, with the interest accruing in a short period, would be equal to the purchase of a new chain, should one ever be wanted."

The West Point Chain—monument to revolutionary imagination and persistence, never challenged by any vessel of the Royal Navy—appeared ready for an honorable discharge.

# Epilogue

---

*In which the West Point Chain proves too valuable for its own good, with much of it soon swallowed up in a fiery furnace*

---

*TIME SWEEPS* history's artifacts into the dustbin.

Forts are razed. Ingenious submersibles are destroyed. *Chevaux-de-frise* rot away underwater. Flaming beacons and fireships go up in smoke. But sixty tons of historic wrought iron chain do not simply disappear.

In truth, Captain Machin's indispensable wartime handiwork represented far too much good quality recyclable raw material to be allowed to simply rust in peace. Just as parts of Hadrian's Wall found their way into many Scots and English border cottages and barns, so did Machin's second Hudson River barrier find new and unforeseen uses in the eager hands of America's foundrymen.

Disposal of the earlier Fort Montgomery chain presented fewer options. The 18th century British military historian Robert Beatson asserted—logically, but with no documentation—that most of that outflanked barrier was taken up by General Sir Henry Clinton's expeditionary force during the fortnight it remained in control of the Highlands. Local tradition echoed Beatson: "The chain was taken from its moorings and put on board some of the ships of war that was then ascending the Hudson."

But Beatson's subsequent assertion in his *Naval and Military Memoirs* that much of that chain was later "shipped to Gibraltar where it was of great use in protecting shipping at the moles," has

175

never been authenticated. In 1893 the British Colonial Secretary at Gibraltar responded to a query from the superintendent of Washington's Headquarters site in Newburgh: "After a careful search of the records of this fortress, no facts can be ascertained relative to the chain."

More than sixty years earlier on August 12, 1830, three rivermen—John Smith, John Morgan and William Malcom—grappling between Fort Montgomery and Anthony's Nose for a lost steamboat anchor, "after three days hard pulling, brought up instead 51 links of the great chain what was stretched across Hudson's River during the Revolution." James M. Duffield brought those links, together with an affidavit from the rivermen, to the offices of the *New York Gazette and General Advertiser*.

"The links," that newspaper reported, "are over a foot in length, and in weight average from 30 to 35 lbs each—they are supposed to be diminished about one-third in weight and size by corrosion. The raising of them was considered very difficult, from the circumstance of some of the links having suffered partial decomposition and subsequent combination with the rocks of the bottom. Several stones weighing from 15 to 20 lbs each, and numerous smaller ones, were brought up with the chain, they being firmly united with it."

Fifty feet of the links examined by the newspaper were subsequently purchased by Edward Allen, a Water Street blacksmith. Some of the others were distributed to small New York museums, including the Naval Lyceum at the Brooklyn Navy Yard, in whose September 1856 catalog they were listed as "Part of the chain at Fort Montgomery." When the Lyceum's collection was transferred in 1888 to the Naval Academy at Annapolis, the links disappeared.

Two other links, presumably from that same river grappling, are preserved in a glass-faced wooden case in the collections of the New-York Historical Society. A lengthy manuscript label written around 1870 by Richard Montgomery Pell identifies them as "two of the fifteen [sic] links of a chain drawn from the bottom of the Hudson opposite Forts Clinton and Montgomery," but gives no date for their retrieval.

Still another corroded link of the Fort Montgomery chain, about one and a half feet long, rests under glass in the historical museum next to Washington's Newburgh Headquarters. It was reportedly recovered from 129 feet of water off Anthony's Nose in 1861 by George W. Wetherell.

Purported Fort Montgomery Chain links, New-York Historical Society (1986).

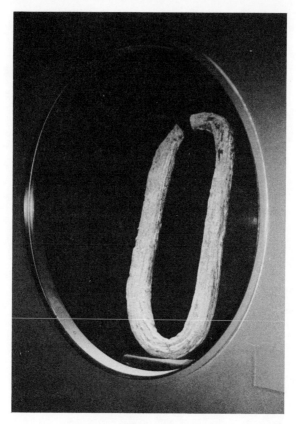

Purported Fort Montgomery Chain Link, Washington's Headquarters,
Newburgh (1985).

Purported Fort Montgomery Chain Links, Stony Point Battlefield State
Historic Park (1986).

Opposite the link is a section of the later West Point Chain boom, plus a large glass case exhibiting a *cheval-de-frise* "pick" complete with heavily-corroded iron "beak." The latter was plucked from the Hudson off Pollepel Island in 1827 by the crew of a lumber sloop whose anchor fouled the remains of one of the 50-year-old frames.

Two links displayed in the museum at the Stony Point Battlefield State Historic Park are labeled, "Believed to be part of the Fort Montgomery Chain." Their provenance is unknown; they actually bear great resemblance to the links joining the salvaged West Point boom section in the Newburgh museum.

*TIME WAS* far kinder to the 800-odd links of the West Point Chain, hauled out of the Hudson above Chain Cove for the last time in the late fall of 1782. During earlier winter retrievals, some sections of both chain and watersoaked boom may even have dropped to the bottom of the 200-foot-deep river, to be replaced in the spring with "spares." One pair of boom logs was preserved in Hudson silt until a grappling operation off the old West Point steamer dock near the Red House by Bishop's floating derrick in 1855 and 1856 brought them to the surface. That massive boom section is now a highlight of the Newburgh museum display.

In the fall of 1783 northern ironmongers eagerly awaited British evacuation of the lower Hudson, while keeping a close eye on the West Point Chain. On September 29, within weeks of Washington's reply to Colonel Pickering regarding the chain's eventual disposal, Mark Bird, 44-year-old ironmaster of Pennsylvania's important Hopewell Furnace in Berks County, petitioned Congress at Princeton to deliver the entire chain to him "at a reasonable price" for resmelting.

Bird planned to pay for the chain out of more than $125,000 the government owed him for "providing military stores"—including flour and cannon—to the Continental Army during the war. One of the Commonwealth's wealthiest revolutionaries, Bird was a member of Pennsylvania's Committee of Correspondence, a representative in the State Assembly, and—like most colonial ironmasters—a dedicated partisan of American independence.

After ten days of consideration, Congress rejected Bird's bid for the chain. As far back as 1778, Richard Henry Lee had predicted that continued "British possession of Canada would inevitably produce" another war, with a fresh struggle to control the Hudson

River. From West Point in April 1783, Brigadier General Jedediah Huntington echoed Lee's thought, writing to Washington with remarkable foresight: "In making military arrangements for peace, a possible war has the first consideration. West Point has been held as the key to the United States.

"The British will, it is presumed," the Connecticut general continued, "keep their eye upon it as long as they regret the loss of the country, or have a passion for power and conquest. West Point ought therefore to be in a complete condition of defence. It may be made a safe deposit where every military article may be kept in good order and repair. And with a small additional expence"— Huntington had a prescient eye for the future—"an academy might here be instituted for instruction in all the branches of the military art."

Such counsel may have suggested to Congress that military preparedness should take precedence over scrap metal speculation; Congress resolved: "That, at this time, it is improper to dispose of the chain."

In 1784 Francisco de Miranda, a Spanish officer who had fought against the British in Florida and later became a leader of the Venezuelan revolution, toured the United States. Observing the giant links piled up at West Point, he wrote: "It cannot be denied that this 'engine' is a praiseworthy effort of the genius, industry and audacity of the country."

The "engine"—and America's residual fear of Great Britain— remained intact. Ambassador John Adams warned from the Court of St. James in 1785 that Britain was ready to "make war immediately against us" should the opportunity arise. The following year Henry Knox—first U.S. Secretary of War—noted to Congress that a chain barrier might again be needed to frustrate any further British attempt to split the young country. He reminded the legislators of the past "demonstrated practicality of fixing a chain or chains across the river" at West Point.

For almost two decades, therefore, the chain remained government poperty, piled high on the Hudson shore near West Point's "Red House." With the establishment of the United States Military Academy in 1802, the rusting iron links were removed to the new Ordnance Compound—also known as the Artillery Laboratory—where they took up valuable space and were probably regarded as a nuisance rather than a monument to revolutionary glory.

Relick of Chain preferved at Weft Point.

Great Chain links in the United States Military Academy Ordnance
Compound (from a stereoscope slide, 1850s).

THIS AGREEMENT made this 25ʳᵈ day of Nov.ʳ 1829, between George Bomford B.ᵗ Col. on Ordnance duty in the service of the United States acting with the consent and under the direction of the Hon. Jno. H. Eaton, Secretary of War, of the one part; and Gouverneur Kemble, President of the West Point Foundry Association in the State of New York of the other part. Witnesseth — First That the said Gov.ʳ Kemble shall manufacture for the military service of the United States, a quantity of cast iron rails for cannon; or other castings of such form and dimensions, as shall be delineated in drawings furnished by the Ordnance Department.

Second — That the Ordnance Department will cause to be delivered to the said Gov.ʳ Kemble a large chain now deposited at West Point, which is to be received in payment for the iron rails.

It is further understood the price of the chain shall be forty five dollars per ton, to be delivered at the place where it now lies; and that the price of the iron rails shall be four cents per pound to be delivered at the West Point Foundry wharf.

The exact weight of the chain not being known at this time, it is understood that its weight shall be ascertained and that the quantity of rails or other castings to be manufactured and delivered, shall be equal in value to the chain at the prices stated.

In Witness whereof the said George Bomford has hereunto set his hand and affixed his seal this 25ᵗ day of November 1829, and the said Gov.ʳ Kemble has set his hand and affixed his seal this 25ᵗ day of November 1829.

Witness to the signature
of Lt. Bomford
W Wade
Witness to the signature
of Gov.ʳ Kemble
W.ᵐ R. Palmer

Geo Bomford B.ᵗ Col. (seal)
on ordnance service

Gov.ʳ Kemble (seal)

Gouverneur Kemble's agreement to melt down the West Point Chain and exchange it for iron rails and castings, 1829.

In 1805 West Point's military storekeeper Major George Fleming casually informed Jefferson's Secretary of War Henry Dearborn that he had given permission to an "outside party" to raise from Hudson River mud whatever cannon—and iron chain—the salvager could locate in "fourteen fathom of water" off the Point. Only half the cannon and a quarter of any other iron recovered would go the United States. That first salvage attempt, however, dredged up little of value.

Two years later during the bitter debate surrounding Congressional passage of Jefferson's Embargo Act to close United States ports to trade with the British and French, Colonel Jonathan Williams proposed to New York City's Fortification Committee that a barrier be stretched across the entrance to the harbor's Upper Bay, under the present Verrazzano Bridge. "The chain which would answer for this purpose," Williams asserted, "is now lying in good order at West Point." Besides the fact that the linkage was half a mile too short, no enemy naval attempt was made on New York City in the War of 1812 that followed.

Almost a quarter century later during Andrew Jackson's presidency, the government finally decided to dispose of the West Point Chain. In the fall of 1829 Colonel George Bomford—"on Ordnance duty in the service of the United States"—was authorized by Jackson's Secretary of War John H. Eaton to execute a scrap metal contract with Gouverneur Kemble, president of the recently established "West Point Foundry" at Cold Spring, a mile upriver from the Military Academy.

Bomford's contract, dated November 29, 1829, called for Kemble and his private ironworks to cast a specific amount of iron cannon rails for the United States, "or other castings of such form and dimensions as shall be delineated in drawings furnished by the Ordnance Department."

In exchange, the War Department agreed to "deliver to the said Govr. Kemble a large chain now deposited at West Point, which is to be received in payment for the iron rails," with the understanding "that its weight shall be ascertained, and that the quantity of rails or other castings to be manufactured and delivered shall be equal in value to the chain at the prices stated."

The value of the 60 tons of chain in the Ordnance Compound— "delivered at the place where it now lies . . . its exact weight not being known at this time"—was established by Kemble at only $45 a ton, less than half the ton-rate the Foundry was then charging the

United States for new castings. No one apparently objected when the total value of the chain was finally fixed at less than $2,000, a tiny percentage of its original $92,000 cost to the government a half century earlier.

Kemble signed receipts at West Point for 36 tons of the chain; before long, the United States had its cannon rails, plus a foundry credit for $14.64.

As section after section of historic West Point links was slowly rafted upstream by barge to the foundry, the honor of the ages went to someone with a sense of history at the new Academy. Some links that might also have been swallowed up in Kemble's furnace were deliberately withheld from that fiery end, and remained within the government's crenelated Ordnance Compound.

On April 15, 1836 Jackson's Secretary of War Lewis Cass even went so far as to authorize Colonel Bomford to "issue a few links of the chain, not exceeding three, to Revolutionary Officers or other persons who desire them"—but again, only in exchange for "an equivalent amount of good iron." There were apparently several takers for those 350-pound three-link souvenir sets.

By the middle of the 19th century, the vast majority of Americans had almost completely forgotten about the West Point Chain. Only a handful of people—perhaps a harbinger of chain fanciers to come—were aware of the relic's historic significance.

The cash value of any surviving links was obvious. In 1855, the New York Floating Derrick Company commenced a private salvage attempt in the river, using a huge grappling iron coupled to a powerful stream hoist mechanism originally developed to erect the Harlem River (High) Bridge to carry New York City's water supply into Manhattan. The derrick inventor, a talented Croton Aqueduct carpenter named William Bishop, eventually formed a company to exploit his new machinery on land and water.

Bishop's initial efforts at West Point created a furor in Washington. On June 25 Army Chief Engineer General Joseph G. Totten urged Franklin Pierce's Secretary of War Jefferson Davis to obtain a legal opinion from Attorney General Caleb Cushing on whether Bishop was about to misappropriate U.S. Government property. The derrick operator was claiming that existing links of the chain, both in and out of the water, were paid for in 1778 by the New York Convention, and still belonged to the people of the state—not the federal government. No one, apparently, was able to locate copies of the original Hughes/Townsend contract.

On July 5, 1855 Totten wrote to Major J. W. Barnard, Superintendent of the Military Academy: "In accordance with a portion of the opinion of the Attorney General the 2nd inst., which, annexed, is copied for your information, you will without delay, cause to be given to the Company engaged in taking up the chain which was thrown across the Hudson for military purposes during the Revolutionary War, and which still remains in the bed of the River off West Point, formal legal notice forbidding them to proceed with their operations."

Barnard responded to the question of who actually owned any links Bishop might find in the river, by reciting fragments of chain history, concluding: "In all this, there is no explicit assertion that the chain was ordered or paid for by the U.S., but the presumption is entirely in favor of the ownership of the chain by the central government, and it is now for those who dispute the fact to show the contrary.

"I can obtain no clue," Barnard said, "to the history of the chain since it was removed from the river. A large quantity of it was stored at this post and remained for years the undisputed property of the U.S. That a portion remained in the river unclaimed has been owing entirely, I imagine, to the fact that its existence was forgotten. I have seen no one at West Point who knew of its existence."

Three days later Barnard added: "Mr. Gouverneur Kemble tells me he has long been aware of a portion of it in the bed of the river, from the fact that vessels occasionally caught their anchors on it. He seems inclined," said Barnard, "to support the statement of Capt. Bishop that the chain ought to be raised as a nuisance—He thinks there may be 30 or 40 tons of it [a wild exaggeration] and that it will yet be worth $30 or $40 per ton.

"As to its being a nuisance which ought to be removed," Barnard continued, "I can only say that the entire ignorance that has prevailed for three quarters of a century ought sufficiently to confute that. Last summer it is true that a vessel did entangle her anchor in it, and this appears to be the way it was discovered.

"Whether there is really enough of it to repay the cost of search and raising seems to me somewhat doubtful. An enormous floating derrick has been now 3 weeks anchored off the Point, and so far as I can learn, nothing has been raised except a piece of small auxiliary chain and some two or three of the buoys [the boom section preserved in the Newburgh museum]. In a more pecuniary point of view, it is likely that its value has been entirely destroyed by rust."

But, Barnard phlegmatically concluded, "I have given the notice to the parties concerned forbidding their future operations."

A few days later, he again wrote Totten: "The floating derrick, after having been absent a few days doing some work at the [West Point] Foundry, has returned and renewed the search for the chain. The notice served by me on them was legal and sufficient, I presume, to support the claim of the U.S., but if it is thought best absolutely to prevent the further search, it may well be necessary to take out an injunction, which I believe requires the agency of the U.S. District Attorney at New York.

"Probably," Barnard noted candidly, "it would be as well to let them continue and be prepared to seize the chain should it be obtained possession of. The opinion of the Attorney General, so far as he has given it, seems however, to leave some doubt as to the propriety of our claim, and I would request immediate instructions on this point, as well as to the *modus operandi* of seizing the property, should that be advised."

In the end, the government apparently permitted Bishop to salvage a few chain links in peace. Passing through both private and government hands—possibly with a brief stay at the Brooklyn Navy Yard—Bishop's remnants were either scattered, melted down, or lost forever.

Perhaps stirred by Bishop's salvage attempts, the Military Academy moved to create an unusual Revolutionary War memorial. In 1857 to honor the original colonies, 12 chain links and a swivel were shifted from the Ordnance Compound to the area that would eventually become known as Trophy Point. The links, resting on billets of wood, were laid out in a circle under the trees and joined with a clevis—one of the 80 U-shaped pinned connectors that made it possible to connect, disconnect, and repair original chain sections. Not far from Chain Cove, the relics soon became an important West Point feature, appropriately noted in all contemporary Academy guidebooks.

Two centuries later, refreshed from time to time with coats of shiny black enamel, that same rugged section of original chain still astounds and delights tens of thousands of West Point visitors annually. More than any symbolic portrait or museum diorama, the actual full-size links reflect all the robust ingenuity of America's revolutionary ironworkers, and offer a dramatic evocation of this nation's tumultuous beginning.

The 13-link chain "sampler" rests in an imposing place of honor

THE GREAT CHAIN

The Great Chain, 1865.

West Point Chain Link Memorial, 1915

West Point Chain Link Memorial, 1941.

Swivel, West Point Chain Link Memorial (1985).

Clevis and pin, West Point Chain Link Memorial; post support at right (1985).

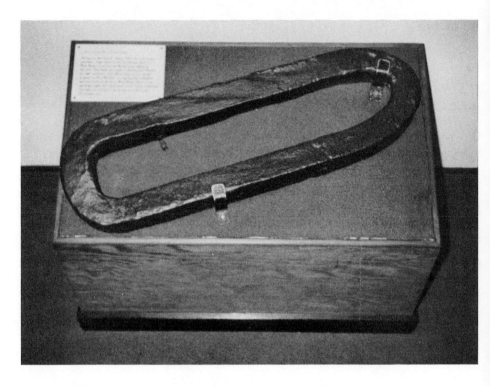

West Point Chain link, Morristown National Historic Park (1986).

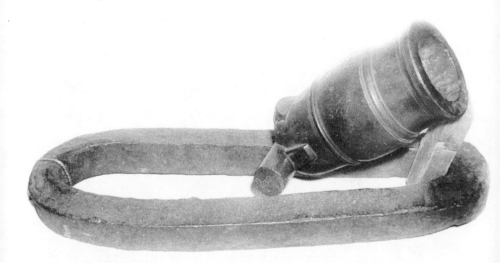

West Point Chain link, with small Revolutionary War mortar, Worcester
Historical Museum (1986).

atop a grassy knoll at Trophy Point, draped over metal posts and guarded by two Revolutionary War fieldpieces. It is a mandatory lecture stop for each new plebe class on its orientation tour of the Academy grounds.

Average weight of the 13 chain links is 114 lbs.; the heaviest weighs 130 lbs. The Sterling Furnace ironworkers and teamsters, Captain Machin's New Windsor artificers—and the half-frozen garrison soldiers stationed at the Point who maneuvered the monstrous chain in and out of the Hudson River every fall and spring for five years—had no easy job.

Length of the rough-shaped links ranges from 28″ to 36″; their average length is 31½″. Based both on their deadweight and location—only a few hundred yards from the original chain installation—the 13 links must be considered authentic.

For 18th century hand-wrought iron, the dimensions of the 13 links are amazingly uniform. Widths range from 9½″ to 10¾″; the average width is ten inches. The 2¼ + ″ thick iron bars, neatly bent around the Sterling Furnace mandrel like huge paper clips and scarfed together to form the chain, have a circumference that rarely varies from 9½″, and is never less than nine inches, or any more than ten.

Based on the specifications of DQMG Hughes's contract, as well as the unprecedented speed with which Noble, Townsend & Company manufactured the chain, any other so-called "West Point Chain" links anywhere in the United States that measure less than 26″ or more than 38″ long—or if they fall within that range, are narrower than 9″ or wider than 11″—or possess a critical circumference varying more than an inch on either side of 9½″—are not part of the original Revolutionary chain but from some other huge linkage.

In addition to the chain section on Trophy Point, only ten other authentic West Point links (plus two swivels and one clevis) are known to exist. They were either souvenirs sawed loose with Colonel Bomford's permission from the pile in the Ordnance Compound, or possibly hauled from the bed of the Hudson in 1856 by Bishop's floating derrick.

One such relic is on exhibit at the Morristown, New Jersey National Historical Park Museum, cataloged as "Industrial Art: Hand-forged link of chain." Thirty-two and a half inches long, 9″ wide, 9″ in circumference, and weighing 104 pounds, the link matches all the Trophy Point parameters.

In 1926 the Morristown link was bequeathed to the Washington Association of New Jersey by Fred A. Canfield. He said it had been discovered in a junk pile at Morristown's Speedwell Ironworks almost a century earlier. In 1933, when administration of the Commander-in-chief's 1779–80 winter residence at Morristown was transferred by the Association to the National Park Service, the link—after 150 years in private hands—again became government property.

Another early chain souvenir rests in the basement collections of the Connecticut Historical Society at Hartford. It was given to the Society in 1841—long before Bishop's salvage effort—by Samuel Bowles, who said he obtained it from Charles Stearns of Springfield, Massachusetts. Bowles related that Stearns "had bought it in New York some years since."

Stearns had actually purchased at least *two* links; in 1832, he presented another to the American Antiquarian Society in Worcester, Massachusetts. When that group moved to its new building in 1909, the link passed into the collections of the Worcester Historical Museum.

Three more links are bolted like a piece of contemporary sculpture to the marble rotunda wall of the old New York State Education Department building in Albany, New York. They may even be one of the "souvenir sets" authorized by Secretary of War Cass in 1836. The three links were presented to the State Library in 1858 by Sterling ironmaster Peter Townsend's great grandson General Franklin Townsend. Destiny would redeem them twice from flames—they naturally survived the disastrous Albany Library fire of 1911.

On September 16, 1949—167 years after the West Point garrison hauled the chain out of the Hudson for the last time—the commander of Royal Navy *H.M.S. Snipe* came ashore in Albany to pay a courtesy call on those three links. Captain C.G. Walker's frigate was the first British warship to pass West Point since 1777.

Two links, still connected by one of the chain's two undamaged swivels, may also be an 1836 souvenir set. They lie half-buried in the pachysandra bordering the portico of the handsome 1764 Redwood Library in Newport, Rhode Island. That chain assembly was donated to the Library in September 1861 by New York merchant Robert Bowne Minturn, scion of an old and distinguished Newport family, who also gave the library part of a West Point boom anchor.

West Point Chain links, State Education Department Building, Albany
(1985).

West Point Chain links at Redwood Library, Newport (1986).

Alice Austen's photograph of her Staten Island living room (1888).

West Point Chain link plus damaged swivel, Boscobel Restoration (1986).

THOMAS MACHIN
1744-1816

Captain of Artillery
and Engineer of na-
tional renown during
Revolutionary War.
Supervised the mak-
ing and laying of The
Great Chain across
the Hudson River
near West Point.

Thomas Machin's grave (1816), Carlisle, Montgomery County, New York.

A link given by Albany politician Thurlow Weed to Hamilton Fish during the Civil War was subsequently presented by the Fish family to the New-York Historical Society. It appears to be temporarily misplaced somewhere in its scattered collections.

Of skimpier provenance but closer to home—lying on the floor of the carriage house museum at Boscobel Restoration just across the Hudson from West Point—is another link attached to a swivel whose head was long ago circumcised. In 1961 that link and swivel were inventoried as part of the collection of the Putnam County Historical Society in nearby Cold Spring, where 36 tons of the chain were resmelted in 1829 in the furnaces of the West Point Foundry.

The Historical Society was founded in 1906; it now occupies the former foundry school. Undoubtedly foundry master Gouverneur Kemble, or some patriotic furnace foreman, sawed off the swivel head and saved the unusual linkage locally for posterity.

After a 150-year journey to the far side of our continent, a pinless clevis ended up several years ago in a Beverly Hills antique shop. Spotted by sharp-eyed West Point Chain buff Gary M. Milan, it is now his most prized Revolutionary War relic—and is the only remnant of Captain Machin's historic linkage currently known to be in private hands. There may be others.

Two additional joined links—now vanished—were at one time in the hands of another Townsend descendant, a Rutgers University chemistry professor named Peter Townsend Austen. They rested for many years atop his heavy living room fireplace stove at 2 Hylan Boulevard on Staten Island, in the historic structure now known as the Alice Austen House. Miss Austen, a famous early New York photographer (a Staten Island ferryboat carries her name), was Professor Townsend's niece. She also lived in the elegant old "Victorian cottage," and her 1888 glass negative of its cluttered living room, showing the two links, is still preserved at the House—now a designated landmark.

Every time an individual souvenir link was cut from the West Point Chain, at least one connection—such as the link in Philadelphia—had to be severed. A 2½″ iron cube, identified as the section removed during such an operation, rests in the collection of the Litchfield Historical Society.

This unprepossessing chunk of rusted iron, smelted more than two centuries ago from Ramapo ore, then triphammered and twisted by Sterling forgemen, and linked by New Windsor blacksmiths, now sits quietly in its glass case in Litchfield, Connecticut. Obviously indestructible, this little piece of chain symbolizes the iron determination of the American people in their epic eight-year struggle for freedom and independence.

# Articles of Agreement

*Articles of Agreement between Noble, Townsend and Company, Proprietors of the Sterling Iron Works in the State of New York, on the one Part, and Hugh Hughes, DQMG [Deputy Quartermaster General] to the Army of the United States, of the other Part . . .*

"*Witnesseth:* That the Said Noble, Townsend & Company jointly, and severally engage to have made and ready to be delivered at their Works to the said Hugh Hughes DQMG, or to the DQMG of the Middle Dept. for the time being, on or before the first Day of April next ensuing the Date hereof, or as much sooner as Circumstances will admit, an Iron Chain of the following Dimensions and Quality.

"That is, in Length five hundred yards, each Link about two Feet long, to be made of the best Sterling Iron, two Inches and one Quarter Square, or as near thereto as possible, with a Swivel to every hundred Feet, and a Clevis to every thousand Wt., in the same manner as those of the Former Chain.

"The said Noble, Townsend & Company, also engage to have made, and ready to be delivered, at least Twelve Tons of Anchors of the aforesaid Iron, and of such Sizes as the said Hugh Hughes or his Successor in Office shall direct in Writing, as soon as the Completion of the Chain will permit.

"In Consideration of which the said Hugh Hughes DQMG, in behalf of the United States, engages to pay to the said Noble, Townsend & Company, or their Order, at the rate of Four hundred and Forty Pounds for every ton weight of Chain and Anchors delivered as before mentioned, unless the General Regulations on Trade, Provisions, &c., which are now Supposed to be framing by deputies from the United States, shall be Published and take effect before the Expiration of Four Months from the Date of this. In which case the Price is to be only Four Hundred Pounds per ton for the said Chain & Anchors.

"The Payments, if demanded, to be made in such Proportion as the

Work shall be ready to be delivered, which shall be determined in ten days after requisition made by a number of Competent Judges, not less than three, nor More than five, unconnected with the Proprietors, or the Works, and if Condemned, to be compleated at the expense of the said Company, who are also to repair, as aforesaid, all failures of their Work, wherever happening, whether at the Works, or River, or in extending it across.

"The said Hugh Hughes also engages to procure of the Governor of this State, for the said Noble, Townsend & Company, an exemption for Nine Months from the date hereof, from Military Duty for Sixty Artificers that are Steadily to be employed at the said Chain & Anchors, still compleated, agreeable to the said Exemption, the said Company complying with the Terms thereof, providing also that the said Company give the said Hugh Hughes, or his Successor in Office, the Refusal, by Letter, of all the Bar Iron, Anchors, &c., made at the said Works in the said Term of Nine Months, at the current Price, unless what is necessary to Exchange for Clothing and other Articles for the Use of the Works.

"It is also agreed by the said Parties, that if the Teams of the said Company shall Transport the said Chain or Anchors, or any Part thereof, to any assigned Post, they shall receive for such Services the same Pay, as shall be given by the United States for the like. The Teams of said Company being exempted from Impress by any of the QM General's Department during the Space of nine Months from the date hereof.

"Lastly, the said Company engage to Use their utmost Endeavours to keep Seven Fires at Forging, and ten at Welding, if Assisted with such Hands as are necessary, & can be spared from the Army, in case of their not being able to procure others, the said Company making deduction for their Labour.

"In Witness whereof the Parties have interchangeably subscribed their Names, this second Day of February, One Thousand, Seven Hundred & Seventy Eight, and in the Second Year of American Independence."

*(signed)* PETER TOWNSEND
& in behalf of Noble & Company

Present
*(signed)* P. TILLINGHAST

Brooklyn N.Y. Sept 18/89

Mr. A. McMahon
    Dr Sir
        In reply to yours of the 16 inst. would say that your the chain that you inquire after, the same was purchased of the govt at a Navy Yard Sale in Brooklyn some two years ago and was used during the Revolution to keep the British fleet from going up the Hudson River. the identity of this chain can be fully established. papers will it seems to that effect the links are about three feet long and two inches thick and in terms of 35 to 40 feet and weigh about 2 tons to the length. I have about 12 tons will sell you one or two lengths or the lot at five (5) cents net cash per pound. the chain can be seen at any time

Yours Respsy
J.C. Abbey

Abbey's initial chain offer to Andrew McMahon, September 18, 1889.

WESTMINSTER MILLS.

WESTMINSTER ABBEY,
*Manager,*
IMPORTER AND DEALER IN

TEAS, COFFEES, SPICES, ETC.,
61 FRONT STREET,

New York, Feby 3 1891

Mr C. F. Gunther
Dr Sir
Yours at hand
in reply would say that
I have about eight (8) tons
of the chain on hand,
have been holding back
on this as there is one or
two parties working on it
but have not done any
thing as yet, if you want
the lot will put it in at
same price as you bought
although I am holding it at
a higher price    dont delay
Respy.    W. Abbey

Abbey offers Gunther the remainder of his spurious "West Point Chain,"
February 3, 1891.

# The Great Chain Hoax

*"O foolish people . . . which have eyes and see not."*
—JEREMIAH V, 21.

THE REMAINS of Captain Machin's iron barrier across the Hudson at West Point represent one of the country's most important historical relics. More than a century after the chain's installation—as interest in the Revolution was reinvigorated by the great Centennial Exhibition in Philadelphia—a pair of enterprising scalawags began to foist a spurious chain on the American public.

John C. Abbey was a 35-year-old New York "odds-and-ends man" with an indisputable sense of American history. This Manhattan junk dealer customarily went under the more colorful Christian appellation of "Westminster"—so named "by his pious father," according to Abbey's 1922 obituary in *The New York Times*—"out of respect for the famous church in London. For 50 years," the obit continued, "it was a byword along the waterfront that you could get anything from a nail to a cannon at Westminster Abbey's old place." Including, it appeared, fully authenticated links of Captain Machin's famous "West Point Chain."

For in the 1880's, Abbey obtained—from the innermost recesses of the 300-acre Brooklyn Navy Yard, he claimed—86 links of a heavy contemporary rolled-iron ground anchor chain. This type of chain, manufactured exclusively in Great Britain, was used to anchor large steamship mooring buoys in worldwide ports that possessed no pier facilities. Chains of this type were brought to New York in the last half of the 19th century to secure the huge dredges used to deepen the major ship channels of Upper and Lower Bay.

Abbey waited a year or so. Then, despite the fact that genuine links of the West Point Chain were available for anyone's comparison only fifty miles up the Hudson at the U.S Military Academy, the dealer began to represent his dramatic-looking scrap metal as newly-discovered links of the famous Revolutionary War river barrier. It was a startling parody of what

Van Wyck Brooks eventually characterized as America's "search for a usable past"; or as a more recent writer suggests in her hagiographic study of George Washington, "the specific human need to achieve a measure of material intimacy with great events of the past."

Before long Abbey had his first bite. On September 18, 1889 he was able to reply to Andrew McMahon, a fellow junk dealer on Manhattan's East River waterfront: "The chain that you enquire after . . . was purchased of the Govt. at a Navy Yard Sale in Brooklyn some two years ago and was used during the Revolution to keep the British Fleet from going up the Hudson River. The identity of this chain can be fully established. Papers will be shown to that effect." Abbey offered the "12 tons . . . at five (5) cents net cash per pound"—all of his entire "historic" chain for $1,200.

McMahon was representing the Chicago sweets manufacturer and inventor of the candy caramel, the wealthy and eccentric Charles Frederick Gunther, erstwhile Confederate Army supplier and Democratic candidate for Governor of Illinois. Gunther was being hailed as the world's largest collector of historical relics, manuscripts and paintings. According to a cynical executive at New York's American Art Galleries, Gunther "would believe anything a seller told him."

At the time McMahon contacted Abbey for Gunther, the candy man was actively amassing thousands of items of Americana to fill his new crenelated block-long Chicago museum, opened to the public in 1889 (and closed ten years later). For the museum, Gunther even purchased the notorious Civil War Libby Prison in Richmond, Virginia, dismantled it stone by stone, and shipped it north in 132 box cars.

In addition to that prison and other historic artifacts, the museum on Wabash Avenue south of the Loop was soon housing not only 18 newly-acquired links of the huge *West Point Chain,"* but also displayed *"Uncle Tom's Original Cabin"* and *"The Skin of the Snake that tempted Eve."*

On February 3, 1891 Abbey reminded Gunther that he was still sitting on "about eight tons of the chain," and offered the remaining links to the candy man "at the same price as you bought. There is one or two parties working on it . . . at a higher price," Abbey warned, "Don't delay." But Gunther passed up any second helping.

Gunther's *Libby Prison War Museum Catalogue* in 1892 described the links as being "made from iron bars two and one half inches square, average length a little more than two feet, and weight about 150 pounds each"— actually a close description of the real West Point Chain links on Trophy Point. But when he reprinted the catalog the following year, Gunther revised that description to better match his Chicago links: "3½ feet long, made of bar iron four inches square."

On September 16, 1893, disturbed by a few publicly-expressed doubts as to what he was actually selling, Abbey sent a letter to the "Gents" at the

"War Departments, Washington, D.C.—I have 25000 lbs of Large Linked Chains said to have been used by Genl Washington at West Point across the Hudson River to prevent the passage of British War ships. I claim that the links weighs upwards of 300 pounds each. this chain was sold by the U.S. Government at auction, and had been in the Navy Yard for a long time.

"A man writes me," Abbey continued, "that your Dept. says the links are 2½ inches square their average length a little over two feet and their weight 140 lbs ea. the Links I have are 3½ inches square, and are 3 feet 9 inches long, and weight 300 pounds ea. I have just weighed a Link and know it is so will you kinly let me know what your Department says about it, and the same will be highly appreciated."

The Department chose not to reply. Emboldened by its silence, Abbey embarked on a more aggressive promotion. On January 8, 1894 he invited a reporter from the New York *Sun* to his five-story warehouse on the east side of Front Street at No. 61, between Old Slip and Cuyler's Alley, only a block from the East River piers. The building facade was decorated with signs: *"Westminster Abbey, Dealer in Guns, Rifles, Revolvers & Military Pistols," "Best Mixed Tea, Wholesale and Retail,"* and *"Sailors Mess & Kits."*

Abbey pointed out three remaining sections—totalling 56 links—of what the reporter later described as a "silver steel" chain, stretched along the warehouse floor. Boldly ignoring the fact that a large part of the same chain had been on public display in Chicago for several years, Abbey unblinkingly told the *Sun* he had just "bid it in several months before at a government auction in the Brooklyn Navy Yard."

Then Abbey innocently described how the chain, originally purchased as "junk," had recently been authenticated by "Mr. Gunther—a collector for the Libby Prison Museum who bought 5,000 pounds—as part of the chain placed across the Hudson at West Point in 1778." Abbey told the reporter that Gunther had recently developed "an authentic history of the chain down to the time it was placed in the Brooklyn Navy Yard, and from there had traced it" to Abbey's Front Street warehouse—a plain but "once aristocratic" four-story brick loft building, on whose topmost floor Abbey cured leaf tobacco.

To support Gunther's "discovery," Abbey referred the reporter to a purported statement by Hilary A. Herbert, Secretary of the Navy in Grover Cleveland's second administration. Herbert asserted, according to Abbey, that he could give "a history of the chain for the fifty years it had been in the Navy Yard."

At the time the *Sun* article appeared, Abbey had been haggling with the well-known industrialist and popular ex-mayor of New York City, Abram S. Hewitt of Ringwood Manor, New Jersey. "Hewitt," the newspaper explained, "is the present owner of the iron mine near the Sterling mines from which the ore came which went into the chain. Mr. Hewitt wanted the chain, but he and the dealer have not agreed upon terms, according to a letter signed by Mr. Hewitt which the dealer showed to the reporter."

Hewitt also ran the family cable business in Trenton. Seventeen years earlier, while serving as a member of the Brooklyn Bridge board of directors, Hewitt had secretly financed J. Lloyd Haigh, a Brooklyn manufacturer caught selling defective wire to the Roeblings for bridge cables.

The *Sun* article concluded with dimensions of the "odds-and-ends man's" links. Although the real West Point Chain was manufactured of unevenly triphammered iron, what lay on the floor of Abbey's warehouse was obviously smooth *rolled* iron. The *Sun* reporter noted ingenuously that while Abbey's description of his discovery "may not be accurate, it is pleasing."

Almost two years later, the New York *World* also picked up Abbey's story. Their reporter, supposedly "attracted by the gilt-lettered name and the medley of goods that overflowed from the shop out on the sidewalk," visited the junk dealer's "queer old curio" warehouse and came away with a fresh newspaper story—a two-column Sunday feature on November 10, 1895. Abbey and Hewitt, according to the *World* reporter, had still "not agreed upon terms." Among other contradictions left over from the earlier *Sun* account, the number of unsold links on Abbey's warehouse floor had somehow increased from 56 to 70.

*IN THE* early 1890s, many of Abbey's inconsistencies were glibly glossed over in a little undated merchandising pamphlet prepared by his Front Street neighbor at No. 27, Francis Bannerman. Born in Dundee, Scotland in 1851 and brought to America as a child, Bannerman had become one of the country's major surplus armaments dealers. Whenever chided for his deadly trade, Bannerman liked to say, "I look forward to St. John's vision of Satan bound, with one thousand years of peace; but they are not yet in sight."

Bannerman decided to buy out Abbey. As the new and somewhat better-organized proprietor of the spurious "West Point Chain" links, Bannerman celebrated the event by issuing a pamphlet entitled *History of the Great Iron Chain Laid Across the Hudson River in 1788, by Order of General George Washington*. It spun a fascinating tale, still naively cited by a handful of historians, of how the "West Point Chain" ended up in the Brooklyn Navy Yard.

According to Bannerman, much of the chain actually escaped Gouverneur Kemble's fiery upriver furnace and lay quietly stored at West Point for almost a century. In March 1864, near the end of the Civil War, almost a hundred links were barged down the Hudson to Manhattan— Bannerman said—where the sections, "18 links to each shot, weighing 5,600 pounds," were loaded on "large windlass trucks, with tackle such as

# HISTORY

OF THE

# GREAT IRON CHAIN,

LAID ACROSS THE HUDSON RIVER
AT WEST POINT IN 1778, BY ORDER OF
....GENERAL GEORGE WASHINGTON....

On exhibition at the Military War Museum, 579 Broadway, New York,

FRANCIS BANNERMAN.

DESK WEIGHT MADE FROM THE CHAIN.

Title page of Bannerman's *History of the Great Iron Chain*, showing links of
the spurious "West Point Chain" and his $2.75 chain desk weight.

The Metropolitan Sanitary Fair—The Department of Arms and Trophies
(New York, April 1864).

Ruins of Long Pond Furnace, Hewitt, New Jersey (1985).

are used in moving heavy machinery," and carted east along 14th Street to the 22nd Regiment Armory for patriotic display at the famous New York Metropolitan Fair.

That giant fair was one of several held in northern cities to raise money for a new War Department bureau, the United States Sanitary Commission, precursor of the Red Cross. The Commission was a group of civilian volunteers soliciting public support for auxiliary army hospitals, recuperation homes and refreshment shelters for sick and wounded Union soldiers. According to Bannerman, the organizers hoped that display of the massive Revolutionary War memento would increase the Fair's patriotic appeal.

There seems no question that at one time the Brooklyn Navy Yard *did* possess a few links of the genuine West Point Chain, possibly as a result of Secretary Cass's distribution policy. On June 29, 1855 the *Albany Weekly Argus* published a letter from Orange County historian Jeptha Root Simms, who asserted that while "any considerable portion of chain is now under the river would seem incredible, 20 years ago there were not a few links of this chain at the Brooklyn Navy Yard; and much of it, as I have been informed, has been worked up by blacksmiths. Museums and the cabinets of antiquarians also have some share of it." Ten years earlier, Simms added, "through the kindness of Colonel E. J. McCarthy of Ulster County, a link of this formidable chain was added to my own cabinet."

Yet in 1895 the Yard wrote to Abbey, "there is no record of the chain in this office. Mr. Magee, the Master Shipwright of the Yard who has been here about 50 years, remembers a similar chain lying in the Ship House. It was sold some years since." In 1932, the Navy again indicated "Yard records do not disclose any data whatsoever concerning this chain."

Even so, there is no doubt the Yard was able to lend some genuine "Links, and a Portion of a Link"—along with 30 other naval mementos—to the two-week April 1864 Metropolitan Fair. Those links occupied a quiet corner of the Museum of Flags, Trophies and Relics, amid more than a thousand more flamboyant military items.

The description in the Museum visitors' catalog is explicit: "No. 807. *Links, and a Portion of a Link of the Great Chain Stretched Across the Hudson at West Point, during the Revolution in 1778, to prevent the British Vessels from Passing.*

"The links were made of Iron Bars," said the catalog, "2½ inches square, average in length a little more than two feet [Abbey's-Bannerman's were three-and-a-half feet] and weigh about 140 lbs. each [Abbey's-Bannerman's weighed 300 lbs.]. The Chain was stretched below the river at its narrowest point between the rocks, just below the present Steamboat Landing; it was hitched to huge blocks on each shore, and was buoyed up by very large logs, about sixteen feet long, pointed at the ends to lessen the opposition to the force of the current.

"The logs were placed at short distances from each other, the chain carried over them and made fast to each by staples. There were also a number of anchors dropped at proper distances, with cables made fast to the chain to give a greater stability; it was made at the Iron Work a few miles distant, and stretched across May 1st, 1776 [*sic*]. Some years since, between twenty and forty tons of the chain were recovered from the bottom of the river where it had sunk [perhaps a confusion with the links sold to the West Point Foundry in 1829].

"More recently one of the large floating boom derricks was sent up from New York, but the logs attached to it were so firmly buried in the mud, that the immense floating power of the derrick was found unequal to the task, and but a small quantity was fished up."

The Metropolitan Fair was a great success, raising over $1 million. At its conclusion—Bannerman's story continues—the 80-odd links of the Great Chain were not returned to the West Point Military Academy, but were carried across the East River for storage in some out-of-the-way corner of the Brooklyn Navy Yard.

Publishing his booklet more than a quarter century after the Fair, Bannerman gambled that no one would remember the general appearance of that handful of genuine links for two weeks in 1864. In fact, the April 4, 1864 *New York Times* and *New-York Tribune,* heralding the event's opening, described in detail its display of trophies, "filled with objects to excite curiousity, patriotism and respect"—from George Washington's uniform and sword, to the purposely shocking "veritable Yankee skull, taken at Bull Run, and manufactured by the rebels into a drinking cup."

But neither newspaper—nor several special Fair issues of the comprehensive, profusely-illustrated *Harper's Weekly* or *Frank Leslie's Illustrated Newspaper*—noted the presence of even a single link of the famous West Point Chain.

Bannerman's pamphlet now leaps ahead two decades, to the time when his "Revolutionary relics" could be safely exhumed. During Grover Cleveland's first administration—says Bannerman—the Navy Department moved to consolidate all its various quartermaster installations into one General Storekeepers Department. The new bureau authorized a board of officers under Commander Robert W. Meade to "visit all Navy Yards to examine all stores, and anything not in use or fit for Naval Service was to be condemned and sold at Public Auction.

"In due time," Bannerman continues, Meade's board "found this old chain and without either knowing the history or having any appreciation for such a valuable relic, ordered it sold at auction, September 4, 1887." Bannerman tells how, 22 years after the end of the Civil War, the unusual links were bid in by his own father, Francis Sr, "who in turn sold the chain along with a lot of other scrap iron to a forge company to be worked over into new iron." (Conflicting stories circulated about Bannerman's father. In the 1920s one biographical dictionary described him as having "died from effects of exposure while serving in the Federal Army during the Civil War.")

A detailed report of that Navy Yard auction—actually held August 30, 1887, five days earlier than Bannerman indicated—*does* exist. It appeared in *The New York Times* under the caption, *"A Navy Yard Sale; Throngs of Buyers From All Over the Country":*

"A sale of old junk and some new articles took place at the navy yard yesterday. The gain to the Government was not made known, but it will not be a large sum. That great interest was taken in the sale was apparent from the crowd that surged about the auctioneer. There were bidders from all over the country, including Mr. Nathan, of Chicago; Simon Belcher, of Cincinnati; N. Gale, of Louisville; A. Weiniske, of St. Louis; August Pollock of Chicago and New York and Brooklyn; and junk dealers, contractors, and wholesale dealers in almost every department of business.

"Some of the truck brought good prices, especially a lot of hawsers and cables. Eleven fog horns, with a letter press and one or two minor articles, brought $113, while a can buoy sold for $2.75. Eighteen drums, which looked and sounded tired out, brought $13. A big pile of flags was knocked down for $35, while 306 spyglasses and binoculars went for $155. An old-fashioned fire engine it was thought would call forth lively bidding, but it sold for $50, and 200 pairs of duck pantaloons only brought 27-½ cents a pair.

"An enterprising bidder purchased 2,800 pounds of hard tack for $38, and 612 shirts of blue cloth sold for $1.65 apiece. Stephen Roberts, a boat builder, purchased 13 Ingersoll lifeboats for $28 each and a yawl for $12. A whaleboat that once belonged to the old *Bear* brought $6. Life yachts sold for $51. Some of the old iron cooking utensils, anchor chains, and other things sold may have had value as souvenirs of the old vessels they have voyaged in, but no mention was made of their antecedents in the catalogue."

The *Times* makes no mention of 86 links of a huge iron chain.

The New York *Sun* covered the same auction with an even longer article—*"Condemned Naval Stores Sold"*—enlivened by the newspaper's charge that one naval officer's wife was permitted to purchase Navy silverware at an inside price in advance of public bidding. Again, no mention of Bannerman's father—or anyone else—bidding on a giant chain.

Bannerman was an excellent promoter. He was convinced that Americans were ready to welcome any links of the miraculously rediscovered West Point Chain. (Even as late as 1913, 89-year-old Anna Bartlett Warner, author of the famed hymn *Jesus Loves Me*, who was still living in the Warner family home on Constitution Island, added to the confusion by claiming in a letter to Stuyvesant Fish that "two-thirds of the old chain lies in the depths just by my boathouse, and at low water many of the timbers to which it was made fast can still be seen.")

Following the myth of the 1887 Brooklyn Navy Yard auction, Bannerman's pamphlet moves on to a description of how John C. Abbey—for some reason, never "Westminster" to the arms dealer—"a frequent bidder at auctions of government property," sensed in 1887 (seven years before the *Sun* article) that the Navy Yard links were part of the original West Point Chain. Bannerman tells how Abbey was able to trace the links to the Brooklyn foundry that had just received them from Bannerman's father. Abbey, he said, bought back all the links not yet melted down.

Bannerman was gambling—again correctly—that no one would bother to look up the original Abbey article in the *Sun* for January 9, 1894.

Abbey—relates Bannerman—then sold sections of his "West Point Chain" to the public "for about 10 years." The links actually received wide distribution from both Abbey and Bannerman. Today scattered all over the country from Vermont to California, they in no way resemble the authentic, chunky, slightly twisted West Point Chain links on Trophy Point.

Bannerman's pamphlet goes on to tell how Abbey sold his first 18 links to Charles Gunther, then "looking around for relics to fit up the Libby Prison Museum, opened in 1889." Ten years later Gunther proudly loaned his links to Omaha's Greater American Exposition—for its *"Largest Chain on Earth Exhibit."*

In 1900—before Bannerman took over the chain from Abbey—Abram Hewitt finally decided to buy 36 links for $432, including cartage. Twenty-six of those links still grace the front lawn of the former Hewitt estate at Ringwood Manor in northwestern New Jersey, now a state park. The area is historic; only four miles away lie the ruins of the Long Pond iron furnace where parts of the Fort Montgomery chain were forged.

Typical of all the Abbey/Bannerman chain links, those at Ringwood are uniform, 46 inches long, 13 inches wide and 12¾ inches in diameter; the wrong size and weight compared to the West Point Chain. Ringwood's smooth, *neatly chamfered* links are not only three times heavier than the rugged links hurriedly forged in 1778 at Sterling Furnace, they are also on average 65% longer, plus an additional 3¾ inches in circumference.

Hewitt, an experienced ironmaster who lived only a few hours' carriage ride from West Point, eventually got around to comparing the links received from Abbey with the links on Trophy Point, and was soon loudly complaining that "Abbey sold the chain to me on false representation."

In nearby Southfields, New York, Macgrane Coxe, another Peter Townsend descendant and a Wall Street lawyer who later became a U.S. Ambassador to Costa Rica and Honduras, also longed to possess a few of the "historic" links. His neighbor Hewitt cautioned Coxe of Abbey's fraud, and suggested that "under the circumstances, it would be very unpleasant"

"Heavy links" of the spurious West Point chain, Ringwood Manor, New Jersey (1985).

## SQUARE LINK CHAIN

The Square Link Chain shown in this illustration gives an idea of the types of Ground Moorings used by the Admiralty for holding H.M. Battleships when moored in harbour.

This form of Chain was also used for the Ground Chain of the Cunard Steam Ship Co.'s moorings in the Mersey for the "Mauretania" and "Aquitania."

Turn of the century Square Link Admiralty Mooring Chain (with round anchor chain at left) manufactured by Brown, Lenox & Co. Ltd., Pontypridd, Wales.

## BATTLESHIP GROUND MOORING CHAIN AND SHACKLE

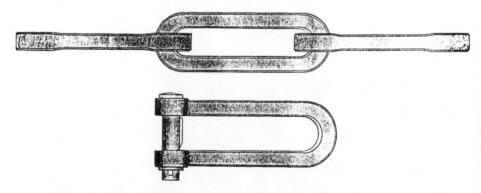

The Links of the largest sizes as used for Battleship Permanent Moorings weigh nearly 6 cwt. each, and the Connecting Shackles 8½ cwt. each

This type of Ground Chain was also supplied by Brown, Lenox & Co. Ltd., for the Permanent Moorings in the Mersey for the Cunard Steam Ship Co.'s 50,000 ton vessels.

Largest (600 lbs.) Brown, Lenox & Co. Battleship Ground Mooring link; note chamfered edges.

for Coxe to apply directly to the "odds-and-ends man." Instead, to cut his own losses, Hewitt offered to sell Coxe 18 of his own links for $226. Coxe settled for ten.

When Coxe died in the late 1920s, his widow Lena gave those ten links to Roscoe W. Smith, present of the Orange Utility Company, in exchange for electrifying her home. Smith later founded the Orange County Museum Village, a local historic restoration at Monroe, New York, where Coxe's ten links are still displayed, unlabeled, on the "village green."

On January 10, 1901 Hewitt sent an angry letter to Abbey, requesting return of his $432, with "all expenses incurred thereon. I have ascertained," said Hewitt, that the chain is "simply what is termed dredging or buoy chain used by the Government for holding vessels above the buoys, and was sold for want of further use." Abbey made no reply.

Almost a half century later, Hewitt's son Edward would recount in a private memoir how a visiting "English iron manufacturer [Sir Lothian Bell] recognized [the chain] as one of the Admiralty buoy chains made by his firm, which had been used in New York harbor." (An *Admiralty chain* had to pass prescribed strength tests at one of several British naval testing stations.) The younger Hewitt also related how he had personally "analyzed the iron of the links and found it to be Lowmoor iron from England." The northwest Lowmoor district still supplies quality iron ore to British foundries.

*FOR SEVERAL* decades, Edward Hewitt kept that embarassing British identification to himself. Contemporary evidence now supports the assertion that Westminster Abbey's "West Point Chain" was not made at Sterling Furnace in 1778, but was manufactured more than a century later in the rolling mills of Brown, Lenox & Co.'s Newbridge Chain and Anchor Works at Pontypridd, 15 miles north of Cardiff, Wales along the Glamorganshire Canal.

From 1806 to recent times, Brown, Lenox has served as a world supplier of huge anchors, cables, buoys, and moorings to naval and merchant shipping, and harbors everywhere. A *History of the Iron, Steel, Tinplate and Other Trades,* published in Wales more than 80 years ago, describes how in 1856 Brown, Lenox manufactured 800 fathoms of 2-5/8″ chain for the mammoth *Great Eastern*—"a size in those days unheard of."

Later, "the firm were busily engaged on a large quantity of mooring chain for holding our modern ironclads; each link was 4½ in. square and 3 ft. long in the clear, weighing over 4 cwt.," a size and weight very close to Abbey's relic. "Powerful hydraulic presses have for the first time been introduced by the firm for the purpose of shaping and welding these huge links, samples of which are proved on the public testing machine at Cardiff to 250 tons without breaking." Such enormous chains were then sold by Brown, Lenox to shipbuilding companies around the world, including several in the United States.

In the midst of all of Bannerman's "historic chain" hoopla, J.P. Morgan Jr bought two links of something misrepresented to him as the West Point Chain. Resembling the pair of links displayed at the Stony Point Museum, they are probably salvaged West Point boom connectors. On February 11, 1916 the financier-collector presented them to New York-New Jersey's Palisades Interstate Park Commission. The Morgan links, with no description, now hang from the huge second floor fireplace of the Bear Mountain Inn, across State Highway 9W from the ruins of Forts Clinton and Montgomery.

One of those Morgan-donated links is longer than the other; the width of both is eight inches and the circumference only six inches. If Morgan truly believed he was buying two genuine links from "General Washington's Watch Chain," the financier, usually an astute and discriminating antique collector, was misled.

In the early 1900's—Bannerman's pamphlet continues—"I purchased the chain." At this stage of the surplus arms dealer's career, he was a wealthy pillar of New York society. He had built a garish and forbidding-looking Scots castle on Pollepel (which he renamed "Bannerman's") Island, to warehouse all his cannon, Gatling guns, rifles and other surplus weapons.

According to another of his promotional brochures, Bannerman was a teetotaler and a "strict observer of the Sabbath." Every room in his castle (today a burned-out ruin) contained "a proverb from the Bible molded in concrete on the wall." Bannerman's publicity related how the dealer "found rest and relaxation in evening games and the study of the Bible with poor boys in Brooklyn near the Navy Yard—especially when his father was in the Navy as engineer during the Civil War." (But the National Archives fail to show Civil War military service by anyone named Bannerman.)

Having bought Abbey's chain, Bannerman continued to peddle it on a much wider scale. Two links, his pamphlet notes, were sold to Colonel Robert Townsend of Oyster Bay, New York, an unsuspecting great-grandson of the original Sterling Furnace ironmaster. Three more went to other Townsend descendants in Danbury, Connecticut and Allegheny, Pennsylvania.

Oyster Bay's Raynham Hall Museum, an erstwhile Townsend residence, still serves as a social gathering place for descendants of that large Long Island family. In a corner of the museum garden off West Main Street, underneath a large sign identifying them as part of the *"West Point Chain,"* lie Colonel Townsend's two links. The Museum sells color postcards of the relics.

"Strange to say," Bannerman commented, his Danbury link buyer "was still in the chain business." He was J.T. Davis, General Manager of Bridgeport's Standard Chain Company. His link became the property of American Chain & Cable Company when that firm absorbed Standard

Purported "West Point Chain links" (probably boom connectors), Bear
Mountain Inn (1985)

Spurious "West Point Chain" links at Raynham Hall, Oyster Bay, New York (1986).

The "heavy links" of Coxe's spurious chain, displayed at Museum Village of Orange County, Monroe, New York (1985).

1922 Smithsonian employee framed by links of the spurious chain [Smithsonian Institution].

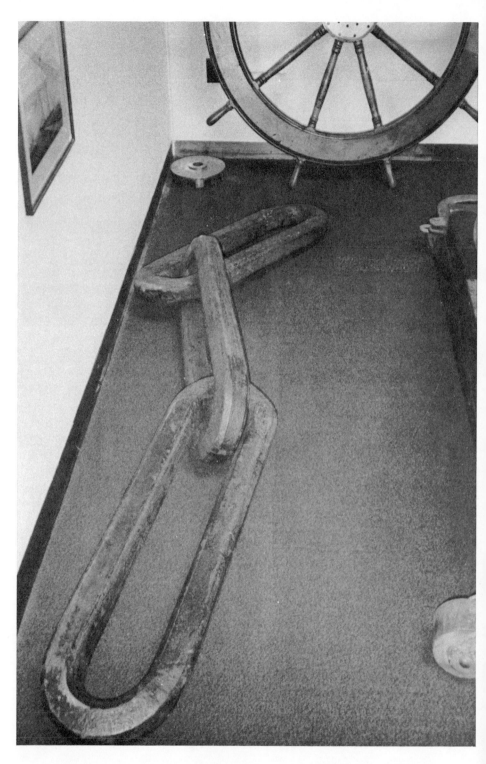

Section of spurious "West Point Chain" links, United States Coast Guard Academy Museum, New London, Connecticut (1986).

Chain in 1916. It was eventually carried off to the new ACCO/Babcock corporate headquarters in York, Pennsylvania.

Another of Bannerman's spurious links, opened, was sold to Daniel Jackson Townsend, a descendent in Niagara Falls, and subsequently presented by his heirs to the Buffalo and Erie County Historical Society, which currently regards it as "one of the most 'historic' articles in our museum."

During the United States Coast Guard Academy's 1933 commencement exercises at New London, six Bannerman links sold many years earlier to still another Townsend descendant were presented to the Academy by the ironmaster's great-granddaughter, Mary Alice Townsend Sackett, and his great-great-grandson, Austen Townsend Sackett. Originally mounted on the stone wall of the Academy's athletic field under a small tablet identifying the memento as having *"stretched from West Point N.Y. to Constitution Island in 1778 to close the Hudson River,"* the links now lie sprawled across the floor inside the front entrance of the training school's museum.

Thirteen of Bannerman's remaining links were sold to Massachusetts millionaire Edward F. Searles, a former interior decorator who married Mark Hopkins's widow, thereby gaining control of the Central Pacific Railroad fortune. Searles approached Bannerman for additional decoration for an elaborate statue of George Washington, commissioned from sculptor Thomas Ball to grace a corner of Searles's Methuen, Massachusetts estate. The rear of Ball's already overladen marble and bronze monument was soon further bedecked with 13 Bannerman links—again one for each original colony.

Sixty years later in 1958, Searles's descendant B. Allen Rowland sold off the huge statue with seven of the *soi-disant* "West Point" links to Forest Lawn Memorial-Park in California. They now serve as a "cemetery feature" at Forest Lawn. The chain, separated from the Ball statue, is installed in Forest Lawn's Glendale "Court of Freedom, beyond the Mystery of Life Garden, where Cathedral Drive becomes the High Road."

The memorial park's *Art Guide* describes the Court of Freedom as a "feature of a continuing program of education, designed to inspire the youth of America with faith in our heritage of liberty under God, dedicated to our country and the men who made it free and have kept it great." Within the Court, Searles's redubbed *"Liberty Chain"* shields a small bronze statue of Washington by the well-known 19th century sculptor John Quincy Adams Ward. The huge Ball work ended up at a different Forest Lawn division, at Hollywood Hills.

Besides the link misidentification, an inscription carved on a twelve-foot square black marble "book" lying open in the Court of Freedom further garbles the true chain story, stating that the links at Forest Lawn were originally strung across the Hudson at Bear Mountain—in 1776!

During the sale to Forest Lawn, Searles's link No. 8 was sawn apart; it now rests on the fireplace hearth of Methuen's Historical Society museum. The remainder of the Methuen links, weighing almost a ton, border the front lawn of Mr. Rowland's Vermont farmhouse.

THE PENULTIMATE paragraph of the Bannerman pamphlet is lifted word-for-word from the last paragraph of the January 9, 1894 *Sun* story about Westminster Abbey's warehouse. It precedes an offer by Bannerman to sell—for $25.00 each—some "HISTORIC GAVELS, the head or hammer made from a piece of the chain, and the handle from the OAK BOWSTEM of the British Powdership *Morning Star,* the remains of which was found in 1896 when excavating near the Battery."

Around the time of the Searles purchase, Bannerman also sold four links to Westchester executive John H. Starin, who then donated them to the Glen Island Museum in Pelham, New York. When that building was demolished in the fall of 1921 by the Westchester County Park Commission to make way for a recreational park, the four links were auctioned by the County for $500.

Successful bidder was British manufacturer Sir Henry S. Wellcome, who outbid the New-York Historical Society. Within a year, Wellcome donated his prize to the Smithsonian Institution in Washington. By then, New-York Historical Society Secretary Oscar T. Barck had grown suspicious of the Bannerman links, and so informed Smithsonian secretary C.D. Walcott—who made no reply.

To close out his inventory of "Great West Point Chain links" in the Military War Museum Bannerman had now established on lower Broadway in New York City, the surplus arms dealer came up with an ingenious and lucrative merchandising idea that neatly disposed of all the "damaged" opened links left behind when past chain sections were sold. Perhaps inspired by the sawn-out chunks, Bannerman began to carve up everything that remained into tiny "handsome souvenir desk weights."

Each link yielded several hundred blanks; the pieces—with their telltale beveled corners—were machined, polished and engraved "SECTION OF CHAIN / USED BY GENL GEO. WASHINGTON, / WEST POINT, N.Y. 1778."

A round "handle"—actually a surplus 1¼″ Civil War canister shot—was welded to the desk weight. Bannerman charged $2.75 for the finished paperweight, and added his eight-page pamphlet. Chopped into such tiny bits, each chain link brought Bannerman a total of almost $350—a considerable improvement over Abbey's original wholesale price of "five (5) cents net cash per pound."

IF ANY doubts still lingered among turn-of-the-century chain link or paperweight purchasers—or even among historians—they certainly appeared laid to rest on June 23, 1906. On that day the local chapter of the Daughters of the American Revolution unveiled a memorial plaque at

Sterling Furnace. Speaker of the day was Macgrane Coxe, who announced, without any evidence from foundry records, that the West Point Chain was actually forged at Sterling Furnace as TWO chains, with heavier links— such as Abbey's, Bannerman's and his own—spliced into the middle!

Coxe's ingenuous explanation, part of his two-hour oration, was later privately printed as a small book. His presentation apparently satisfied all the 1906 Daughters and everyone else. "As a matter of fact," Coxe carefully explained, "as the work progressed it was realized that, since the strain on the chain would be greater on it at some portions than at others, it would be advisable to have some of the links heavier than the contract called for, and accordingly some were made of iron as large as 3½ inches square and measuring as much as 3½ feet in length."

Coxe's curious account defied all physical principles of strain and attachment; even an engineering novice would presume the exact opposite. Coxe also ignored the simple observation made in July 1776 by Gilbert Livingston and William Paulding regarding the proposed Fort Montgomery chain: "It will certainly be of no use to have one part thicker than another." Coxe served briefly in the early 1890s as President of the Sterling Iron & Railway Company—which operated several of Ramapo's dying furnaces. Undoubtedly he knew better.

In the years that followed Coxe's address, Colonel Henry D. Paxson of Philadelphia began a quiet study of the various conflicting chain claims. Paxson's first step was to demolish a local assertion that part of the original chain had been fabricated and shipped to the Hudson Valley from iron furnaces at Durham Pennsylvania—almost a hundred miles from West Point.

In a November 10, 1900 letter from the Pennsylvania historian General W.W.H. Davis to B.F. Fackenthal Jr, president of the Thomas Iron Company in Easton, Pennsylvania—a letter later collected by Paxson— Davis advised, "The Durham furnace has no standing. It will almost break Mr. Laubach's heart, but the truth of history must prevail" (Charles Laubach was a local historian who aggressively asserted the Durham connection). "In my research I became satisfied of another thing," Davis continued, "that the links which Mr. Hewitt paid a big price for, and was many years getting, never belonged to the West Point Chain. I believe he has been imposed on."

Fackenthal picked up the thread a dozen years later when he warned Paxson on January 31, 1913: "You are treading on dangerous ground in writing on the great chain which stretched across the Hudson river. However, I am glad, because it will give you a splendid opportunity to correct the many errors into which some of our historians have fallen.

"The first edition [1876] of General Davis's history [*History of Bucks County*]," Fackenthal went on, "says the chain was forged at Durham, which is entirely wrong. I know that the information was one of those offhand statements by Charles Laubach, who so often made declarations of that sort, and then left it for some other historian to prove that his statement was or was not correct."

Ten days later, Paxson, undoubtedly inspired by Fackenthal's observations, pursued Francis Bannerman in New York with a letter filled with questions relating to the spurious chain. The arms dealer fobbed Paxson off with a copy of his pamphlet, and also offered him "part of some of the logs forming the *Chevaux de Freise.*" In June Paxson also wrote Macgrane Coxe, only to hear from Coxe's secretary that "Mr. Coxe regrets that there are no more copies of *The Sterling Furnace and the West Point Chain*, and he is unable to send you one."

Paxson never published the results of his researches. Many years later, in 1937, Fackenthal read an ambivalent paper to the Bucks County Historical Society which appeared, surprisingly, to underwrite Coxe's original claim. "The contract with Noble, Townsend & Company was later changed," said Fackenthal, following Coxe, "and links of much larger size and weight were ordered for the middle of the stream where the strain was greatest."

That illogical assertion of different-sized links was continued by subsequent writers on the West Point chain. Without exception, they have swallowed misgivings regarding comparative size, shape and appearance. Some researchers were willing to acknowledge problems with certain details, but none cared to sail into the wind of received "historic fact." Even the respected engineer and historical researcher Charles Rufus Harte wrote shortly after World War II: "The appearance of some of the large links is certainly a bit suspicious," but refused to acknowledge use of a rolling mill.

Harte even went so far as to assert that—in the midst of a desperate Revolution—chain production was slowed while the neat rolled "chamfers on the 3½″ bar [almost 40 feet of chamfering to each of several hundred links] were done with a hand hammer."

A decade earlier, C.B.F. Young, a Columbia University engineering instructor, requested Hewitt family permission to conduct metallurgical experiments on one of their Ringwood Manor links. When permission was refused, Young machined and polished a Bannerman paperweight, and published eight photomicrographs in an iron trade magazine.

Ken Holloway, retired Chain and Smiths Manager of the Welsh Pontypridd works, helped the present writer understand Young's photomicrographs—by describing traditional 19th century Brown, Lenox processes for manufacturing ground mooring chain links: "Iron 'scrap' of known quality was piled into 'box piles,' risen to welding temperature and forged into slabs under the stream hammer. Those slabs were again raised to welding temperature and forged into a larger slab, which is passed through rolls to reduce it to bar size and shape. I was able," Holloway continues, "to watch this process of making square chain right up to the second World War, and for a good number of years thereafter."

In 1937, Professor Young had determined that the "iron was forged first in several pieces, then bundled together and welded into one large piece." While such an analysis in no way describes the original Sterling chain's raw materials—or any 1778 forging process—Young still failed to draw the obvious conclusions.

BANNERMAN DIED in November 1918 at the end of World War I, exhausted—said *The New York Times*—by his dedicated efforts to supply the British government with second-hand armaments "worth almost three million dollars." *The Times* added (somewhat uncharitably for an obituary): "It was charged in Congress last summer that Mr. Bannerman was trying to sell the United States Government for $450,000, thirty six-inch guns bought by him from the Navy for about $78 apiece."

Westminster Abbey outlived his more enterprising Front Street associate by four years. *"WESTMINSTER ABBEY DEAD,"* read the headline over his obituary in *The New York Times* on June 11, 1922. The sub-headline read: *"Old Front Street Ship Chandler Whose Warehouse was Famous."* "Westminster Abbey," said *The Times*, "died last Sunday in the Broad Street Hospital at the age of 69. The news came out yesterday when his shop, located at 208 Pearl Street of recent years, reopened after being closed for a week."

It took three more decades for the truth to catch up with the spurious chain links, and the entire Abbey-Bannerman-Coxe myth to unravel.

In the late 1940s Edward Hewitt privately printed his opinion that the fraudulent artifact was an "Admiralty buoy chain," but at the same time he told one researcher that "the public regards it as part of the West Point Chain, and it had better be left this way."

In the 1950s a sharp-eyed Smithsonian curator announced that the four "West Point chain" links donated to the Institution by Sir Henry Wellcome and placed in the Arts and Industries Museum were not forged from 18th century hammered iron—where a single hot spongy lump has been physically pounded to consolidate the metal's crystalline structure and squeeze out bits of entrapped slag—but were uniformly rolled, re-rolled, chamfered, and welded by some very heavy ironworking machinery.

While the revolutionaries did possess primitive waterpowered equipment capable of rolling and slitting narrow wrought iron strips, the heavy duty steam machinery required to handle massive rolled iron and steel items was not developed for almost a century. Domestic railroad rails, for example—poor by comparison to the imported British product—were first rolled in Maryland in 1844.

After its disconcerting "discovery," the Museum discreetly consigned the controversial links to a Suitland, Maryland warehouse. Said the Smithsonian: "Although the National Museum staff during the period of the acquisition of the four chain links seemed to have satisfied themselves as to their authenticity, we do not share this view today."

A decade later that news—much delayed, but "loaded with dynamite," according to one Chicago researcher—reached the Windy City, where Gunther's 18 links of 19th century Welsh mooring chain were still being hailed by the Chicago Historical Society as "reflecting the spirit of our ancestors who united to gain their freedom." In the 1920s the Society had almost gone bankrupt trying to purchase the entire Gunther Collection from the "Candy Man's" heirs. For years thereafter, Gunther's links were listed as one of the Society's "weightiest and most interesting exhibits" and paraded through Chicago during national holidays on a huge flatbed truck.

Learning of the Smithsonian's decision, the Chicago Historical Society edited its accession records to acknowledge: "There is some dispute as to whether this chain was actually used at West Point on the Hudson River." A 1973 issue of the Society's bulletin *Chicago History* candidly refers to those Windy City links as "another Gunther fraud." For several decades, they lay in a huge heap, resembling a piece of loose abstract sculpture, on the sidewalk behind the Society's permanently sealed rear door. A 1987 renovation of that forecourt area dumped them in an unlabeled monkey-puzzle pile, adding an unusual accent to an otherwise attractive semicircular ornamental yew border.

So should you wish to look upon Captain Machin's wonderful West Point Chain, skip all those curious sections of Welsh buoy linkage at Forest Lawn, Ringwood Manor, Museum Village, Oyster Bay, the Coast Guard Academy, the Smithsonian warehouse, the Vermont farmstead—and the Chicago, Buffalo and Erie County, and Methuen Historical Societies.

Go to West Point.

And since more than a few missing links of original chain must have passed in and out of private hands in one part or another of the United States since 1829—and survived the scrap metal drives of two World Wars—you might even consider renting a metal detector.

1921 Chicago Memorial Day Parade float displaying the Gunther links of the Historical Society's spurious *Great Revolutionary War Chain stretched across the Hudson to protect West Point, 1776* (sic). [Courtesy: Chicago Historical Society]

Gunther's 18 links, unidentified, lying on the sidewalk behind the Chicago Historical Society, 1985.

SPENCER GUN FACTORY
CANNON WAREHOUSE
1556-1562 BERGEN STREET
BROOKLYN

STOREHOUSES
MILITARY GOODS
BANNERMAN'S ISLAND ARSENAL
HUDSON RIVER
Opposite Cornwall, N.Y.

LIEGE-BELGIUM
79 RUE LAIRESSE

ERIE BASIN STORES
WATER FRONT
BROOKLYN

Cable Address "Bannerman"
Use A. B. C. Code, 4th Edition
also Lieber's and Western
Union Codes

ESTABLISHED 1865

TELEPHONE 1754 SPRING

# FRANCIS BANNERMAN
## ORDNANCE
## WAR RELICS
## MILITARY GOODS

OFFICE, MUSEUM AND SALESROOMS
501 BROADWAY

*NEW YORK*, Feb. 11, 1913.

Henry D. Paxson,

    804 Morris Building,

        Philadelphia, Pa.

Dear Sir:-

    We have your favor of the 10th and can just answer
your questions by sending you a little phamplet that we had
made up some years ago. You will note on page 8 that we disposed
of the last thirteen links of the chain to Mr. E. J. Searles of
Methuen, Mass.

    As you will note by our letter that our Arsenals are sit-
uated on Polopel's Island which was *me of the line* the place of defences of the
Hudson in the Revolutionary War period. We have part of some of
the logs forming the Chevaux de Freise.

        Yours truly,

        *Francis Bannerman*

F.B/M.C.

Bannerman's reply to Paxson's letter, 1913 [American Antiquarian Society].

# Bibliographical Notes

*Primary sources of the American Revolution, including full libraries of correspondence, journals, memoirs, Congressional and state public records, newspapers, speeches, and sermons, as well as many 1775–83 books and pamphlets, are well known to most professional historians. Non-academics (like myself) who may be interested in casting a wider net will find the sources of this study indicated here, or in the text.*

The initial title-page epigraph is from a 1776 letter by Captain Daniel Joy to Samuel Howell, in the *Pennsylvania Archives, Vol. IV, 1st Series* at Harrisburg.

## INTRODUCTION

Robert Graves's belief in the overwhelming significance of the American Revolution is from the *Foreword* to his adaptation of Sergeant Roger Lamb's original memoirs, *An Original and Authentic Journal of Occurences During the Late American War* (Dublin, 1809). Graves's fictionalized work is titled *Sergeant Lamb of The Ninth* (London, 1940).

The observation by Thomas Paine is from *The American Crisis, V* (Lancaster, Pennsylvania, 1778). Ezra Stiles's comment is in *The United States Elevated to Glory and Honor* (New Haven, 1783). The British pamphleteer's criticism was reprinted in the *Boston Gazette*, May 27, 1776. In his classic study *The Hudson River: A Natural and Unnatural History* (New York, 1969), Robert H. Boyle properly notes the absence of a characteristic hanging "sill" at the end of the Hudson fiord. North American population estimates for 1670 and 1770 are drawn from the U.S. Census Bureau's *Historical Statistics of the United States, Series Z* (Washington, 1961).

Sir Henry Clinton's observations on the strategic value of the Hudson River are in his three-volume manuscript memoirs, *Historical Detail of Seven Years Campaigns in North America from 1775 to 1782* (part of the Clinton

Papers in the William L. Clements Library at the University of Michigan). Howard Peckham served as director of that magnificent research library for 25 years; his observations on the value of eyewitness history are quoted from his Introduction to *Historical Americana* (Ann Arbor, 1980). The relatively early perceptive British lament—"a defeat is ruin"—was reprinted in the *Boston Gazette*, May 27, 1776. The idealization of Washington is from Horatio Hubbell's *Arnold, or the Treason of West Point: A Tragedy in Five Acts* (Philadelphia, 1847).

The estimated North American strength of the Royal Navy during the second year of the Revolution is based on Viscount Howe's September 18, 1776 return to Admiralty Secretary Philip Stephens, among the Admiralty papers in London's handsome new Public Record Office at Kew. The figures are supplemented from a June 24, 1776 report by an anonymous French agent in London to Foreign Minister Comte de Vergennes, and are found in *Volume 516* of *Correspondence Politique*, Archives du Ministère des Affaires Étranger, Paris.

The September 30, 1609 *"Halve-Maan"* log entry by Hudson's mate Robert Juet is recorded in the third book, *Voyages and Discoueries of the North parts of the World, by Land and Sea* of Samuel Purchas's *Purchas His Pilgrimes* (London, 1625).

The observation, "A land whose stones are iron," was made by Corresponding Secretary of the Rhode Island Sons of Liberty Silas Downer, in his remarkable July 25, 1768 oration dedicating the great elm "Tree of Liberty" outside Olney's Tavern in Providence. Downer's speech, delivered from a "Summer House" high in the tree, received wide immediate distribution as a pamphlet; it foreshadowed the concepts and even many phrases of the Declaration of Independence.

Scholars engaged in American Revolutionary research remain in incalculable debt to Peter Force's (1790–1868) incomplete but monumental *American Archives* (Washington, 1837–53), the important source of many orders, letters, and reports otherwise uncredited here—many of whose originals have now disappeared. The oversized nine-volume, double-columned multi-million-word *Series 4* and *5* was accurately culled from Force's personal collection of nearly 23,000 historical books, 40,000 pamphlets, 250 volumes of newspapers, 1,200 maps and views, 429 volumes of original manuscripts, and 360 volumes of transcripts—all gathered over 35 years and purchased by the Library of Congress in 1867.

That huge printed set, available at major libraries, reprints thousands of priceless documents from the earliest Revolutionary period and provides an invaluable shortcut through widely scattered manuscript archives and related microfilm.

The full work planned by Force, a newspaperman, avid manuscript collector, and one-time mayor of Washington, was designed to gather all relevant historical materials from the discovery of North America through the year 1789. It was sponsored by the federal government, until funding was eliminated by William L. Marcy, Secretary of State under Presidents Pierce and Buchanan.

Force's *Series 1, 2,* and *3* were outlined, but never begun. His six-volume *Series 4: A Documentary History of the English Colonies in North America from March 7, 1774 to July 4, 1776*—particularly *Volume II*—contains the important correspondence quoted extensively throughout this study, between the New York Provincial Congress/Convention and the Continental Congress. Much of this material is also available in the *Journals of the [New York] Provincial Congress* (Albany, 1842), and *Papers of the Continental Congress* in the National Archives at Washington. Force also prints pertinent committee and military reports to both those bodies.

Force's (incomplete) three-volume *Series 5*, commencing with the Declaration of Independence and originally planned to end with *The Definitive Treaty of Peace with Great Britain, September 3, 1783* never got beyond December 31, 1776, thereby tantalizing generations of scholars who have sought in one convenient place detailed documentation on the later years of the Revolution. *Series 5* contains many references to the clandestine work of the New York Convention's Secret Committee.

Almost as impressive as Force's *American Archives* is John Clement Fitzpatrick's 39-volume edition of *The Writings of George Washington From the Original Manuscript Sources, 1745-1799* (Washington, 1931–1944). The bulk of Washington material cited here, mainly correspondence between the Commander-in-chief and his officers, is drawn from this series. The remainder is from the *Washington Papers* (Washington, 1964), the complete 124-reel microfilm collection of all the manuscript material in the Washington Presidential Papers at the Library of Congress.

Francis B. Heitman's *Historical Register of Officers of the Continental Army* (Washington, 1914) proved essential in identifying minor officers. Generous credit should also go to Edward Manning Ruttenber's handsomely-printed *Obstructions to the Navigation of Hudson's River* (Albany, 1860), although Jeptha Root Simms's *Frontiersmen of New York* (Albany, 1882) challenges many of Ruttenber's interpretations.

Ruttenber's century-old book contains many useful clues to primary sources still "lost" in the 1860's, but which have since surfaced in various historical collections. Ruttenber's Albany publisher Joel Munsell affected the Revolutionary War *"Long f"* for the *"Round s"* throughout the 1860 volume, an ancient English typographic custom (whose passing Franklin noted as early as 1786). Despite the crotchet, this title, *No. 5* in *Munsell's Historical Series*, remains an elegant and important little book.

*CHAPTER I: Romans's Fort*

*Quod vide* material on Bernard Romans and his failed attempts to complete Fort Constitution is excerpted from my own *Bernard Romans: Forgotten Patriot of the American Revolution* (Harrison, New York, 1985). Besides the general sources already noted above, much documentation for that study (and this one) is drawn from our great contemporary version of Force's *American Archives*—the equally ambitious and massive Department of the Navy (Naval History Division) *Naval Documents of the American Revolution*, edited by William Bell Clark (Washington, 1966, etc., currently eight volumes covering the progress of the war through 1777 alone!). Other Romans materials can be found in the *Calendar of Documents Relating to the War of the Revolution* (Albany, 1868).

The New York Committee of Safety's warning to the Continental Congress on British strategy to split the states along the line of the Hudson River was reiterated to John Hancock by William Duer on November 28, 1775. Comte Guillaume Deux-Ponts's surprise that the British failed to harrass the French army crossing the Hudson in 1781 is recorded in his *My War in America* (Boston, 1868). Reverend Timothy Dwight's characterization of the Hudson Highlands is from *Volume III* of his *Travels in New-England and New-York* (New Haven, 1822).

Colonel Putnam gives Clairac as his inspiration for chandeliers on Dorchester Heights in *Memoirs of Rufus Putnam and Certain Official Papers and Correspondence* (Boston, 1903). Washington's complaint to Hancock regarding the dearth of patriot military engineers is from Fitzpatrick. Charles Carroll of Carrollton's observation on the same subject to the Maryland Committee of Safety is in Force *Series 5.*

Notes on the Continental Congress debates over Romans's plans are from John Adams's and Richard Smith's *Diaries* in the Massachusetts Historical Society and the Library of Congress, respectively. Jefferson's observation on the strategic importance of the Hudson River is in *Volume I* of his *Papers* (Princeton, 1950).

The 1672 comment on the natural defensive strength of the Popolopen area is from a June 16 letter to a "Capt. DeLavall & Mr Steenwyck" in *Volume XIII* of Edmund B. O'Callaghan and Berthold Fernow's *Documents Relative to the Colonial History of the State of New-York* (Albany, 1881). The Congressional Committee to the Northward's report to John Hancock is in the National Archives. The New York Committee of Safety's caustic remark, endorsed on the bottom of Romans's own March 18, 1776 salary petition, is from *Volume I, Calendar of Historical Manuscripts Relating to the War of the Revolution* (Albany, 1868). Robert R. Livingston's letter to Thomas Lynch of South Carolina is in the New York State Library Archives.

General Horatio Gates's comments on the evacuation of Boston are from his *Papers* in the New York Public Library. The record of Washington's Roxbury council of war is with the *Continental Congress* papers. The April 1776 description of conditions at Fort Constitution has been drawn from both the *Journal of Charles Carroll of Carrollton* (Baltimore, 1876) and *Volume 22* of Benjamin Franklin's *Papers* (New Haven, 1982).

*CHAPTER II: Bushnell's Submarine*

All of David Bushnell's personal narratives on the development and operation of his *Turtle* are either from the inventor's 1787 memoir to Thomas Jefferson—in *Volume 34* of the *Jefferson Papers* at the Library of Congress—or in Ezra Stiles's *Papers* at the New Haven Colony Historical Society in that city.

A less than half-size, considerably misleading model of *Turtle* is displayed in the Research Library and Museum of the U.S. Submarine Force's Thames River Base at Gale's Ferry, Connecticut. That library holds scant material on Bushnell, but does contain a vast store of original material on two other famous cutthroat competitors of the submarine industry—the early Fenian John P. Holland (who *also* dreamed of sinking the entire British navy) and Simon Lake—all awaiting future Ph.D. candidates.

A full-sized replica of *Turtle* was actually built in 1976 by Connecticut shipwright Fred Frese and journalist Joseph Leary, and successfully operated under water to celebrate the bicentennial of both Bushnell and the American Revolution. This exciting copy of the world's first military submersible is now on display at Essex's Connecticut River Foundation Museum, not far from the spot where the Yankee inventor tested his original craft two centuries ago.

Dr. Benjamin Gale's letter to Franklin, and Franklin's subsequent request to Silas Deane for additional information on Bushnell, is from *Volume 22* of the Franklin *Papers*. Samuel Osgood's letter to John Adams is in the latter's *Papers* at Boston's Massachusetts Historical Society. All of Dr. Gale's direct letters to Deane are from *Volume II* of the Connecticut Historical Society *Collections* (Hartford, 1836).

James Brattle's espionage report rests in British Admiralty records. Captain Daniel Joy's "copycat" submarine suggestion to Samuel Howell and the Pennsylvania Committee of Safety is in the *Pennsylvania Archives.* Tutor John Lewis's "secret" Latin note on *Turtle* to Ezra Stiles is in Stiles's *Literary Diary* (New York, 1901).

The Connecticut Council of Safety's £60 grant to Bushnell is recorded in *Volume XV* of the *Connecticut Records* in Hartford. Information on Ezra Bushnell's service on the privateer brig *Defence* is recorded in *Volume I* of Louis F. Middlebrook's *History of Maritime Connecticut during the American Revolution* (Salem, Massachusetts, 1925). George III's remark to Parliament is found in Merrill Jensen's edition of *American Colonial Documents* (New York, 1955). Thomas Stone's comments on the residents of Staten Island are from *Volume 12* of Baltimore's *Maryland Archives;* John Adams's similar remarks are in a July 11, 1776 letter to Abigail in the Adams's *Family*

*Correspondence* (Cambridge, Massachusetts, 1963).

The *MS.* of Sergeant Ezra Lee's description of *Turtle* and his September 6–7, 1776 underwater attack is at the Yale University Library. General Parsons's request to General Heath for a sloop to carry *Turtle* back into New York City from its tests on Long Island Sound is with the *Heath Papers* at the Massachusetts Historical Society. Sgt. Lee's target is identified as *H.M.S. Eagle* in the *Diary of Captain Samuel Richards* (Philadelphia, 1909). General Heath's comment on the loss of *Turtle* is from his *Memoirs of Major-General Heath, Containing Anecdotes, Details of Skirmishes, Battles, and other Military Events, during the American Revolution* (Boston, 1798).

Washington's comments on Bushnell and the military value of *Turtle* are from *Volume 15* of the *Jefferson Papers* in the Library of Congress. Franklin's original July 22, 1776 letter commending Joseph Belton to the Commander-in-chief has drifted overseas to the Kunstsammlungen der Veste Coburg Collection, in Coburg, Germany; in April 1777 Belton solicited Congressional funding for another "secret weapon," a musket based on a European "superimposed charge" design perfected during the previous century, supposedly capable of firing eight rounds with one loading. In less than three weeks, Belton received an army order for 100 such muskets but there is no indication they were ever supplied. A year after the Revolution, Belton attempted without success to sell the same gun design to the British Army.

Timothy Dwight's eulogy of Bushnell is from *Book VII* of his long narrative poem *"Greenfield Hill,"* dedicated to John Adams and published in New York in 1794.

## CHAPTER III: *Fort Washington's* Chevaux-de-Frise

Washington's use of "ragged boys" to describe his young volunteer troops is reported in *Volume I* of Edward Everett Hale's *Memories of a Hundred Years* (New York, 1902). By his own account, New England clergyman William Gordon enjoyed Washington's confidence at critical moments during the Revolution. Five years after the Treaty of Paris, Gordon published his four-volume *History of the Rise, Progress, and Independence of the United States of America* (London, 1788); Washington's letter regarding the poor quality of the army's firearms is in *Volume II*.

Isaac Sears's comment on the undependable revolutionary spirit of New Yorkers is from *Volume I* of Gideon Hollister's *History of Connecticut* (New Haven, 1855). General Charles Lee's defense plans for New York City are in *Volume IV, Journals of the Continental Congress.*

The *"Profile and Plan"* illustration of the *cheval-de-frise* is a map inset from William Faden's *The Course of the Delaware River from Philadelphia to Chester* (London, 1779). The 1777 British description of Delaware River obstructions is from *Vol. XL* of *Proceedings of American Antiquarian Society* (Philadelphia, 1855). Joseph Plumb Martin's ("Private Yankee Doodle's") account of the Delaware *chevaux-de-frise* is from *A Narrative of Some of the Adventures, Dangers and Sufferings of a Revolutionary Soldier, etc.* (Hallowell, Maine, 1830).

Josiah Quincy's letter to Washington regarding *chevaux-de-frise* for Boston Harbor, and Arnold's letter to the Congressional Committee in Canada, are in *Volume I* of Jared Sparks's *Correspondence of the American Revolution* (Boston, 1853).

Israel Putnam's *"Shevrord fres"* reference is from a letter to General Gates at New York's Pierpont Morgan Library; *"Shiver de freeses"* is in a July 30, 1776 letter from New Yorker Peter Elting to his brother-in-law Richard Varick, then aide-de-camp to General Schuyler at Albany, quoted in Thomas Jones's *History of New York During the Revolutionary War* (New York, 1879).

The British concept of landing in Washington's rear was reported by London's *St. James's Chronicle* on October 3, 1776. Congressman William Duer's letter to the Secret Committee is among the Robert R. Livingston Papers in the Library of Congress. Lafayette's January 1778 comment on Duer is from the Henry Laurens *Papers* in the South Carolina Historical Society at Charleston.

Widely scattered reports of the New York Convention's Secret Committee proceedings are in the (Albany) New York and (Hartford) Connecticut State Libraries, the Free Public Library in Newburgh, and the Library of Congress. They can also be found among the *Jay Papers* at Columbia University.

Figures on Salisbury cannon production and distribution are from archives in the Connecticut State Library. Robert Livingston's complaint about his ironworkers is from *Volume II* of the *Public Papers of George Clinton, First Governor of New York* (New York, Albany, 1899–1914); all the original manuscript materials in that collection were transcribed before the unfortunate 1911 New York State Library fire which destroyed most of the originals.

I found Edward Countryman's incisive analysis of revolutionary "political society"—varying ideological concepts at different levels of the movement—in *A People in Revolution* (Baltimore, 1981) most illuminating. Most of Ambrose Serle's comments in this study are excerpted from his *Journal* (San Marino, California, 1940).

Thomas Jefferson's letter to Francis Eppes describing the August 3, 1776 naval action above Dobbs Ferry is in *Volume I* of the *Jefferson Papers* (Princeton, 1950). The colorful newspaper account of that event is from the August 12 *New-York Gazetteer*, in the Rare Book Collection of the New York Public Library. Lieutenant Colonel Kemble's observation on the completed *cheval-de-frise* is from his wartime *Journal* (New York, 1884).

Mifflin's letter to Washington on the *chevaux-de-frise* is in *Volume I* of Sparks's *Correspondence*. Washington's order to Colonel Rufus Putnam is in the Marietta College Library, Marietta, Ohio. General Heath's description of the *chevaux-de-frise* below Fort Washington is from his *Memoirs*.

All Royal Navy logs quoted in this study are from Admiralty Records in the Public Record Office at Kew. Captain (later Admiral) George Collier's letter is in London's National Maritime Museum. That museum also kindly provided the author with the 16th-century shipbuilders' formula (used until 1854), for calculating the tonnages of *H.M.S. Phoenix* and *Rose*—based on theoretical cargoes of wine tuns weighing 2,240 lbs. each (ship length –3/5 breadth × breadth × ½ breadth ÷ 94). John Nicoll's disappointment over the escape of the enemy frigates is in *Volume I* of the Clinton *Papers*.

Washington's concern over the safety of civilians in New York City is from *Volume II* of *Correspondence of the Provincial Congress;* the Commander-in-chief's August 19, 1776 broadside is in the New-York Historical Society. General Heath's comment to Washington on the downstream return of *Phoenix* and *Rose* is in *Volume I* of Sparks's *Correspondence*. John Jay's "scorched-earth" proposal for southern New York State is from an October 6, 1776, letter to Robert Morris, printed in *American Book Prices* (New York, January, 1917). His resolution questioning the timing of American independence is set down in *Volume I* of the *Journals of the Provincial Congress*.

Colonel Israel Hutchinson's report to Heath is with the *Heath Papers*. The British post-invasion analysis of revolutionary fortifications on Manhattan Island is from the papers of Lieutenant Colonel Stephen Kemble in the New-York Historical Society *Collections* (New York, 1883). The order removing New York City's bronze bells and brass door knockers is in *Volume I* of the New York Convention's *Journals*.

Ambrose Serle's expressed resentment to Lord Dartmouth regarding the transported British convicts who filled revolutionary army ranks is in Benjamin F. Steven's *Fascimile Manuscripts* (London, 1889). Captain Henry Duncan's report of the "liberation" of New York City is from his *Journals* (London, 1902).

Admiral Howe's communications are among Admiralty Papers. The testimony of Hudson River pilot John Yates against William Hickey on June 24, 1776—in Force *Series 4, Volume II*—was followed by Hickey's execution two days later. Captain Hamond's report to Vice Admiral Molyneaux Shuldham is in *Volume I* of *The Private Papers of John, Earl of Sandwich* (London, 1932). Hammond's own *MS.* journal is in the Library of the University of Virginia at Charlottesville.

Robert R. Livingston's copy of his letter to Congressman Rutledge is in the New York State Library at Albany. Lee's comment on the defense of Fort Washington is in *Volume II* of Gordon's *History*. William Demont's treacherous confession, contained in his 1792 Royal pension application, also appears in Jones's *History of New York During the American Revolution*.

Demont cynically adds: "Had I served my God as I have done my King he would not Thus have Forsaken Me."

Washington's correspondence with Greene prior to the fall of Fort Washington is in *Volume II* of Gordon's *History*. The description of that fall by the British officer aboard *Emerald* was enclosed in a letter, now in the Warwick Record Office, to Basil Fielding, 6th Lord of Denbigh in Warwickshire, from his relative Lieutenant William Feilding (sic) serving with the Royal Navy in Nova Scotia. Anthony Wayne's outspoken comment to War Secretary Richard Peters is in the Emmet Collection of the New York Public Library.

George III's proclamation of the two-day fast for the British Isles in December 1776 is reprinted in Force, *Series 5, Volume II*.

*CHAPTER IV: Stirling's Beacons and Hazelwood's Fire Ships*

The Congressional resolutions, Continental Army orders, and New York Convention proceedings on signal beacons and fire ships are recorded in Force, *Series 4*. The original Navesink beacon location is now inside the New Jersey State Park Service Historic Site at Navesink Highlands, high above the Sandy Hook Section of the Gateway National Recreation Area. The Todt Hill site of the Staten Island relay beacon is surrounded by one of the best-kept residential secrets in New York City—hundreds of very expensive homes with magnificent views of Lower Bay, plus a local country club. The report to Clinton on the accidental beacon firing is in *Volume V* of the *Clinton Papers*.

Joseph Bass's detailed description of the August 16, 1776 fire ship attack on *Phoenix* and *Rose* first appeared in the May 1826 *Worcester* (Massachusetts) *Journal*. The commander of that attack was mistakenly identified in the August 20, 1776 *Pennsylvania Evening Post* as a "Captain Fosdyke." This was undoubtedly Thomas Fosdick, a sergeant in Captain Nathan Hale's company, who volunteered to serve under Bass with four of his fellow Connecticut infantrymen.

Hale notes his soldiers' service in a letter to his brother Enoch *(see below)*, but also misidentifies Fosdick as one of the skippers in the attack, adding that "the gen'l has been pleased to reward their bravery with forty dollars each, except the last man who quitted the Sloop, who had fifty. Those on board the Schooner received the same."

Frederick Philipse's (undated) August 17 manuscript letter to his wife is in the Collections of Sleepy Hollow Restorations (now Historic Hudson Valley), Tarrytown, N.Y. Nathan Hale's August 20, 1776 letter to his brother is in George D. Seymour's *Documentary Life of Nathan Hale* (New Haven, 1941). Adjutant-General Joseph Reed's caustic October 18 reply to Governor Trumbull on the poor performance by the Connecticut galleys is in Force, *Series 4, Volume II*. General Heath's letter to Washington regarding additional fire ship activity against the British fleet is in *Volume I* of Sparks's *Correspondence*. Captain Collier predicted the subsequent fire ship attacks in New York harbor in an unaddressed letter, now in London's Maritime Museum.

The British comment on the New York City fire is from Dodsley's *Annual Register* (London, 1779); Lieutenant Colonel Kemble's observation is from his wartime *Journal*. The notes on the capture and execution of Nathan Hale are from the *Diary of Frederick Mackenzie* (Cambridge, 1930), and the *Journal of Rear Admiral Bartholmew James* (London, 1896).

*CHAPTER V: Fort Montgomery's Chain*

The history of early harbor chains is from Captain George Peacock's *Treatise on Ship's Cables with the History of Chains* (London, 1873), and Thomas W. Traill's *Chain Cables and Chains* (London, 1885). As recently as 1940, Great Britain was stretching huge hastily-fabricated defensive chains and booms to block key harbors—while Nazi anti-submarine nets across Norway's Altenfjord signally failed to protect the Tirpitz from Royal Navy midget submarines.

General Sullivan's report to Washington on blocking Portsmouth harbor is in *Volume I* of Sparks's *Correspondence;* Lieutenant Colonel Kemble's comment on that chain is from his wartime *Journal* (New York, 1884).

The image of a chain strung across the Hudson River has always delighted American children; Susan Cheever in *Home Before Dark* (Boston, 1984), recalls a "huge iron loop embedded in the parapet of an abandoned castle on a cliff above the water, that supposedly held one of the chains that kept the British from sailing up the river during the Revolutionary War." This was near her Scarborough home (15 miles south of Fort Montgomery) where the Hudson is 10,000 feet wide.

Thomas Palmer's suggestion to skid Fort Montgomery construction timbers down the frozen Hudson is noted in John A. Roberts's *New York in the Revolution as Colony and State* (Albany, 1897). Palmer's summer 1776 Fort Montgomery sketch map is with other New York State Secretary of State documents in Albany.

Lieutenant Henry B. Livingston's suggestion to place a chain/boom at Con Hook is in the *Washington Papers*. John Hancock's Congressional letter on March 26, 1777 appointing George Clinton a Brigadier General with command of the Highlands, is in Harvard's Houghton Library.

Most of General/Governor Clinton's wartime correspondence is published in the *George Clinton Papers* (New York, Albany, 1899–1914). Burgoyne's July 1777 letter to Secretary of State Lord George Germain, mentioning the Fort Ticonderoga boom, was published in London's annual *Gentleman's Magazine* for that year; Sergeant Roger Lamb (who served under Burgoyne) abstracted the reference in his 1809 *Original and Authentic Journal.*

The Livingston/Paulding letter on the Fort Montgomery chain, and the Yates/Livingston letter defaulting on payment for iron delivery, are on microfilm at the Franklin D. Roosevelt Library at Hyde Park. Philip Livingston's August 30, 1776, letter to Abraham Yates is in the Bloomington (Indiana) University Library. The note on undelivered chain bars, from William Smith, is in his *MS. Memoirs* in the New York Public Library. Although Smith, an able New York jurist and mugwump of the Revolution, actually helped draft New York State's first constitution, he eventually fled to England.

Wesley S. Griswold's *The Night the Revolution Began* (Brattleboro, 1972) catalogs Machin among the Boston Tea Party participants as an "immigrant laborer from England." The rate of flow of the Hudson River through the Highlands was extrapolated by the author from U.S. Department of Commerce *Tidal Current Tables of the Atlantic Coast of North America* (Washington, 1979). The London newspaper report on the Fort Montgomery chain and the power of the Hudson River tides is from the *St. James's Chronicle*. The anonymous London letter predicting the failure of British strategy in America is quoted by Sir George O. Trevelyan in *Volume II, Part II* of his *The American Revolution* (New York, 1926).

Governor Clinton's letter to Washington on the successful installation of the chain is in *Volume I* of Sparks's *Correspondence*. General McDougall's urgent communication to the Marine Committee is in Volume 161 of *Letters From General Officers to the Continental Congress*, at the National Archives. The round-robin letter to Washington from his five generals is in the *Washington Papers*.

The Ringwood Furnace invoice for the boom hardware originally intended for use at Fort Montgomery is in Washington's Newburgh Headquarters museum. The grudging Tory appreciation of the role of the American Commander-in-chief is from the *Journal of Nicholas Cresswell, 1774-1777* (New York, 1924). The anonymous two-page 1777 Tory espionage report, covering Hudson defenses and obstructions at Fort Montgomery, Fort Constitution, and Pollepel Island, is among the Sir Henry Clinton papers in the Clements Library at the University of Michigan.

Putnam's warning to Governor Clinton about reinforcements for the Highlands is in *Volume II* of Sparks's *Correspondence*. The gallows confession of spy Daniel Taylor is in *Volume II* of the *Clinton Papers*.

New York editor Hugh Gaine's report on British troop behavior after the fall of Fort Montgomery was printed in his October 11, 1777 *New-York Gazette and Weekly Mercury;* the comment on Gaine himself is from the February 19, 1777 *Pennsylvania Journal*. Major Abraham Leggett's prison *Narrative*, edited by Charles I. Bushnell, was privately printed in New York in 1865. Charles Stedman belonged to a Welsh troop that served under Cornwallis; his grandiloquent description of the burning of the revolutionary fleet is from his *History of the Origin, Progress and Termination of the American War* (London, 1794). The romantic tale of wounded General James Clinton's feverish 16-mile escape from Fort Montgomery is from Ruttenber's *Obstructions*. Although present federal, state, and local disinterest discourages visitors from treading hallowed ground at the unreconstructed site of Fort Montgomery, it is still possible to weave one's way through the scrub and woods off U.S. 9W to explore the gently rolling remains of the fort's cannon platforms and parapets, high above the Hudson River.

The British comment on the chain's destruction at Fort Montgomery is both from Stedman's *History* and Dodsley's *Annual Register, or a View of the History, Politics and Literature for the Year 1777* (London, 1778)—an incredibly astute yearly evaluation of the political and military aspects of the Revolution both in England and the United States. Established by Edmund Burke in 1758, the *Register*—heavily plagiarized by at least nine 18th and 19th century historians—reflects considerable revolutionary bias. The reaffirmation of the chain's supposed cost is from John Almon's *The Remembrancer; or Impartial Repository of Public Events for the Year 1777* (London, 1778).

The revolutionary newspaper account of the burning of Kingston is from the October 23, 1777 Fishkill *New York Packet*. The deprecatory comment on General Vaughan is from *Volume III* of Sir John W. Fortescue's *History of the British Army* (London, 1902). The characterization of Captain James Wallace is from an article prepared during the 19th century by John Know Laughton for *Volume XX* of George Smith's (British) *Dictionary of National Biography*, a standard reference work in most American libraries. Sir Henry Clinton's characterization of Howe's failure to support him on the upper Hudson is from his MS. memoirs in the Clements Library.

With Washington preparing for a bitter winter at Valley Forge, he could detail only a handful of reportedly disorderly dragoons to accompany the self-important president of Congress home to Boston retirement; the Commander-in-chief's apologetic note to Hancock is in *Volume V* of Jared Sparks's *Writings of George Washington* (Boston, 1834–37).

The bleak description of the Fishkill winter barracks is from Lieutenant Thomas Anburey's *Travels Through the Interior Parts of America, 1776-1781* (London, 1789). Colonel Philip van Cortlandt's account of the revolt of General Poor's New Hamsphire Continentals is from his *Memoir*, printed in the May 1878 issue of the *Magazine of American History* (New York). A study that helped me fathom the great gulf between Revolutionary War enlisted men and their officers was Charles Royster's thoughtful *A Revolutionary People at War* (New York, 1979).

Washington's realistic comment to Lafayette is also from Sparks's *Writings of George Washington*. Governor Clinton's December 20, 1777 letter to Washington recommending a new chain and boom is in *Volume II* of Sparks's *Correspondence*.

*CHAPTER VI: Pollepel Island's* Chevaux-de-Frise

General Schuyler's letter to the New York Convention proposing alternate Hudson sites for *chevaux-de-frise* obstruction is in his *Letter Book* at the New York Public Library. The text of the New York Convention resolution to obstruct the northern entrance of the Highlands is in *Volume I* of the *Clinton Papers*, as is Clinton's year-end litany of complaint to the Convention, and the carpenters' contract.

John Adams's comment on the corrupting effect of commerce is from his April 16 1776 letter to Mercy Warren, in *Volume I* of the *Warren-Adams Letters* (New York, 1917). John B. Livingston's letter urging his brother to join with John Jay and buy a privateer is among the New-York Historical Society's *Papers Relating to Naval Affairs*. Charles Carroll of Carrollton's comment on the Pollepel Island *chevaux-de-frise* is in a letter to his father, at the Maryland Historical Society in Baltimore.

The 1777 petitions from the carpenters at Fort Constitution and the shipyard workers at Poughkeepsie—part of the collections of the New York State Secretary of State—are printed in *Volume I* of the *Calendar of Historical Manuscripts Relating to the War of the Revolution*. John Nicoll's complaint to George Clinton regarding excess cutting of timber is in *Volume IV* of the *Clinton Papers*.

*CHAPTER VII: Machin's West Point Chain*

The exchange between General Putnam and Governor Clinton is in the *Appendix* to *Volume I* of Sparks's *Correspondence;* Hamilton's letters to Washington about Putnam are in *Volume II*.

General Putnam's and Governor Clinton's comments on de la Radière; the New York State Legislature's resolution to create the new chain; and DQMG Hughes's urgent request for cash, with Governor Clinton's relay to Gates, are all from *Volume II* of the *Clinton Papers*. Jacobus van Zandt's 1776 suggestion to install the first Fort Montgomery chain at West Point is in *Volume I*. Captain Graydon's observation on colonial chauvinism is from his *Memoirs of a Life* (Harrisburg, 1811).

Clinton's July 15, 1776 letter to Washington, suggesting a chain of fire ships at the spot where Machin's second iron chain was installed two years later, is in *Volume I* of Sparks's *Correspondence*.

On occasion the revolutionaries, a bit unfairly, referred to the British as "Rebels." Three days after Washington's reinvigorating victory at Trenton, Governor Clinton used that contemptuous description in a letter to Colonel John Hathorn. On Machin's long, narrow map, just beneath the village of Peekskill, one of the engineer's legends follows suit.

The Rotterdam consul's comment on the quality of North American bar iron is in the Colonial Office's *Consular Reports to the Secretary of State* at Kew. Praise by the anonymous "New-Englandman" for North American ironmaking (attributed by Carl Bridenbaugh to Rhode Island patriot lawyer Silas Downer) is from a front page article attacking Grenville's American Revenue Acts in the August 18, 1764 *Providence Gazette.* A number of Thomas Machin manuscript items, including some curious letters from Peter Woodward to "Tommy"—relating to sex and the Continental soldiery—are in the collections of the New-York Historical Society.

The exchange value of the pound sterling—"lawful money," as George Washington was still calling it in 1783, compared to Congress's Continental dollar—is based on the $/£ conversion table on page 52 of the Commander-in-chief's own expense ledger, *Accounts, G. Washington with the United States, Commencing June 1775, and ending June 1783* in the National Archives.

Several of Captain Thomas Machin's expense accounts—with all charges carefully separated between the United States of America and the State of New York—are in the collection of the New-York Historical Society.

The 1776 war materials output of the Sterling Iron Works is given in a petition from Peter Townsend to the New York Convention in *Volume I* of the *Calendar of Historical Manuscripts Relating to the War of the Revolution,* as is Noble, Townsend's complaint about their "absconding" workmen. DQMG Hughes's February 3, 1778 report on his negotiations with Townsend is in *Volume II* of the *Clinton Papers,* Henry Wisner's warning letter regarding Mr. St. John is in *Volume III.*

Israel Putnam's curious exchanges with Washington and Gates following the fall of Fort Montgomery are in *Volume I* of Sparks's *Correspondence.* Robert R. Livingston's January 14, 1778 letter to the Commander-in-chief—and the latter's March 12 reply—are in *Volume II.*

Dr. Thacher's description of the installed chain is from his lengthy *Military Journal During the American Revolutionary War* (Boston, 1823). McDougall's letter with the Afro-American waiter's report is in *Volume IV* of the *George Clinton Papers* (New York, 1899–1914); General Pattison's observations are in Clinton *Volume V.* Henry Laurens's caustic comments on Congress are in his August 27, 1778 letter to John Huston in the New-York Historical Society's *Deane Papers* (New York, 1888).

Benjamin Gilbert's description of racing across the boom to escape a thunderstorm is from his *Diary* at the New York State Historical Association, Cooperstown, N.Y. The anonymous British espionage report on the chain anchorages is from an undated *Description of Obstructions in Hudson's River* among the Sir Henry Clinton Papers at Michigan's Clements Library; Benedict Arnold's comment on the weakness of the chain is from a letter in the same collection. Lord Germain's frustrated comment regarding the revolutionary army is in the *Germain Papers* at the Clements Library.

Livingston's letter to Washington proposing Benedict Arnold as West Point commander is in *Volume II* of Sparks's *Correspondence;* Putnam's letter to Washington after his stroke, and Benedict Arnold's letter requesting an Erskine map to guide Major André's notorious ride through Westchester County, are in *Volume III.*

The strange assertion that Arnold was able to remove a link of the chain is found in Benson J. Lossing's *Field-Book of the American Revolution* (New York, 1875). Portions of Marquis Barbé-Marbois' *Complot d'Arnold et de sir Henry Clinton contre les États-Unis d'Amérique et contre le général Washington* (Paris, 1816) were translated the following year for the annual *American Register; Or, Summary Review of History, Politics and Literature* (Philadelphia 1817). Sir Henry Clinton's October 11, 1780 report to Germain regarding his readiness to move on West Point is in the Clements Library, as is his similar letter of April 5, 1781.

In *Volume IV* of his 1788 *History of the Rise, Progress, and Establishment of the Independence of the United States of America*—in which he assesses the potential impact of Arnold's treachery—Reverend William Gordon becomes the earliest of at least nine 18th and 19th century historians who place themselves in transparent debt to Dodsley's *Annual Register* (London, 1782)—see note to *Chapter V,* above. Dodsley: *"Such a stroke could not have been recovered. Independent of the loss of artillery, magazines, and stores, such a destruction of their whole disciplined force, and of most if not all of their best officers, must have been immediately fatal."* Gordon: *"Such a stroke could scarcely have been recovered. Independent of the loss of artillery and stores, such a destruction of their disciplined force, and many of their best officers, must have been fatal."*

General Duportail's considerations of chain defensive strategy are from an *MS.* translation by Lieutenant Colonel Donald Dunne in the U.S. Military Academy Library. In addition to supplying talented volunteers like Duportail, the French crown contributed money, arms, military supplies, and logistical ground and naval support that were all absolutely essential to the eventual success of the Revolution. Even so, it took the Society of the Cincinnati a century and a half to acknowledge French assistance, finally offering membership to descendants of those volunteers—as representatives from a "14th State."

General Heath's report to Washington concerning the British sleighs in northern Manhattan is in *Volume II* of Sparks's *Correspondence.* Baron Cromot du Bourg's observation on the efficacy of the Chain is from his 1781 *Journal,* reprinted in the *Magazine of American History* (New York, 1880); Rochambeau's army, of course, did not cross the Hudson "at the foot of the Catskills, where the wail of the wildcats drifts through the undomesticated hills, and the rumble of thunder means that the ghosts of Henry Hudson's crew are playing at bowls"—as Barbara Tuchman wrote in

*The First Salute* (New York, 1988)—but below Peekskill at Verplanck and Stony Point.

Cornwallis's April 10, 1781 complaint to Major General William Phillips about his footling southern campaign is from his *Correspondence* (London, 1859). Joseph Plumb Martin's 1783 comments on the chain are from his *Narrative;* the historic "Yankee pumpkin vine" reference is from a letter by E.W. Claff in the September 17, 1855 *Albany Weekly Argus.* Colonel Pickering's letter to General Knox is in his *MS.* letter book in the National Archives.

## EPILOGUE

The unsupported assertion that sections of the Fort Montgomery chain wound up at the Rock of Gibraltar is found in Robert Beatson's multi-volume *Naval and Military Memoirs of Great Britain from 1727 to the Present Time* (London, 1790). An unsigned 19th century memoir in the New York State Archives in Albany asserts the chain was indeed taken aboard British "ships of war." The two salvaged Fort Montgomery chain links in the New-York Historical Society were a 1928 gift from Mrs. Louis T. Hoyt.

Edward M. Ruttenber documents the salvage of the Fort Montgomery chain link, West Point boom section, and piece of *cheval-de-frise* in his *Catalogue of Manuscripts and Relics in Washington's Head-Quarters, Newburgh, N.Y.* (Newburgh, 1890). The recovery of the *cheval-de-frise*—"in order to free the anchor, the Sloop's hands were obliged to cut from the frame one of the timbers with a massive iron spike on one end"—was reported in the *Westchester Herald* for November 13, 1827.

General Huntington's letter to Washington is in *Volume IV* of Sparks's *Correspondence.* Francisco de Miranda's praise for the chain is from his *Diary* (New York, 1928).

John Adams's expressed fear of a new war with Great Britain, in a July 19, 1785 letter to John Jay, is on microfilm *Reel 11* of the *Adams Papers.* Secretary of War Henry Knox's 18th-century plea to maintain the West Point Chain was quoted 35 years later by Roswell Park in his *Sketch of the History of West Point* (Philadelphia, 1840); Park also noted that "several [links of the chain] still remain at the Military Academy." Another early description of the Trophy Point Memorial may be found in Joseph H. Colton's *A Guide-Book to West Point* (New York, 1844). Colonel Williams's August 17, 1807 suggestion to stretch the West Point Chain across the entrance to New York harbor is reported in *Volume 5* of Isaac Newton Phelps Stokes's *The Iconography of Manhattan Island* (New York, 1915).

General Totten's letter to USMA Superintendent Barnard regarding the Bishop derrick is in the National Archives in Washington; copies of Barnard's replies are from the *Superintendent's Letter Book #3* in the West Point Library. The California Revolutionary War buff and collector who recognized the peripatetic West Point Chain clevis as an "antique" is Dr. Gary M. Milan of Beverly Hills. The cube of wrought iron reportedly cut from an opened link of the chain was given to the Litchfield Historical Society *ca.* 1890 by Mrs. J. A. Vanderpoel.

## THE GREAT CHAIN HOAX

Van Wyck Brooks's seminal essay *"On Creating a Usable Past"* appeared in *The Dial* a year after the United States entered World War I; Karal Ann Marling's observation on the "need for material intimacy" is in *George Washington Slept Here* (Cambridge, 1988).

The story of the insatiable Chicago collector "Candy Man" Charles F. Gunther is covered in detail in *Volumes I, II* and *VII* of the Chicago Historical Society's periodical *Chicago History*. A colorful description of Gunther's chain purchase (which the Society often referred to as "The Great Putnam Chain") was published in the Omaha Exposition's *Time Saver and Catalog of America's War Museum* (Omaha, 1899).

The site of Westminster Abbey's lower Manhattan warehouse at No. 61 Front Street—as well as two entire blocks of Front Street itself—has now been eradicated by a huge glass-faced Water Street financial office tower. The new 52-story building also looms over the erstwhile location of Bannerman's arms depot at No. 27 Front Street, near Coenties Slip (now the site of a tiny, treeless park containing New York City's Vietnam War Memorial).

The U.S. Navy's inability to locate any Brooklyn Navy Yard records on authentic or spurious West Point chain links is recorded in an 1895 letter to Westminster Abbey from the Yard's equipment officer Commander Edwin White, and a 1932 letter from Captain P.B. Dungan to Roscoe W. Smith. The 19th century description of the Yard's authentic links is from the *Catalogue of Flags, Trophies, and Relics relating to the Revolution, the War of 1812, the Mexican War, and the Present Rebellion, Exhibited at New York for the Benefit of the U.S. Sanitary Commission* (New York, 1864).

Related coverage from *The New York Times* and New York *Sun* for 1887 and thereafter—as well as the earlier April 1864 Metropolitan Fair coverage by *The New York Times, New-York Tribune, Harper's Weekly* and *Frank Leslie's Illustrated Newspaper*—is available on microfilm in major libraries.

Abram S. Hewitt's letter of complaint to Westminster Abbey is among his papers at the Cooper Union (N.Y.C.) Library. His son Edward Ringwood Hewitt privately laid the Abbey fraud bare in his pamphlet on early Hewitt family life, *Ringwood Manor, The Home of the Hewitts* (Trenton, 1946).

Personal comments on Francis Bannerman, Jr are from booklets published at different times by his surplus arms firm. The observation stressing his interest in "developing the moral and religious side of boys' nature" is from *Vol. 19* of the *National Cyclopaedia of American Biography* (New York, 1926). Bannerman's obituary is in *The New York Times* for November 28, 1918.

The Buffalo and Erie County Historical Society published a brief description of their severed link in a 1925 booklet entitled *The Book of the Museum*, with text drawn from Macgrane Coxe's 1906 explanation. Mrs. Charles A. Sackett's 1933 gift to the Coast Guard Academy of six of her father's links was reported in the June and September 1933 issues of *U.S. Coast Guard* magazine (Annapolis).

Edward Francis Searles, purchaser of 13 Bannerman links, was a turn-of-the-century Massachusetts interior decorator with an irrepressible penchant for adolescent Greek catamites. In 1958, when Searles's grand-nephew sold Ball's ornate George Washington statue and chain to Hollywood's Forest Lawn Cemetery, six of the spurious links remained behind in New England. *The Searles Saga* by Sister St. Martina Flinton of the Presentation of Mary (Methuen, Massachusetts, 1976) tells the whole strange story.

Macgrane Coxe privately printed his 1906 oration to the Daughters of the American Revolution, as *Sterling Furnace and the West Point Chain* (New York, 1906). Coxe's and Bannerman's 1913 letters to Henry D. Paxson are in the Paxson collection at the American Antiquarian Society in Worcester. B.F. Fackenthal's 1937 address, *"The Great Chain at West Point,"* was published in *Volume VII* of the *Bucks County Historical Society Journal.*

Charles Rufus Harte was a Connecticut civil engineer who published several papers on early iron mining and manufacturing in the northwestern corner of that state. His comment on "hand chamfering" the Abbey/Bannerman links is in his monograph *"River Obstructions of the Revolutionary War,"* published in the *62nd Annual Report* of the Connecticut Society of Civil Engineers (Hartford, 1946). C.B.F. Young's photomicrographs of the polished Bannerman paperweight appeared in the metal trades magazine *Iron Age* (New York, June 3, 1937).

In a 1985 letter to the author, the Department of the Navy's Naval Historical Center at the Washington Navy Yard noted its failure to find a reference to either production or use of the Abbey/Bannerman chain at the Brooklyn Yard. This led directly to the author's further research in Great Britain, based on comments in Charles Wilkins's *History of the Iron, Steel, Tinplate, and Other Trades of Wales* (Merthyr Tydfil, 1903).

These bibliographical notes, therefore, should properly conclude with an expression of deep appreciation to Haydn Osborne, Secretary of the Pontypridd Works of Brown, Lenox & Co. Ltd. in Wales, and Ken Holloway, Pontypridd's retired Chain and Smiths Manager—as well as to Sir Robert Haslam, Simon Melhuish-Hancock and Jane Francis of the British Steel Corporation—for their generous assistance in helping the author determine the origin of Abbey/Bannerman's spurious "West Point Chain," and its final identification as a 19th century Welsh artifact.

# Index

# Index to Appendix B

## *"The Great Chain Hoax"*

# More History Books From Carol Publishing